ISRAELI BOUREKAS FILMS

SEPHARDI AND MIZRAHI STUDIES
Harvey E. Goldberg and Matthias Lehmann, editors

ISRAELI BOUREKAS FILMS

Their Origins and Legacy

Rami Kimchi

INDIANA UNIVERSITY PRESS

This book is a publication of

Indiana University Press
Office of Scholarly Publishing
Herman B Wells Library 350
1320 East 10th Street
Bloomington, Indiana 47405 USA

iupress.org

© 2023 by Rami Kimchi
Publication of this book was supported by funding from the
Publishing Committee of Ariel University, Israel.

All rights reserved
No part of this book may be reproduced or utilized in any form or by any means, electronic or mechanical, including photocopying and recording, or by any information storage and retrieval system, without permission in writing from the publisher. The paper used in this publication meets the minimum requirements of the American National Standard for Information Sciences—Permanence of Paper for Printed Library Materials, ANSI Z39.48-1992.

Manufactured in the United States of America

First printing 2023

Cataloging information is available from the Library of Congress.

ISBN 978-0-253-06341-0 (cloth)
ISBN 978-0-253-06342-7 (paperback)
ISBN 978-0-253-06344-1 (e-book)

CONTENTS

Preface vii

Acknowledgments ix

Introduction 1

1 Birth of the Bourekas: *Sallah* and Its Innovations 13

2 A Thematic Analysis of Bourekas 28

3 Mizrahi Self-Representation Films 58

4 Bourekas and Classical Yiddish Literature 87

5 The Dynamics of Continuity between Two Disparate Cultures 107

6 Bourekas Legacy: Post-Bourekas and Neo-Bourekas 127

Notes 147

Bibliography 167

Index 179

PREFACE

Bourekas films—the only original Israeli film cycle,[1] consisting of some of the most popular Israeli films ever made—have been experiencing a boom of exposure during The last two decades. Produced between 1964 and 1977, these films have gained an outsized presence in Israeli contemporary cultural discourse: a popular television series was dedicated to them (*A Black and White Movie*, 2011); two stage musicals were adapted from original Bourekas scripts and ran successfully on Israeli stages (*Sallah*, 2008, 2014, 2021; *Snooker*, 2013); a book (by me) was published about them (*The Israeli Shtetls*, 2012); and newspaper articles have discussed the film cycle's heritage and legacy.[2]

The name of the cycle, *Bourekas*, derives from a popular Sephardic-Mizrahi pastry that has its origins in Turkey. The phrase "Bourekas film" was apparently coined by the director Boaz Davidson and first entered Israeli cinematic discourse outside of any gastronomic reference in an interview Davidson gave to Yael Ontokovsky in 1975, following the commercial success of his first Bourekas film *Charlie and a Half* (*Charlie Vahetzi*, 1974). Davidson did not yet speak of Bourekas *films* but rather of a "Bourekas culture". The phrase denoted what was, in his view, the "primitive," vulgar culture of Mizrahi immigrants to Israel: "I objected in the strongest way to 'the Bourekas culture,' but then I suddenly realized what an idiot I was. We live here in a jungle of Bourekas, in a jungle of ethnicity, and we are surrounded by a jungle of accents and languages" (Ontokovsky 1975, 57; my translation).

In *Orientalism*, Edward Said (1978, 30) quotes Antonio Gramsci to describe how a researcher's awareness that he himself is a product of a historical process—one that has left infinite intellectual and emotional traces in his consciousness—is a necessary prerequisite to any serious career as a cultural critic. My own study of Bourekas films emerges from just such a personal awareness; the traces that sunk into my consciousness as a child in Israel are essential to it.

When I was about ten years old, I was first exposed to the popular comedies and melodramas that I would only later come to know as Bourekas films. The films enchanted me. I was drawn to what Ella Shohat (2010, 122) later defined as their "carnivalesque logic" and anarchistic atmosphere.

However, it never crossed my mind then that there was supposed to be a connection between my modern Sephardic Jewish family, who emigrated from Egypt to Israel in 1950, and the people I laughed at on the screen, with their poor material culture and their emotionally and intellectually narrow, premodern Jewish world. From my vantage point as a child, their reality was one that belonged to some kind of Others that I could only vaguely identify as Israeli traditional Jews.

Only years later did it dawn on me that the authors of the films were aiming to represent me and my family. This awareness led to a great cognitive dissonance. On the one hand, it was quite clear that both the producers of the films and most of their audiences saw the reality portrayed in the Bourekas films as a legitimate representation of Mizrahim in Israel. But by the same token, I clearly felt that my family, like other Mizrahim that I knew, embraced a material culture and a set of values, norms, and codes of behavior completely different from what was attributed to the Mizrahi communities in the Bourekas films. This dissonance became more acute in college when I was exposed to the works of classical Yiddish writers, which described the Jewish shtetls (rural towns with a large Jewish minority population) in eastern Europe. It seemed to me then that there were similarities between the world that came to life in these works and the world of the Mizrahi neighborhood as portrayed in Bourekas films.

The aim of this book is to plant my intuition in academic soil. My study of the Bourekas attempts, first of all, to define this cinematic cycle by separating it from other groups of Israeli films, more clearly delineating its features. Second, I aim to examine the connection between Bourekas and the texts of classical Yiddish literature—in particular, their portrayal of life in the Jewish shtetls of eastern Europe. Lastly, I trace the Bourekas legacy in contemporary Israeli cinema. I hope that the findings from these avenues of research eventually lead to a comprehensive explanation of the Bourekas' central place in Israeli culture, their enormous popularity and commercial success, and their impact to the Israeli cinema of today. In a way, I hope to evoke in this book something of a child's fascination with Bourekas as entertainment alongside the adult recognition of what they really meant for Israeli discourse as a cultural phenomenon.

ACKNOWLEDGMENTS

The major and final stages of this work were supported by Ariel University, Israel, while the initial stages of it were supported by the Department of Near Eastern Studies and the Frankel Center for Jewish Studies at the University of Michigan; the Jewish Memorial Foundation, New York; and the ISEF Foundation, Israel. My thanks to all for their generous support.

Much gratitude to Yehuda Shenhav and Ella Shohat, whose work and activism have been inspirational to me and drove me to take interest in the Bourekas in the first place. To my dear friends and colleagues Yaron Shemer, Sami Shalom Chetrit, and Gilad Zukerman, whose researches were a guiding principle for me.

The long and winding road that led me to this book started at the University of Michigan. I would like to express much gratitude to Anita Norich, Carol Bardenstein, Catherine Benamou, and Shahar Pinsker, from whom I learned so much that was relevant to this study, for their guidance in the initial stages of it.

Thanks to Ilan Avishar, Anner Preminger, Yaron Eliav, Ilan Tamir, Albert Pinhasov, Orzion Bartana, Amit Goren, Menachem Einy, Izhak Goren-Gurmezano, Yigal Cohen-Orgad, Michael Zinigrad, Yehuda Danon, Yehuda Ne'eman, Yossi Goldstein, Yoel Cohen, Rafi Man, and Gabriel Ben Simhon, my colleagues and friends, for their empathy and support.

Thanks also to my editors, David Lobenstine, Katie Van Heest, Elisheva Lahav, and Micaela Ziv. Appreciation to Harvey Goldberg and Matthias Lehmann, the series editors at Indiana University Press, especially to Harvey, whose wisdom and support accompanied me so gently along the way. I appreciate the interest Gary Dunham, editor in chief at Indiana University Press, showed after he reviewed my manuscript, and I am grateful to him and to the editorial assistants Ashante Thomas and Anna Francis for being responsive to my requests and for their dedication in bringing this work to fruition.

Thanks also to the photos rights holders Yoni Hamenachem, Assa Dorat, Moshe Edri, and Gidi Dar for their kindness and generosity and to the staff at the Tel Aviv Cinematheque Library, the Beit Ariella Library in Tel Aviv, and the Tel Aviv University Library.

My most profound thanks to my family, my children Danielle and Michael Kimchi, and their mother, Carmel Gottlieb Kimchi, for their sacrifices and support and to Jacques Kimchi and Henriette Azar-Kimchi, my beloved parents, who unfortunately did not live to see it come true.

ISRAELI BOUREKAS FILMS

INTRODUCTION

When the Hollywood musical *Fiddler on the Roof* (Norman Jewison, USA, 1971) told the story of a Jewish peasant who struggles to adjust to modern times, capturing the hearts and imaginations of millions all over the world, some spectators may have identified the film as a creative adaptation of *Tevye the Milkman* by the Yiddish writer Shalom Aleichem. They may also have noticed that the hybrid space, a conglomeration of rural village and urban entity that the film depicts as Tevye's residence, is in fact a Jewish shtetl—a small, rural town in nineteenth-century eastern Europe in which Jews were a large minority. However, it seems that only a handful of people knew that Haim Topol, the Israeli actor who played Tevye in the film, had only seven years earlier—wearing a similar outfit, adorned with the same beard, and dwelling in a comparable hybrid space—played the eponymous role in *Sallah* (Ephraim Kishon, Israel, 1964), the first and archetypical father in Israeli cinema's only original cycle: Bourekas films.

As has been the case for many national cinemas of recently formed countries, Israeli cinema has been strongly influenced by the ideology of the nation's elite, especially as it relates to the struggle for the country's independence and the status of different collectives within its borders. That ideology, for Israel's ruling class, is Zionism. As such, an expedition into the Bourekas must begin with a sketch of Zionist history, an account of the international conflict that preceded Israeli independence, and a brief recounting of the ethnic national conflicts that have persisted within its borders over the years that followed.

The Zionist project, of which Israel is a product, was born in Europe in the late nineteenth century. First promoted as an ideal solution to European anti-Semitism, Zionism's core idea as the national movement of the Jewish people was to revive nationalistic feelings among European Jews, encouraging their emigration to the Land of Israel (Palestine), which had for centuries dominated the Jewish diasporic imagination as the nation's cradle and homeland. Its final goal would be the establishment in Palestine of a Jewish nation-state in the European model.

However, living in the height of a colonial epoch, most Zionist leaders ignored the fact that Palestine was already inhabited at this time by Muslim Arabs—a reality that became an increasing problem on the road to realizing the Zionist project. As European Jews immigrated to Palestine in larger numbers beginning in 1904,[1] they faced a violent reaction from Palestinian Arabs, who on May 1, 1921, fatally attacked unarmed Jewish immigrants in Jaffa.[2] The shock of the Jewish Yishuv[3] turned this pogrom into the starting point of the Jewish-Palestinian conflict. Subsequently, Palestinians were largely perceived in Zionist thought and discourse as "the enemy." In the warfare against them, such colonialist concepts as orientalism and nativism were deployed alongside real weapons (Shohat 2010).

In the beginning, the Zionist movement did not regard non-Ashkenazi Jews as an ideal target audience for the Zionist project. The non-Ashkenazi Jewish population was small in numbers (amounting to only one-tenth of the world Jewish population at the beginning of the twentieth century), mostly non-European, and culturally different from the dominant Ashkenazi group. Yet after the Holocaust, when most of European Ashkenazi Jewry was annihilated, the non-Ashkenazi population became a natural reserve people for the Zionist project. Starting in the late 1940s,[4] and encouraged by the Zionist establishment, Jews who would later be called Mizrahim started to immigrate in greater numbers to Palestine. They did so willingly at first and then as refugees fleeing persecution in their home countries, which grew increasingly nationalistic in response to the Jewish-Arab conflict in Palestine, among other reasons (Chetrit 2004; Shenhav 2003).

The Israeli establishment welcomed these immigrants and thought of using them to populate Israel's countryside, which remained abandoned and empty after the War of Independence (1948). Mizrahi immigrants were settled mainly on the periphery and along the borders, sometimes serving as a buffer between Israel and neighboring hostile Arab countries (Chetrit 2004; Shohat 2010). The distribution of labor and properties was often discriminatory against them (Swirski 1981). Although the same colonialist discourse and orientalism that were part of the Zionist propaganda against Palestinians were sometimes used to suppress Mizrahim, they were not considered an "enemy" but an inner Other instead.

As a national movement, Zionism promoted a national, so-called authentic culture—Hebrew culture. Israeli cinema was born in 1933 as a part of this Hebrew culture, and although small in scale,[5] it would soon become an important component of nationalist Zionist discourse in the prestate

Jewish Yishuv. Functioning as an ideological state apparatus from its beginning, Israeli cinema intensively reflected the official national-Zionist dogma and offered its perspective on the Jewish-Palestinian conflict (Schweitzer 2003; Zimmerman 2001). At the same time, it echoed the power dynamics within Jewish society, reflecting the point of view of Zionist Ashkenazi elites. It was particularly revelatory of the "natural" and "peaceful" subjugation of the Mizrahim to the dominant Ashkenazi hegemony, as these films typically cast Ashkenazi figures as leading characters and Mizrahi figures only in supporting roles (Kimchi 2012; Shohat 2010).

However, in the early 1960s, films that were regarded by some critics as deviating from the idealized portrayal of Zionist ideology began to appear. Among these new films were some that placed Mizrahi figures in leading roles and highlighted the ethnocultural-social conflict between Mizrahim and Ashkenazim in Israel. This group would later be called Bourekas films—after a popular local Mediterranean pastry—and some of its films would eventually be counted among the most popular Israeli films ever made.

Bourekas films dominated Israeli cinema from 1964 until 1977 and have remained relevant to its history ever since. Comprising a variety of film types, mainly comedy and melodrama, Bourekas[6] cannot be approached as a single film genre; however, the new themes they offered, as well as their new paradigmatic representation of the Mizrahi community that reflected the ideological and political discourse of the time—particularly their portrayal of a fundamental conflict within Israeli society and offering a solution to it—render the Bourekas a discernible film cycle (see Schatz 1981, 14–42).

Centered on disadvantaged Mizrahi immigrants in poor neighborhoods on the outskirts of Israeli metropolitan areas, Bourekas films introduced new content to the Israeli cinematic discourse. This originality, however, was not appreciated. In the Israel of the 1960s, where the Ashkenazi Zionist elites enlisted the arts in support of their project of building a new European national identity (Chinski 2002), the focus on an Israeli Mizrahi hero seemed almost subversive. Moreover, cinema critics of the time, for whom the ultimate cinematic model was that of the modernistic European cinema of the auteur, were professionally biased to see these somewhat clumsy, low-budget folk comedies and melodramas reflecting the popular cinema logic of "documents of wish fulfillment" (Nichols 2001) as inferior cinematic texts. Bourekas films were belittled by critics of the time and received with derision.

Nevertheless, this degrading critical reception did not seem to detract from the overwhelming popularity of Bourekas films. *Sallah* (1964), the first and archetypical film of the cycle, is undoubtedly the most popular Israeli film ever made.[7] It is dealt with here at length, since its release forever changed Israeli cinema, offering a new metanarrative and giving birth to a distinctive representation paradigm of Mizrahim, which became the identifying mark of Bourekas films. The Bourekas films that followed were also extremely popular, and although the last one was produced in 1977, they remain mind-bogglingly popular in Israel, as can be seen in new DVD and online releases and in repeated screenings on Israeli television on national holidays and special occasions. In a way, Bourekas films became a cult phenomenon in Israel. The films are publicly celebrated as cultural products that echo the true original Israeli spirit.[8]

Perhaps as an enduring effect of the cycle's initially poor critical reception by reviewers, few academic studies have addressed the Bourekas. In reviewing existing scholarship, one can identify two main critical approaches. The first, which echoes European modernist cinematic discourse (Metz 1974; Pasolini 1974), presents a persistent refusal to discuss Bourekas as a viable subject for academic critical analysis. In the studies of critics in this group, such as Yehuda Ne'eman (1979, 1999) and Moshe Zimmerman (2001), Bourekas are dismissed outright; their moral and esthetic content is deemed to be so inferior that it warrants no serious critical attention (Ne'eman 1979).[9]

In contrast, critics whose works utilize postcolonial theories, such as Ella Shohat (1989, 2001, 2010), Hannan Hever, Yehouda Shenhav, and Pnina Motzafi-Haller, (2002), and Yaron Shemer (2013), treat the films with critical seriousness. Adapting the colonizer-colonized paradigm to the Israeli sphere, where the Ashkenazi Zionist elites are identified as the colonizer and Mizrahim as the colonized, they see Bourekas as "colonialist texts which echo colonialist stands originally created to justify relationships between the First World and the Third World, and which were reproduced within the Zionist discourse to explain the relationships between Ashkenazim and Mizrahim, sometimes while comparing the Mizrahim to Arabs and Blacks" (Shohat 2010, 106). However, while emphasizing the demeaning orientalist representation of Mizrahi neighborhoods/communities in the films, this approach fails to convincingly explain the box office success of Bourekas, especially among Mizrahi audiences.[10]

Neither group has suggested a clear Bourekas corpus or a generic definition of the group. Rick Altman (1999) claims that American film scholars frequently do not bother to offer a generic definition of groups of films they intuitively comprehend as recognizable. This tendency appears to apply as well to Israeli studies of Bourekas films: the prevailing assumption among scholars is that these films do, in fact, constitute a recognizable group, yet none has sought to define this group or to systematically identify what makes a film a Bourekas film.

This book is the first and (so far) only book in English wholly dedicated to Bourekas films. It pursues postcolonial studies on the Bourekas and attempts to answer some of the questions that this research has raised to date: What classifies a film as Bourekas? Which films make up the Bourekas film corpus? How can one explain the wide appeal of Bourekas films in Israel and the fact that this group encompasses some of the country's most popular films? What has remained of the Bourekas legacy in present-day Israeli cinematic discourse?

Critics claim that narrative is the focus of the popular film (Cutting 2016). A distinction must be made, though, between *fabula* (i.e., the story and its various components) and *syuzhet* (i.e., the way the story is being told) (Propp [1968] 2003; Shklovsky [1917] 1965). Bourekas films have quite a bit in common when it comes to fabula. For example, many times pairing has a central place in the film's narrative. But in terms of syuzhet, there is a lot of variety. Not only do the events and their order vary, but the genres range from melodrama to comedy to musical.

What makes the Bourekas films a cycle then, beyond the sociopolitical aspects mentioned, are not the plots but rather three diegetic facts: the fact that the film is focused on a Mizrahi character or family; the fact that, in the vast majority of cases, the space in which the story takes place is a neighborhood, town, or transit camp inhabited primarily by Mizrahim; and the fact that this Mizrahi space and its characters are focalized through the eyes of a non-Mizrahi director. I therefore base my analysis on the following three elements: the nature of the Mizrahi protagonist/family depicted, how the space of the Mizrahi neighborhood is presented ontologically and culturally, and the impact of Ashkenazi focalization on the diegesis.

My main claim is that Bourekas films, in a way that is reminiscent of *Fiddler on the Roof*, adopted the situations, conflicts, motivations, cultural atmosphere, and setting of the late nineteenth-century Jewish shtetl as it was paradigmatically represented in the writings of three classical Yiddish writers—Mendele Mocher Sforim (1835–1917), Y. L. Peretz (1851–1915), and Shalom Aleichem (1859–1916)—integrating these features into cinematic texts. However, unlike *Fiddler on the Roof*, Bourekas films project this Ashkenazi paradigmatic representation of the shtetl onto the Israeli suburban reality of the 1960s and 1970s populated mainly with Mizrahim—thereby creating a product that culturally corresponds with what Homi Bhabha (1994) called "a mottled entity." My research has led me to the hypothesis that the Ashkenazi directors of Bourekas films portrayed the community and space of the Israeli Mizrahi neighborhood according to paradigms that closely correspond with those used by classical Yiddish writers who portrayed the east European Jewish shtetl in a highly critical light, and, in so doing, projected the premodern "inferior" Jewishness of the shtetl's Ashkenazi Jews in those paradigmatic representations onto the Mizrahim.

As such, Bourekas, I find, are part of an effort intended to support the progressive "Sisyphean challenge of westernization . . . and albinism" (Chinski 2002, 68) taken on at first by the old Ashkenazi Jewish elite in eastern Europe[11] and continued by the Ashkenazi elite in Israel. Within this project, the term "Blacks"—the common moniker for Mizrahim, as the Others in the Israeli sphere—is meant to attach the desired whiteness to Ashkenazi elites and establish their status as colonial rulers.

The removal of the whitened supremacy from its normative elevated status will not be achieved only by the returning of the oppressed to the arena, argues Bhabha (1998). A truly subversive move will attempt to expose within the mantle of whiteness the elements that struggle with each other, the forgetfulness it imposes on itself, and the violence it creates as it transforms itself into a transparent and transcendental power of authority. In that sense, this book is indeed subversive for, through its discussion of Bourekas films—which it presents as a site for the implementation of strategies designed to achieve and preserve the whiteness of the Ashkenazi elites—it indicates that Bourekas film production was, among other things, an outcome of internal struggle within the camp of whites: between Hebrew Zionists, Ashkenazim who sought to negate Yiddish culture, and those who were loyal to it. It also reveals that Bourekas served as a site for the realization of the *negation of exile*—a strategy used by the elites to suppress and impose on Ashkenazi immigrants to Israel the forgetting of Yiddish culture and become ethnically transparent.

Since my argument about Bourekas films attaches crucial importance to the director's influence on the film, I partly use auteur theory. Since its emergence in the 1950s and even more so since the 1970s, auteur theory has been the subject of harsh methodological criticism. However, it still prevails and functions as a major theory in film analysis (see Malou-Strandvad 2012;

McIntyre 2012; Sellors 2010). My approach adapts it to a limited extent, also providing a platform for one of the two types of critique directed toward it—the poststructuralist (Barthes 1977; Foucault 1969; Gerstner and Staiger 2003) critique—which engages a view that indicates that films do not present their author's personalities only but, at the same time, are "written" by a series of historical and cultural assertions. Emphasizing the author's control over the film should thus be dialectically understood and take into account the complex and dynamic relationships between artists (film directors), institutions, and certain cultural and sociopolitical circumstances (see Naremore 2005). I adopt this assessment to analyze the approach of Bourekas directors to the representation of the people and spaces in their films.

Semiotic studies of cinema argue that film text signifiers possess at least two functions: the recreation of a comprehensive, realistic space (the metonymical and indexical functions) and the representation of abstract features (the metaphorical function) (Barthes 1977; Metz 1974; Wollen 1972). These studies also devalued the effect of the human author's personality on the text and highlighted the role of cultural tendencies and modes, existing textual paradigms, and previous texts done in the same category in the production of a new text. On the other end, François Truffaut's auteur theory regards the director as a film's only "author" and considers the film to be the result of such rhetorical measures as the director as a subject deems necessary during the film's production, whether consciously or subconsciously (Truffaut 1976 [1954], 1967; Unger 1991, Heb).

This book attempts to combine both theories. I consider *all the signifiers* of the filmic text—both metaphoric and metonymic—as the result of *conscious and unconscious rhetorical measures taken by the director of the film as a representative of his culture and class*. This approach stresses the importance of the fact that while the communities that stand in the center of Bourekas are Mizrahi ones, all directors and producers of the films are of Ashkenazi cultural backgrounds.[12] This negation of the self-representation of Mizrahim stands at the center of my approach to the cycle and, in a way, asserts my conclusions concerning the cycle's corpus, characteristics, origins, and legacy.

Targeting a relatively small audience of Hebrew speakers, Israeli cinema is hardly an industry at all, even nowadays. In the days of the Bourekas, it was even smaller. Until 1964, when *Sallah* appeared, only thirty-two Israeli feature films had been produced, and not all of them found their way to screens.[13]

The Bourekas film corpus, according to the criteria suggested, comprises eleven films produced between 1964 and 1977. These all share a particular shtetl-like paradigmatic representation of an Israeli Mizrahi neighborhood and community focalized through the agency of a director with an Ashkenazi cultural background. This Ashkenazi cultural background is necessary for the creation of a Bourekas film; I confirm this through the fact—proven in chapter 3, where the book compares Bourekas films with films centered on Mizrahi characters and neighborhoods made by Mizrahi directors—that Mizrahi characters and neighborhoods focalized through a non-Ashkenazi director do not produce a Bourekas film.

Seeing Bourekas films as textual phenomena, and utilizing a structural comparative analysis, this book further suggests that the distorted representation of Mizrahim—which bears a strong resemblance to classical Yiddish writers' representation of the shtetl's population—was unconsciously implemented by Ashkenazi Bourekas directors, for whom it was the traditional way of representing a premodern Jewish community. I also contend that this adoption of Yiddish cultural elements by Bourekas films into their diegesis rebelled against the Zionist negation of exile[14] ideology and reflected a new balance—one that was more favorable to Yiddish culture, between the concurrent Zionist institutional oppression of Yiddish and forces striving for the meaningful presence of Yiddish culture, than that common in the Zionist sphere prior to the era of Bourekas production.[15] I further contend that this hybridity of Bourekas films—which are at the same time Israeli/Mizrahi and diasporic/Ashkenazi—is the primary reason for their success in Israel and for their continued legacy nowadays, since it satisfies in different ways the political, sociological, and psychological needs of both Mizrahi and Ashkenazi audiences in Israel.

Discussing Bourekas from the point of view of the conflict between a marginal group and a hegemonic one calls for postcolonial discourse. From this perspective, the Bourekas are texts that reflect the dialectic relationships between the colonizing Ashkenazi elite and the colonized Mizrahim and texts embedded with the Ashkenazi conflict of identity, caused by their traumatic encounter with Mizrahim, who became encoded as Others.

To explain this strength of Bourekas, I draw on works of postcolonial discourse such as those of Homi Bhabha (1994, 2002) and his ideas on the complex relationships of inclusion and isolation between colonizer and colonized. Using this perspective, I argue that despite seeing Mizrahim through a demeaning orientalist prism, Bourekas films are not unequivocally unfavorable toward Mizrahim, as claimed by previous critics, but rather offer the Mizrahi spectator a complex message, incorporating disparate motifs of inclusion (the portrayal of Mizrahim as Jews, i.e., part of the Israeli nation) and isolation (the Mizrahim orientalist portrayal that denounces them as premodern).

To strengthen my explanation of the Bourekas' success among Ashkenazi audiences, I further examine the role of Bourekas in Zionist discourse through Bhabha's (1994, 66–85) discussion of colonial mimicry. The effect of the colonized mimicking the colonizer is a camouflage, claims Bhabha (following Lacan). The colonized do not harmonize with the new identity (of the colonizer) that they mimic, nor do they totally become it; rather, it is used to partially cover their original identity. It is not a situation of completely covering a certain background but of producing a "mottled entity" (85). The Bourekas—which define the community presented in them as Israeli Mizrahi but portray it as if it were an archaic/diasporic Ashkenazi one—can be seen as texts through which colonial mimicry is implemented through representations of Mizrahim mimicking Ashkenazim and looking ridiculous while doing so. This phenomenon seems to flatter Zionist Ashkenazi elites and therefore facilitate the process presenting the Mizrahi neighborhood as a mottled entity and Mizrahi characters as ridiculous Ashkenazim mimickers of ratifying their relatively new status as colonizers of the Israeli sphere.

In the final chapter, I show that my findings allow for a repositioning of Bourekas films as a phase in Israeli cinema's quest to resist the limiting discourse of the *negation of exile* and to openly reflect the true spectrum of ethnicity and cultural diversity in Israel. The Bourekas represent a stage in which Israeli cinema was already prepared to portray cultural/ethnic diversity while challenging the borders of the Zionist ethos of Hebrewness but in which Ashkenazi filmmakers, affected by the negation of exile ideology, were still compelled to express their diasporic Jewish pre-Zionist ethnic culture (Yiddish) by projecting it onto others, even while twisting and demeaning it.

I further maintain that the Bourekas formula has *not* disappeared from current Israeli cinematic discourse and that films depicting a mottled reality—in which an Israeli Mizrahi space/community is partially covered by a diasporic Ashkenazi one—are still being produced in Israel. I categorize these films as neo-Bourekas or post-Bourekas. The first category that I delve into, the neo-Bourekas, includes films that naturally, and seemingly with little awareness, reproduce the paradigmatic representation of the Mizrahi community in Bourekas films, with some adjustments to reflect the period and place in which the story takes place. Examples of this are *Colombian Love* (2004), *Turn Left at the End of the World* (2004), and *Aviva, My Love* (2006). The *post-* label is applied to films that describe Mizrahi communities partly using the Bourekas representation paradigm of Mizrahim in the original cycle while deliberately and consciously exaggerating or twisting one or more features of that paradigm. Taking an ironic stance, these films reproduce the Bourekas even as they criticize them, casting some doubt on whether this mottled reality does indeed exist in Israel's reality. Examples of these films are *Lovesick in Housing Complex C* (1995), the internationally successful *The Band's Visit* (2007),[16] and the local hit *This Is Sodom* (2010).

Overall, I maintain that the Bourekas paradigm is being kept alive in Israeli cinema through its appearance in contemporary neo- and post-Bourekas films and that the Bourekas formula may continue to persist in mainstream Israeli cinema as long as three conditions prevail: (1) veteran Ashkenazi elites remain in power in Israel, (2) the polarity between Ashkenazim and Mizrahim continues to be a dominant force in Israeli society, and (3) the negation of exile ideology maintains some restrictive power. If these elements hold, Ashkenazi elites, as colonizers of the Israeli sphere, will continue to find in the Bourekas paradigm a means of manipulating the Mizrahim and will, dialectically, be manipulated in turn by Mizrahim to strengthen their distinctive Ashkenazi identity and ratify their colonial rule by covertly injecting Yiddish culture into filmic representations of Israeli Mizrahi reality.

The Poststructuralist Approach to the Auteur Theory

This book adopts a structuralist approach, viewing films as narrated texts.[17] This fundamental understanding permits the use of similar analytical tools and methods to analyze both cinematic texts (the Bourekas films) and written fictional texts (stories and novels in classical Yiddish literature), although each medium produces meaning through distinct processes: literature via written language and cinema via the process of signification, using visual and vocal signifiers that vary in nature and source.[18]

As indicated, in part the book adopts what is known as auteur theory. My approach to auteur theory and the director's persona, alongside being influenced by poststructuralist critique, is affected by the discourse of identity politics. To paraphrase Deleuze and Guattari's (1975) discussion of minor literature it can be said that the politics of identities connects the personal to culture and politics and gives it a collective presence and visibility (see Shenhav 2001) but shifts the center of gravity from the individual as a psychological persona to the cultural and political textures of power and normalization (Foucault [1954] 1987).

The science of psychology, with its emphasis on individual personality, likewise increases consciousness of the fact that action and individual personality are familiarly constructed by cultural and social context. Advanced studies in the field (see Shoda and Cervix 2007) argue that the "science of the individual" has failed so far precisely because it has tried to explore the individual.

Bourekas are popular films. Propp ([1968] 2003) has already shown that popular texts owe more to the cultural repetitiveness of paradigms than to their particular so-called author. Integrating these approaches with Barthes's (1977, 79–124) poststructural one and auteur theory, I suggest that what Andrew Sarris (1971, 132) called the "élan of the director's soul," which creates the inner meaning of a film, especially in popular films, is not of a particular, individual subjective nature but instead reflects mainly the director's sociocultural identity. The substance that is reflected in the inner circle of the auteur is not quite the director's individual persona but the culture he or she promotes and the structures that keep appearing in it, as well as the ideology of the class he or she belongs to.

The book's hypothesis is that a popular film is, in a way, a tool through which the true sociocultural identity of a director, which is sometimes not evident in everyday life, is exposed. Film thus becomes a mirror for class and culture—inflected conflicts that the director and other members of the same culture and class experience. Accordingly, the book attributes major significance to a director's cultural identity, also paying attention to the mythos and other structures that appear in that culture's history. At this junction, the study is close to postcolonial studies that focus on ethnic and diasporic cinema; these include the works of Stuart Hall, Michael Martin, Hamid Naficy, Peter Bloom, and Yaron Shemer. The book shares with them the presumption that films expose their director's sociocultural identity.

Auteur theory is here adopted only in this narrow sense. I see the director of the popular film—very much like the storyteller or the shaman of ancient societies mentioned by Barthes—as giving up his or her own personality and letting the structures of his or her particular culture, as well as the ideology of his or her class, pass through him or her into the film. The study denies the influence of the popular film director's individuality (as an author) on the film text and focuses instead on how certain structures continue to return in a certain culture through art (film) and the people who create it (directors) (Barthes 1977, 79–124).

As a result of this approach, the book is not interested in directors' biographical personas; unless they include information about their cultural identity, Bourekas directors' biographies, previous films, styles, narratives of their careers, and interviews with them are all of little relevance to my study. However, adopting auteur theory principally by accepting the director as the author of a film, I use the term *cinematic author*, drawn from the literary-critical term "implied author" (Booth 1961, 77–97), to relate to the aspect of the director reflected throughout the film's rhetoric: his or her cultural identity as it is echoed through cinematic tactics and rhetorical means utilized in the film.

Following Barthes, I suggest that film is a text that reflects the cultural identity—whether Mizrahi or Ashkenazi—of the director as an author. In Israel's early film history, it was the Ashkenazi directors, members of the hegemonic cultural elite, who set the tone and created a "default" cinematic representation of Mizrahim. Bourekas films are the first instances in which Ashkenazi directors turned deliberately to Mizrahim and constructed film narratives around their communities and neighborhoods.

In Bourekas films, I find that the paradigmatic representation of the shtetl—established as a literary genre through which Ashkenazi Jews made sense of themselves as a marginal ethnocultural group in eastern Europe—changes shape. When the relatively newly settled Ashkenazi elites in Israel depict the ethnocultural group of Mizrahim through its prism, the result is a marginalizing of the Mizrahim. Ultimately, the Bourekas are an attempt, however veiled and even at times subconscious, to cast Mizrahim as abject and to shore up the nascent, and thus comparatively unstable, identity of the Ashkenazi Israeli.

All of this and more is explained in the coming chapters. In chapter 2, I describe a Bourekas corpus and analyze it thematically, while chapter 3 is dedicated to comparing Bourekas to the films in Israeli popular cinema most closely related to them—the popular Mizrahi self-representation films. Chapter 4 explores Bourekas homology to classical Yiddish literature, and chapter 5 explains how and why the transfer from Yiddish classical literature to Bourekas happened, offering new explanations for the box office success of Bourekas. Chapter 6 deals with the Bourekas legacy in Israeli contemporary film discourse and presents two new Israeli films cycles: neo-Bourekas and post-Bourekas

However, I begin in chapter 1 by answering a preliminary question: How and why did it all start?

1

BIRTH OF THE BOUREKAS

Sallah *and Its Innovations*

Between the first Israeli feature film in 1933—*Oded the Wanderer (Oded Hanoded)*—and the early 1960s, Jewish filmmakers, first in Palestine as a part of the Yishuv and then in Israel after 1948, produced fewer than three dozen fiction features (Schnitzer 1994, 30–62). This group of films, although small in number, is revealing: they were decidedly ideological and conformed to the beliefs of the Israeli elites who were distributing Zionist dogma (Zimmerman 2001, 13).

Louis Althusser (1971, 127–189) argues that in order to secure the production systems and to maintain its domination, the ruling class of a state distributes its ideology through what he calls an "ideological state apparatus." In the modern period, this apparatus can include, among other elements, schools, families, the media, and the arts. Early Israeli cinema[1] served as a vital part of the state of Israel's ideological apparatus.

Israeli cinema in those days offered a barometer of the Israeli-Palestinian conflict from a Zionist point of view, but it also echoed Zionist notions about Israel's Jewish society. It was particularly successful in distributing the imagined Zionist utopia of harmony between Ashkenazi Jews, Israel's dominant Jewish ethnic group, and the marginalized Mizrahi Jews. These films propagated the idea of a "natural" inferiority and subjugation of the Mizrahi population to the dominant Ashkenazi group. Largely underrepresented in these films, Mizrahim were typically cast in supporting roles in their rare appearances (Shohat 1989, 124–125, Stier-Livny 2019).

Israeli cinema's enthusiastic conformism to Zionist dogma ended with the release of Ephraim Kishon's film *Sallah* (*Sallah Shabati*, 1964).[2] The plot of this unusually popular and successful movie[3] was built on conflicts between Mizrahim and Ashkenazim and featured a Mizrahi character in the leading role. Critics also noted that *Sallah* deviated from a simple reflection of Zionist ideology by mocking fundamental Zionist symbols (e.g., the kibbutz [collective settlement] and the *halutz* [pioneer]), presenting such central Zionist institutions as the Jewish National Fund as corrupt,[4] and echoing non-Zionists' capitalistic ideas.[5]

This chapter reexamines the innovations replicated in *Sallah* vis-à-vis early Israeli films. Due to *Sallah*'s place in Israeli cinematic history as a herald of the Bourekas film cycle, this analysis stands to shed crucial light on what Bourekas films actually are, along with emphasizing the role that Bourekas films played in Israeli Zionist nationalist discourse.

Sallah is a film about an immigrant. The protagonist, Sallah Shabati, is a forty-something-year-old Mizrahi Jew born in an Islamic country. The film begins as he arrives in Israel with his wife and eight children. On arrival, they are all transferred to a *ma'abara* (transit camp for new immigrants). The officials there, all Ashkenazi Jews, inform Sallah that this is only a temporary solution for a short time until his housing is ready. This turns out to be a lie, as Sallah and his family are actually expected to stay in the ma'abara for a long time.

From this point on, the film depicts Sallah's fight for permanent housing, which is also a fight against state institutions and the officials who try to thwart him, and the efforts of his large family to adapt to the new country. In the end, both efforts are successful. After Sallah fails to use the local corrupt politicians to secure a permanent home, he finds a more efficient solution: organizing a boycott among the inhabitants of the ma'abara to protest *against* moving to permanent housing. The authorities react, as he anticipated, by "forcibly" transporting the camp's entire population to the accommodations they were promised. Sallah's other main efforts also end with unexpected success: at the conclusion of the film, Sallah's eldest daughter is about to marry her beloved, an Ashkenazi native Israeli kibbutz member; Sallah's eldest son, meanwhile, is set to marry an Ashkenazi Israeli native young woman on the same kibbutz.

In many respects, *Sallah* is indeed different from the films that preceded it, and it marks a significant departure from Israeli cinema of the 1940s, 1950s, and early 1960s. The film diverges from the earlier films' conformity to the Zionist ethos by forgoing some of the cinematic paradigms that its predecessors use to echo Zionist ideology through and by twisting others.

At the center of Zionist ideology of that time lay the idea of Hebrewness. The Zionist movement believed that it could and should change what it saw as the warped nature of the Jewish diasporic human being and convert a Jewish diasporic subjectivity[6] into a specifically Hebrew one.[7] The Jewish diasporic sense of self was seen by Zionists as structured on the traits attributed to Jews in European anti-Semitic discourse. That kind of Jew was characterized by fear (of open spaces, among many other things), urbanity, aggression, physical weakness, idleness, fraud, and femininity (Gertz 1999, 382–87). In sharp contrast, the characteristics of the new and evolving Hebrew human being were perceived as almost the polar opposite—courage, productivity, physical strength, firmness, and control over open spaces. In accordance with this ethos, one of the main aspirations of early Israeli cinema, as an ideological state apparatus, was to present Hebrew subjectivity as the identity of the Zionist Ashkenazi elite and as the desirable identity of every Jewish emigrant to Israel. Early Israeli cinema also often used the level of assimilation to Hebrew subjectivity of its characters as a way to portray their status in Israeli society (Gertz 1999, 381).

Early Israeli films placed at their discourse's center a dichotomy of Jewish versus Hebrew; they attached Hebrew subjectivity to characters representing Zionist elites and affixed Jewish diasporic subjectivity to "Zionist-to-be" characters, such as new non-Zionist immigrants to Israel and Holocaust survivors. The Zionist-to-be characters, who typically began these films embodying a Jewish diasporic subjectivity, had to earn their Hebrewness. The common trajectory of these early Israeli films was thus a coming-of-age journey that ended in the Zionist-to-be characters turning from Jews into Hebrews.

Attaching Hebrew subjectivity to members of the Zionist elite was achieved through the use of a variety of cinematic tactics, including integrating them into cinematic images of Zionist tropes, such as "Hebrew labor" and "making the desert bloom"; presenting members of the Zionist elite as in control of open spaces; and presenting the Zionist elite as accentless, native Hebrew speakers, implying that they are Sabras (i.e., native-born Israeli Jews). Symbolizing that a Zionist-to-be character—a new immigrant or a Holocaust survivor—had already conquered his Hebrew subjectivity was accomplished using the same cinematic tactics.

Sallah offered a departure from this fundamental dichotomy of Jewish versus Hebrew in early Israeli films and raised doubts about the very existence of Hebrew subjectivity in 1960s Israeli society. By examining various cinematic tactics employed by *Sallah*, one can appreciate the innovations of this groundbreaking film. *Sallah* departed from early Israeli cinema's habit of reproducing Hebrew subjectivity through connecting characters to Zionist tropes. Although in some cases it adopted the scenery and actions used in early films to reproduce Zionist tropes, a closer look reveals that instead of simply reproducing the tropes, the film ridicules them and in the process also undermines the characters' Hebrew subjectivity. One of the Zionist tropes that *Sallah* subverts, for example, is that of Hebrew labor.

Zionism's concept of Hebrew labor reflects the argument put forth by certain Zionist thinkers that Jews should abandon their traditional occupations, such as trade and finance, and return to productive labor—especially to farming—as a necessary step on the road toward becoming a healthy and "normal" nation.[8] Early Israeli films reflected this idea by creating narratives in which Jews of the Diaspora symbolically acquire Hebrew subjectivity by cultivating the soil of the Land of Israel and through constructing scenes that show Hebrew men and women working willingly and happily in the fields.[9] *Sallah*, however, undermines the concept of Hebrew labor as a national or collective value.[10] The film's main character is a defiant immigrant who is not positively engaged with Hebrew labor in any stage of the film. The way Sallah relates to work marks him as startlingly different from, for example, the adolescent figures of emigrating Holocaust survivors depicted in early Israeli films.[11]

Sallah indeed begins the film like these young men and women: troublingly idle and fraudulent.[12] However, quite unlike the immigrants in these earlier films, who come of age and replace these traits with a new, distinctively Hebrew diligence and productivity (Gertz 1999, 383), Sallah does not change over the course of the movie and does not seem to suffer for his stubbornness. On the contrary, through its narrative, the film hints at the fact that his "weaknesses" pay off. By the end of the film, Sallah's financial issues, as mentioned before, are solved through his successful pretense that he will vigorously resist any attempt to move his family out of their current home in the transit camp, through which he cleverly manipulates government officials into moving his family to a new, modern flat.

Sallah also integrates its main character into scenes that produce a twisted and grotesque visual equivalent to the Zionist trope of Hebrew labor. There are scenes in the film that could have easily reproduced this trope metonymically, but instead undermine both it and Sallah's Hebrew subjectivity. When Sallah is sent as a day laborer to help the forestation of a hilly landscape, for example, instead of bravely cultivating the land—as early films so often had their characters do in this kind of setting[13]—Sallah evades work and runs away from the planting location as soon as he can. The extreme long shot that ends the scene shows Sallah, who at this point has been fired by the foreman, abandoning his shovel and running jubilantly through the open plowed field toward home.

Furthermore, even the kibbutz members portrayed in the film, those typical representatives of Zionist elites who at that time symbolized for many the perfect example of the new Hebrew human being, are presented as behaving in ways that severely contradict the Zionist ideal of labor. While the trope of Hebrew labor reflects the Zionist ideal of self-sufficiency, in the film, the people on the kibbutz consistently try to persuade other people to do their work for them.[14] The kibbutz secretary goes out of his way to persuade the unwilling Sallah to carry his wardrobe to his new office; a kibbutz member who rides a tractor and seems to be in charge of a farming branch begs the kibbutz secretary to hire a day laborer assistant for him; and the young kibbutz members, Ziggy and Bat-Sheva, do not really work but instead manage the work of others, giving orders and instructions to salaried employees. Finally, instead of working in productive agriculture as the Zionist ethos dictates, kibbutz members are occupied with what the prevailing anti-Semitic discourse views as typical Jewish activities: articulating and interpreting the kibbutz laws and regulations (at the kibbutz's general assemblies), engaging in commercial negotiation (with Sallah, both about the value of his labor and about the value of his daughter), and counting money in Yiddish (not insignificantly, when the secretary counts the money he pays Sallah to "buy" his daughter from him, he speaks in Yiddish, which was connected at this time with a pre-Hebrew Jewish diasporic subjectivity).

Sallah reproduces and degrades also the important Zionist trope of "making the desert bloom." One of the central scenes in the film shows a group of new Jewish immigrants busily planting a pine tree forest on what looks like a deserted piece of land. There are a few twists, however, to this ostensibly straightforward realization of making the desert bloom. First, the government official who sent Sallah to this job makes it sound like a hard labor punishment rather than a profound Zionist duty. Second, the film sequence cuts between long shots depicting the other workers planting the trees as asked and a medium shot of the eponymous protagonist sitting on the ground, his body slack as he ineffectively uses his shovel to slowly dig a hole much deeper than needed, which effectively swallows the seedling—all while humming an Arab tune. Sallah seems to be doing his

Figure 1.1. *Sallah* (1964). Two pre-Hebrew Jews in a closet. The kibbutz secretary (Shraga Friedman) pays Salah (Haim Topol) the dowry fee for his daughter and counts the bills in Yiddish. Photo: Asher Molet.

best to abandon the land, basically returning it to its original condition of neglect. And then, in the course of the work, two couples, both wealthy Jewish American sponsors, separately visit the location. As a government official welcomes each couple, he sets up an official sign with their family name on it and tells each couple in its turn that the area is about to become a forest carrying their name. This act of fraud perpetrated by government officials subverts the integrity of making the desert bloom, revealing it to be an empty phrase, a notion invented largely to squeeze money from wealthy American Jews.

Sallah subverts another tactic used by early Israeli cinema to show its characters' evolution toward acquiring Hebrew subjectivity: linking the characters' degree of control over open space to their level of assimilation into their new Hebrew identity. Instead of using this equation to present its characters as Hebrew, or at least on the road to becoming Hebrew, the film uses the tactic to present its figures as defiantly pre-Hebrew human beings with slight hope of or interest in changing. Sallah is presented both metonymically, by the rhetoric of the cinematic sequence, and through narrative events, as a person who fears open spaces.

One extreme long shot is especially revealing. Here, two party delegations come to bribe him and are searching for an empty place to "close the deal." Sallah, it seems, would prefer to retire to a quiet corner inside the ma'abara, but they put their arms aggressively around his shoulders and lead him, unwilling and fearful—by the nose—up the hill and out of the "closed" transit camp, into the open space of the Israeli countryside. Sallah otherwise leads his life in closed and sheltered locations—the transit camp and the kibbutz yard—which he rarely leaves. The occasions on which Sallah does leave these enclosed spaces and crosses into real open space cause him to become disoriented and end with his disappointment and retreat. In the forestry scene, soon after getting fired, Sallah eagerly departs from this hilly open area. The final, extreme long shot of the scene shows him running from the open space back to the shelter of the transit camp.

Unlike the Holocaust survivors in early Israeli cinema—who sometimes go through a phase of being afraid of open space (Gertz 1999, 390–393)—Sallah's regression to his base instincts, as well as his fear of open spaces, is permanent. While the pre-Hebrew figures of early Israeli cinema aspired to cross over into the open space and control it (a goal usually fulfilled by the film's end), Sallah's wish—also fulfilled—is the opposite: to move to a smaller and more protected space. Ultimately, Sallah longs to replace the relatively large space of the transit camp with a small, stuffy flat in a modern housing complex.[15]

Furthermore, in *Sallah*, the kibbutz members, who represent the Zionist elite, are also presented as pre-Hebrew through particular relationships with space. Shots of the kibbutz secretary and accountant are mainly indoors: in the kibbutz dining room, in their tiny office, in the chicken coop, and even inside a closet. The indoor locations in which these two leaders of the kibbutz operate become stuffier and narrower as the film goes on. This narrowing of their physical surroundings occurs as they move further and further away from Zionist ideology. In the dining room, the widest space of all, the two leaders conduct the kibbutz's general assembly and discuss kibbutz regulations; in the chicken coop, they negotiate the purchase of Sallah's daughter with him—an acute digression from Zionist ideology, to say the least, and inside the closet, the secretary pays Sallah for his daughter and counts the bills in Yiddish—a language connected to the pre-Hebrew Jewish diasporic subjectivity (Kimchi 2013, 164–188).

In early Israeli cinema, the thorny question of subjectivity was even hinted at through the Hebrew accents of its characters.[16] The films used the nonaccented native Hebrew speech of their Zionist Ashkenazi characters to point to their Hebrewness. In *Sallah*, by contrast, with the exception of the two young kibbutz members, Ziggy and Bat-Sheva, all the Zionist elites' representatives speak accented Hebrew that testifies to their immigrant status, hinting at the same time that they are pre-Hebrew in the eyes of the author;[17] these include state officials, political party activists, Sallah's daughter's suitor, the kibbutz secretary, and the kibbutz accountant.

Though all of these details might paint *Sallah* as subversive, the film is shown to have some conservative characteristics too. By casting a Mizrahi as its leading character, *Sallah* ended a period characterized by severe underrepresentation of the Mizrahim in Israeli cinema, but it did not radically change the early Israeli cinema tradition of presenting the Mizrahim as inferior and subordinate to Ashkenazim. Instead, the film maintains and reproduces this hierarchy by creating a dichotomy between modern and premodern figures, keyed to Ashkenazim and Mizrahim, respectively. Sallah and his family are clearly in the latter category; their premodernity is evident in their ignorance and disorientation in the face of modern phenomena—everything from the modern flat and its equipment to Israel's democratic party system and the kibbutz's modern distribution of labor. While visiting his future flat, Sallah seems unaware of what mailboxes are, and he is amazed by the miraculous mechanism of modern water faucets. On Election Day, he proves his total ignorance of the democratic system when he puts the ballots of all the parties who bribed him in his voting envelope.

That Sallah the character clings to a premodern way of life is shown by his belief in superstitions and an extremely patriarchal worldview. He consistently avoids speaking to women and bluntly ignores their status, which is often higher than his. He completely ignores, for example, the kibbutz accountant, although she is his employer; whenever she addresses him, he castigates her by saying that he does not speak to women. Sallah's attitude toward the women in his family is no better. He yells at his pregnant wife, insisting that she bring him a son this time. He sits on the only armchair at home while leaving the footstool to his worn-out, nursing wife and treats his beautiful daughter, Habuba, as a valuable object of exchange. He forbids her to meet up with Ziggy, the poor kibbutz member with whom she is in love, and simultaneously bargains for her bridal price with a much older, wealthier taxi driver.

Birth of the Bourekas | 21

Figure 1.2. *Sallah*. Bat-Sheva (Gila Almagor) at a kibbutz gathering of members—an ultramodern utopian social structure. Photo: Asher Molet.

At the same time, and beyond the heavy irony the film directs toward them, the Ashkenazi Israeli figures embody modernity. The film goes to great efforts to connect the Ashkenazi kibbutz members with modern apparatuses or spaces that metonymically imply their modernity. They are seen eating in a modern dining room, riding a tractor, and working in an ultramodern chicken coop. The Ashkenazi kibbutz members also maintain a hypermodern utopian social structure and hold an enlightened attitude about women, which is emphasized by the high status of the female accountant on the kibbutz and by the (initial) refusal of the kibbutz leaders to negotiate with Sallah on his daughter's price ("Women are not possessions," the kibbutz accountant scolds Sallah). Although a member of the lower middle class, the Ashkenazi urbanite who courts Habuba drives a taxi, and even Sallah's old, poor Ashkenazi neighbor owns a symbol of modernity: a mechanical cuckoo clock that Sallah fears.

In *Sallah*, different types of Ashkenazim represent different levels of assimilation to modernity. The kibbutz members, who represent Zionist

Ashkenazi elites, no doubt rank at the top of the modernity pyramid, while other Ashkenazim seem to be less modern. The taxi driver, who is also studying to be a cantor, appears to cling to a lower rung of modernity. Sallah's Ashkenazi neighbor, who lives in a wooden hut, appears to have no profession (he earns his living from election bribery), sustains a more traditional Jewish way of life (he is seen leaving the camp's synagogue with Sallah), ranks even lower on this modernity pyramid. Nevertheless, these figures are all higher on the modernity pyramid than Sallah and his family.

It cannot be denied that the film includes a remarkably wide range of Ashkenazi figures: kibbutz members from eastern Europe, Sabras, lower-middle-class city people, bourgeoisie of central European origin, newcomers to Israel, and ambitious party politicians. This variety is in sharp contrast to the dearth of Mizrahi characters. Although Sallah is the main character, he and his family are the film's sole Mizrahim, and the viewer learns little about them aside from their ethnic status; it is as if their "Mizrahiness" dictates all their other social and personal characteristics, rendering further elaboration unnecessary.

The result is that *Sallah*, although innovative in crucial ways, simultaneously replicates early Israeli films' ideas about the inferiority of the Mizrahim relative to Ashkenazim and about the higher social status of the Zionist elites relative to other groups of Ashkenazim.

Sallah as an Ideological State Apparatus

Seen against the background of early Israeli cinema's ideological conformism to Zionism, *Sallah* could be considered a revolutionary film. A catalog of the film's traits make it seem almost anarchistic: adopting a few of early cinema's paradigms and cinematic tactics but using them subversively to undermine parts of the Zionist ethos; ridiculing central Zionist utopian spaces and figures, such as the kibbutz and kibbutz members, and presenting both as "pre-Hebrew"; and ending the long years of severe underrepresentation of Mizrahim in Israeli cinema by presenting, for the first time, a Mizrahi character in the lead role. But although *Sallah* erodes the Zionist utopia of Hebrewness presented by early Israeli cinema and implies that this ideal is far from Israeli reality, the film ultimately is neither antigovernment nor anti-Zionist nor even "a-Zionist"; on the contrary, *Sallah* was ultimately a part of the Israeli ideological state apparatus and thus was meant to reproduce and distribute the ideology of the Zionist elites. *Sallah*'s great accomplishment, however, is in heralding a new stage in Zionist discourse, which shifted slightly the desirable image of the Zionist Israeli.

Analyzing the film against the background of early Israeli cinema emphasizes the fact that *Sallah*'s biggest shift from previous films is its divergence from these films' utopian representation of Hebrew subjectivity. The film questions the very possibility of Hebrew subjectivity's existence as an active identity within the borders of Israeli society of its time. Unlike previous films that dealt with immigration to Israel, *Sallah* presents its immigrant hero as a person who is at peace with his original Jewish diasporic subjectivity, which he does not aspire to replace. The film repeatedly tears the Hebrew mask from the faces of the characters who pretend to embody the new Hebrew subjectivity (including such characters as the kibbutz members, who represent mythological Zionist figures), to discover the old Ashkenazi diasporic identity that they still hold underneath it. *Sallah* ultimately alleges that Hebrew subjectivity is not the real identity of the Zionist elite in Israel and that Jewish diasporic subjectivity is still the only real identity of all Jewish immigrants to Israel, including most of Zionist Ashkenazi elites, who are immigrants themselves. This negation of Hebrew subjectivity within the Israeli sphere enables *Sallah* to avoid using the dichotomy of Jewish versus Hebrew as a tactic for character portrayal.

If we look deeper, however, we see that what led *Sallah* to destabilize Hebrew subjectivity was not any revolutionary impulse on the part of the film's writer and director but rather his natural tendency to express his cultural identity and to view the Zionist sphere of his time through its norms, dichotomies, and conflicts. Ephraim Kishon was a Shoah survivor who immigrated to Israel from Hungary in 1949. He was raised in Budapest by Jewish parents who were well assimilated into modern European culture, but he had grandparents who still lived in a remote provincial Jewish shtetl and spoke Yiddish (London 1993, 17). The conflict between modern and premodern diasporic Jewish embodied subjectivities was central to the content of his Jewish cultural identity.[18] One can speculate, therefore, that the modern/premodern Jewish dichotomy in *Sallah* is a reflection of Kishon's experience of a fundamental conflict within the contemporary Jewish community and family.[19]

But *Sallah*—although loaded with Kishon's negation of Hebrew subjectivity and offering a new dichotomy of premodern versus modern—would not have been a successful film if these elements had not matched the deep interests of the Zionist Ashkenazi hegemony of the time. *Sallah* offered a necessary compromise for Israel's elite in a changing cultural and demographic landscape. From the perspective of Israel's Zionist elites, the dichotomy of Jewish versus Hebrew was a perfect means of portraying Israeli society, as long as it was presented in a Zionist utopian way, just as it was presented by early Israeli cinema—a sphere that included very few Mizrahim, if any. This was a cinematic rhetoric that reproduced and distributed the society's hierarchy desired by Zionist elites, emphasizing their pedigree over other groups in Israel. It stressed the superlative status of Sabras of Ashkenazi origin and veteran Zionist Ashkenazi Hebrew speakers, who made up the Zionist elite; it also subordinated non-Zionist Ashkenazi immigrants who spoke Yiddish and were still struggling with their Jewish diasporic subjectivity.

This cinematic rhetoric ceased to be effective, however, when the movies, which by the early 1960s began to be commercially financed through box office returns rather than subsidized by the state,[20] could no longer ignore the huge potential Mizrahi audience (about 40 percent of the population at the time). The film industry was obliged to give a larger place to Mizrahi characters. The problem was that in shaping these Mizrahi characters, Israeli filmmakers could not dodge the fact that in contemporary Israeli society, some of the Mizrahim were obviously more "Hebrew" than most of the new, non-Zionist Ashkenazi immigrants.[21] Furthermore, certain Mizrahim were even more advanced in their assimilation of Hebrew subjectivity than some members of the Zionist elite.[22] Under these new terms, a dichotomy based on assimilation to Hebrew subjectivity could not have reproduced the hierarchy desired by Zionist elites. On the contrary, sticking with this former dichotomy could have led to a film in which the Mizrahi figures ranked higher in the cultural hierarchy than members of the Zionist elite and Ashkenazi non-Zionist immigrants. The Eurocentric Zionist hierarchy pyramid could not bear this negation.

Three reforming strategies were available: this dichotomy could be abolished, the essence of Hebrew subjectivity could be changed so that Ashkenazi Zionists could be seen as more assimilated than Mizrahim, or a new dichotomy could be invented—one that differentiated between the various Israeli Jewish figures so that the Zionist's desired hierarchy would be reproduced. Remarkably, *Sallah* uses all three strategies.

Sallah abolishes the dichotomy Jewish vr. Hebrew by representing Hebrew subjectivity as a phantom. The film hints at the idea that Hebrew subjectivity is an imagined subjectivity, one that simply covers over the Jewish

Figure 1.3. *Sallah*. A dichotomy between premodernity and modernity. Sallah (Haim Topol) and the social worker (Gila Almagor). Photo: Asher Molet.

Ashkenazi diasporic subjectivity secretly remaining underneath. However, this same presentation stresses a notion that is even more desirable to the Ashkenazi Zionist elite; it changes the content of Hebrew subjectivity and promotes the belief that Hebrew subjectivity cannot be acquired without having a fundamental layer of Jewish Ashkenazi diasporic subjectivity underneath it so that, at its heart, Hebrew subjectivity is the natural extension of Ashkenazi Jewish diasporic subjectivity and cannot be achieved by people who lack an Ashkenazi cultural background. On top of this, *Sallah* also replaces the Jewish-versus-Hebrew dichotomy with a binary of modern versus premodern. By characterizing its Jewish Israeli characters according to their levels of assimilation to modernity and their relationship with it, *Sallah* reproduces the hierarchy desired by the Zionist elite. Although mocked in the film because of their camouflaged Jewish diasporic subjectivity, kibbutz members and Ashkenazi Sabras (who represent Zionist Ashkenazi elites) are presented in *Sallah* as ultramodern; Ashkenazi new immigrants are less modern; and Mizrahim, like Sallah and his family, by contrast, are entirely premodern.

Sallah—the First Bourekas Film

Sallah was not the first Israeli film to pit modernity against premodernity. This dichotomy was already in use in early Israeli cinema, but there it was used to distinguish between Jews and Arabs. The source of this dichotomy was colonial orientalist discourse, which dictated the portrayal of the Arab as either a noble savage (as in the film *They Were Ten* [1961]), or as an oriental object, an inseparable part of the oriental landscape (as in *Oded the Wanderer* [1933]).[23] However, the hero of *Sallah* seems to be only insignificantly inspired by colonial discourse. This character—created by a cinematic author who embodies a Jewish diasporic identity—is neither a noble savage nor an oriental object; he is very much alive and very Jewish. His portrayal echoes the characteristics of the traditional diasporic Jew, according to prevailing European anti-Semitic discourse. His premodernity, in other words, is distinctively Jewish.

When compared to early Israeli cinema, *Sallah* appears subversive and highly critical toward Israeli Zionist elites, revealing their hidden pre-Hebrew Jewish diasporic subjectivity and revealing their partial implementation of the Zionist ethos and partial assimilation to its values. A deeper look, however, reveals that *Sallah*—much like early Israeli cinema before it—functions as an ideological state apparatus in the service of Zionist elites. *Sallah* is ultimately not subversive and does not reflect a decline in the authority of Zionist ideology or in the power of Zionist elites.[24] Instead, the film evidences an adjustment made by Zionist elites as a response to changes in Israeli society: dictating the replacement of Hebrewness with modernity as a central Zionist value. From this perspective, *Sallah* marks a turning point in Israeli film history—a junction at which a new Zionist ethos of modernity appears alongside old dogmatic Zionist elements of early Israeli cinema that are represented in a way that twists and undermines the values for which they stand.

Over the following decade, a cycle of folk comedies and melodramas were produced in the long shadow of *Sallah*. Termed *Bourekas*, they are characterized, much like *Sallah*, by vivid representations of Mizrahim as a Jewish premodern community and the Ashkenazi characters as ultramodern. However, these films do not employ the cinematic tactics used by *Sallah* to reproduce a twisted Hebrew subjectivity; in fact, they do not deal with Hebrew subjectivity at all. Instead, they represent a world in which modernity is the sole value and a society in which groups are evaluated solely according to their level of modernity. Since this focus on Mizrahim and their representation as a premodern Jewish community is what distinguishes Bourekas from early Israeli cinema movies, it is necessary to examine and analyze this representation on our way to discovering just what Bourekas films are. The next chapter does exactly that.

2

A THEMATIC ANALYSIS OF BOUREKAS

THE PREVAILING ASSUMPTION AMONG ISRAELI FILM SCHOLARS IS that some Israeli popular film comedies and melodramas constitute a film genre they have named Bourekas, yet no one has sought to seriously define this group or to systematically identify what makes a film a Bourekas film.[1]

The first critiques of Bourekas films appeared in the late 1970s as part of modernist discourse on Israeli cinema.[2] This critique stressed Bourekas films' thematic and aesthetic deviation from the two groups of films that preceded them—the national heroic genre and the bourgeois comedy—and pointed to a link between Bourekas themes and the Zionist ideological arena; however, the critics who took part in this first group generally invoked moral judgments, condemning the Bourekas' unrefined cinematic qualities and what they saw as the ignoble intentions of their cinematic authors.[3]

The way these critics denounced Bourekas films in the 1970s stems from their tendency to examine them in light of the modernist, artistic European cinema of the 1960s, and especially from the perspective of the French New Wave films that they looked up to as ideal cinematic models.[4] The tendency to judge the Bourekas—a group of mostly unpretentious, folk, commercial melodramas and comedies that reflected the popular cinema logic of "documents of wish-fulfillment" (Nichols 2001)—against films that regard cinema as a noble form of art stressed their populist, unrefined features, making them look particularly unattractive.

Hence, the writings of this first group of critics on the Bourekas are characterized by a few aspects that should be reexamined. First, it seems that such a critical approach—having a fixed idea of what a film should be—is a priori judgmental. Reviewers prejudiced in this way might focus on the film's poor fit with the model against which it is being judged and therefore overlook what the film really has to offer; this, combined with an inclination toward moral judgments, made this group extremely hostile to Bourekas. Indeed, it soon happened that the term *Bourekas* became, among this group of critics, a signifier used to label any popular Israeli film that seemed to possess aesthetic and ideological faults.[5] Nissim Dayan (1976) writes about the film *Lupo in New York* (1976), which he considers to be a Bourekas film, "The plot of *Lupo* is so staggering in its idiocy that you do not believe your eyes." He continues, lambasting the film for its stereotypes, "Once again, the worn-out scene returns, of a Moroccan police officer who speaks with a funny accent" (Dayan 1976, 51–52). Yehuda Ne'eman titled his article on Bourekas films "Cinema: Ground Zero" (1979), and Meir Schnitzer (1994, 16), in his comprehensive history, *The Israeli Cinema*, writes with both judgment and irony about the "messy production of ethnic comedies that were called the Bourekas films." As recently as 2001, Moshe Zimmerman (2001, 391) wrote that the appearance of Bourekas films was an outcome of "a vulgarization that was made in one aspect of the Israeli commercial cinema of the mid-1960s."

Apart from accusing the Bourekas of being works of low aesthetic value, modernist critics also condemned them for showing low cultural and moral values. Ne'eman, for example, disregarding popular films' function as cultural products,[6] accuses the Bourekas of manipulation, deceit, and the facilitation of the anesthetization of the citizenry's social criticism. In his article "Cinema: Ground Zero," he attacks the producers of the Bourekas, saying that their sole intention was to betray a delusional worldview and to depict false assurances that class mobility and social climbing were available in Israel at the time and that they were an accessible solution to filmgoers' social and economic hardships.

One can also find a tendency in Bourekas modernist critique to denounce the films as a mere reflection of a non-Zionist, capitalistic ideology. Reflecting the *modernization approach*'s view of Mizrahim as a disadvantaged class collective, these critics somewhat simplistically see the Bourekas through the struggle between opposing social ideologies in Israel of the time.[7] Ne'eman (1979), for example, denigrates the Bourekas as representing a diminution of true Zionist socialist values and spirit, pointing to them as a sign of the penetration of the capitalistic "implementation" spirit into the originally socialist ethical Zionist arena.[8] Ne'eman does not find the Bourekas subversive but believes that they naively mirror degradation in the ideology of the Zionist elites at the time. Their deviation from Zionism's original socialist ideology is therefore, in his eyes, evidence of the decadence of the Israeli Zionist socialist establishment, which by the mid-1960s had abandoned, he feels, true socialist Zionist values.

Nitzan Ben Shaul shares this perspective with Ne'eman, saying that the Bourekas predicted the rise of the capitalist, right-wing Likud Party, which swept the national elections in 1977. However, Ben Shaul refines the judgmental tone of Ne'eman's analysis and regards the appearance of the Bourekas more as a natural cultural evolution than an indication of the Zionist elite's ideological decadence. He also clearly indicates that the echoes of capitalistic ideology in the Bourekas are only part of a larger phenomenon that characterizes Israeli cinema of the time (Ben Shaul 1999).

This first wave, so to speak, of Bourekas critics suggested some fallible Bourekas definitions that leave key films out of the corpus. For Ne'eman (1979), Bourekas are films that intend to flatter their folk spectators by creating stories that falsely promise class mobility and social mobility via interclass marriage in Israel, a definition that leaves *Snooker* (1975)—a prominent Bourekas film in which there is no social mobility via interclass marriage, since the hero marries a girl from his own neighborhood—out of the corpus Ben Shaul suggests a Bourekas definition that leaves out films that aren't comedies (e.g., *Fortuna* [1966], *Salomonico* [1972], and *Kazablan* [1973]) and includes, on the other hand, a wide range of totally different films.[9]

The hostility with which modernist critics regard Bourekas films also prevents them from reaching a comprehensive and persuasive explanation of the films' appeal to the Israeli audience. Their charm, claims Ne'eman, comes from their false promise to Mizrahi filmgoers for social and economic success and social mobility via "intermarriage."[10]

To accept this explanation for the films' success, apart from leaving out such an important film as *Snooker*, one must believe that the Mizrahi audience was, at best, naive and susceptible to persuasion. Research, however, suggests that a significant portion of Mizrahim were politically well aware during this period and were not persuaded by discursive Zionist attempts to present Israeli society as egalitarian and socially fluid. According to Sami Shalom Chetrit (2004, 72–160), for example, in the 1950s the Mizrahim began a political struggle against what they saw as their oppression by the Ashkenazi establishment; this struggle reached its peak during the 1970s, the height of the Bourekas, with the organized protests of the Mizrahi folk movement known as Ha'panterim Ha'shkhorim (the Black Panthers).[11] However, Ne'eman's account is perhaps more problematic due to the fact that the audiences of the Bourekas were not made up entirely of Mizrahim.[12] The question then remains, If the false promise of full assimilation of the Mizrahim into Israeli society was indeed the drawing power of the Bourekas, as suggested, what attracted the Ashkenazim to the Bourekas?

Ya'akov and Nathan Gross's (1991, 258–59) accounting for the popularity of Bourekas differs slightly. They suggest that the attraction of Bourekas lies in the "folklorist magic . . . the folk humor, the typical figures, the food, the prayer, and also the goodness and folk wisdom" (259). However, what they ignore is the fact that the audiences came from at least two distinct ethnic groups (Ashkenazim and Mizrahim), each with its own traditions and cultures. So which group's folklore is really presented in the Bourekas? And why was it attractive to viewers belonging to the other group?[13]

The second group of critics that dealt with Bourekas offered a postcolonial, critical-discursive perspective that sees these films as "texts which echo colonialist viewpoints originally created to justify relationships between the First World and the Third World, and which were reproduced within the Zionist discourse to explain the relationships between Ashkenazim and Mizrahim" (Shohat 1989, 120). Compared to the modernist perspective, postcolonial critique of the Bourekas is free of value or moral judgments. The postcolonial approach also stresses the films' ethnic aspect instead of class struggle, and it sees them as echoing the official Zionist ideology, which it regards as both Eurocentric and orientalist.

Shohat raises some perceptive new points on Bourekas. She claims that Bourekas, like Zionist narratives, use orientalist discourse to define anew the Mizrahi Israelis as inferior to the European Ashkenazi Israelis—Eurocentrism in action. In other words, instead of seeing the Bourekas—as the first group of critics does—as a discursive tool that encourages social escapism,[14] which seeks to convince viewers that the socioeconomic gap between Mizrahim and Ashkenazim is temporary and subject to change, she sees the Bourekas as orientalist texts with the essential mission of convincing viewers that Mizrahim are inherently inferior to Ashkenazim. Chetrit also interprets Bourekas as orientalist Zionist propaganda for Mizrahim, intended to convince them that they are to blame for their low socioeconomic status. For Chetrit (2004, 134), Bourekas are "films in which the Mizrahi figures go from blindness to light, thanks to their Ashkenazi brothers."

Hannan Hever, Yehouda Shenhav, and Pnina Motzafi-Haller (2002) present a slightly different view. They see the films as texts shaped by the modernization approach,[15] which regards Mizrahim as a premodern ethnic group that should be modernized by the state and through contacts with Ashkenazim. The Mizrahim, they claim, are understood through the metaphor of a family; likewise, their progress toward modernity is expressed using the family paradigm: while the first generation of Mizrahi immigrants (the parents) will never achieve modernity, the second generation (their children) will become modern through the new knowledge they acquire in modern Israel and will eventually become a homogenous part of the country (Shenhav, Hever, and Mutsafi 2002, 301).[16]

Orly Lubin also sees an echo of Zionist ideology in Bourekas films but thinks that more relevant than the modernization approach is their resonance with the negation of exile, which refers to Zionist discourse's rejection of all that is considered pre-Zionist and "exilic" in Israeli culture. She claims that all representations of Mizrahim in Israeli cinema (including the Bourekas) are shaped to echo the Zionist demand for all new immigrants to deny their previous, exile-based cultures to assimilate into a new Israeli society. The Mizrahim represented in Israeli cinema repeat—through their journey toward being modern Israelis—the master Zionist narrative of exile and redemption (Lubin 2002, 178).

Shohat is the only scholar of what I call the postcolonial group who attempts to seriously classify the Bourekas as a film cycle. However, despite the tremendous significance of her work in this context, it leaves several issues unresolved. First, perhaps because of the diachronic approach of her study, she does not offer a definitive Bourekas film corpus; nor does she describe the films cinematically. In a relatively late article, she formulates a kind of generic definition that excludes noncomedic films from the Bourekas cycle[17] but, at the same time, presents *Fortuna*, a noncomedic melodrama, as an archetype of Bourekas films (Shohat 1999, 52). One may conclude from this ambiguity—even contradiction—that Shohat sees the Bourekas as a kind of hybrid film genre that combines elements of melodrama and comedy. Nevertheless, she does not clarify what can be interpreted as definitional imprecision.

Shohat insists that Bourekas serve as Eurocentric, orientalist propaganda and that they harshly and specifically denigrate Mizrahim. With that argument, the Bourekas' popularity among Mizrahi viewers is inexplicable: Why would Mizrahim adore films that present them reductively? In response, she suggests that the Mizrahi viewers were entranced by the carnivalesque representation of Ashkenazi figures of authority. To accept this explanation for the Bourekas' success among Mizrahi viewers, however, one must believe that the Mizrahim watched these films selectively, noticing only this aspect while ignoring the degrading ones. Shohat lets this paradox go unexplained.

To summarize, it seems that the main contribution of both schools—modernist and postcolonial critique—to research on the Bourekas is the suggestion that a particular representation of the Israeli lower-class, Mizrahi neighborhood, community, and family is essential to a Bourekas film. Nevertheless, none of these critics has supplied a definition or a definitive corpus of Bourekas; nor have they successfully explained their enormous popularity and commercial success in Israel.

What is now necessary is a full rendering of the boundaries of the Bourekas as a film group and a thematic analysis of the corpus to point out the films' shared features. Partly relying on what previous critics have indicated, but using their concepts more consistently and adding new ones, the efforts to classify that follow move the study toward a comprehensive definition of the Bourekas films and a convincing explanation for their success.

A Bourekas Corpus

Because the Bourekas film group comprises comedies, melodramas, and musicals, it can hardly be approached as a film genre. However, since the Bourekas offer new themes and, what I consider, following the postcolonial perspective, a particular new representation of a Mizrahi community that reflects the ideological and political discourse of the time—and because Bourekas display a fundamental conflict in Israeli society (the Ashkenazi-Mizrahi conflict) and offer a solution—it does indeed constitute a discernible film *cycle* (Schatz 1981, 14–42).

Critics of both schools claim that Bourekas films lost their social function beginning in the middle of the 1970s, and particularly after 1977, when the Likud Party came to power (Ben Shaul 1999; Ne'eman 1999; Shohat 1989). As a result, I have selected 1977 as the last year for the production of such films. Out of about one hundred Israeli films that found their way to the screen during this period,[18] only forty-three of them found an audience larger than 250,000 spectators[19]—a threshold that all Bourekas films meet easily. With that in mind, this study proposes the following corpus of eleven films:

> *Sallah* (*Sallah Shabati*), dir. Ephraim Kishon, 1964
> *Fortuna*, dir. Menachem Golan, 1966
> *Aliza Mizrahi*, dir. Menachem Golan, 1967
> *Katz and Carasso* (*Katz ve'Carasso*), dir. Menachem Golan, 1971

Salomonico, dir. Alfred Steinhardt, 1972
Kazablan, dir. Menachem Golan, 1973
Charlie and a Half (*Charlie Va'hetzi*), dir. Boaz Davidson, 1974
Snooker, dir. Boaz Davidson, 1975
Rabbi Gamliel (*Hacham Gamliel*), dir. Joel Silberg, 1975
You Can Work It Out, Salomonico (*Yih'ye Tov, Salomonico*), dir. Alfred Steinhardt, 1975
The Tzanani Family (*Mishpahat Tzanani*), dir. Boaz Davidson, 1976

Due to what I see as the lack of clear definition and lack of consistency, previous critics consider some other films that are not listed in this corpus to be Bourekas; however, they have specifically categorized all of the above as such. Moreover, a substantial group contained within this corpus consists of films that previous critics see as Bourekas classics—movies that can serve as templates for other Bourekas films or best demonstrate the group's essential characteristics.[20] These include *Sallah* (*Sallah Shabati*), which critics regard as the most archetypical of the Bourekas films; *Fortuna*, which Shohat (1999) describes as archetypical Bourekas for its orientalist motifs; and *Katz and Carasso* (*Katz ve'Carasso*), which, according to Ne'eman (1979), best demonstrates the "social escapism" of Bourekas.

In addition, the corpus includes films by Boaz Davidson, whom critics consider the prime Bourekas director:[21] *Charlie and a Half* (*Charlie Va'hetzi*), *Snooker*, and *The Tzanani Family* (*Mishpahat Tzanani*).

Bourekas' Representation of Mizrahim

The Bourekas' most typical innovation, as it emerges from the analysis of *Sallah* (see chapter 1), is a particular and stylized representation of the Mizrahi protagonist, neighborhood, community, and family as Jewish premodern entities. Thematic features of Bourekas will thus be found through an analysis of this representation in the films.

Regarding what can be termed *the paradigmatic representation of Mizrahim in Bourekas films*, one might begin with the fact that the Bourekas represent the Mizrahi neighborhood as an isolated place. A few cinematic strategies back up this choice. First, the films avoid identifying the extratextual rural locations in which the stories take place. In *Sallah*, for instance, it isn't clear where the ma'abara (transit camp) in which Sallah lives is located. Similarly, in *Rabbi Gamliel*, the moviegoer cannot glean enough data to locate the town where the heroine lives in the extratextual sphere of Israel.

In addition, when it comes to the urban context, the cinematic authors make efforts to disguise the extratextual locations of the Mizrahi neighborhoods, preventing conclusive recognition. In *Charlie and a Half*, although the film was shot in the Shabazi neighborhood of south Tel Aviv, the cinematic author makes sure that well-known symbols of Tel Aviv (the Shalom Tower, the promenade, the shoreline, etc.) are not a part of the cinematic text; this is true also for cinematic representation of the Mizrahi urban neighborhoods in *Kazablan*, *Snooker*, *The Tzanani Family*, and *Salomonico*.

Second, the cinematic authors of Bourekas make sure that the Mizrahi neighborhood is perceived as disconnected, or at least far away, from other places. As for the rural locations, in *Sallah*, the ma'abara is surrounded by fields and open spaces, giving the impression that it is located somewhere far from Israel's large cities. In *Rabbi Gamliel*, the fact that the town is located near a quarry gives the impression of a rural, disconnected, isolated place.

Regarding Bourekas' urban locations, efforts are made to present the Mizrahi neighborhood as cut off from other sections of the metropolitan area. Tel Aviv is a relatively small city—one can walk or bike almost everywhere—yet in *Charlie and a Half*, it is obvious that in order to reach neighborhoods that are more "urban" than that of the Mizrahi protagonist (e.g., the city center) or, rather, more upscale (e.g., Charlie's Ashkenazi girlfriend's neighborhood), one needs to use a car.

The feeling that the Mizrahi neighborhood is disconnected from the rest of the world is created also by an architectural distinction between the Mizrahi neighborhood and the spaces around it. In *Sallah*, the architecture of the ma'abara is quite different than the housing complex to which Sallah finally moves or that of the nearby kibbutz. In *Charlie and a Half*, the dusty half-urban streets of the Mizrahi neighborhood are different than the city streets and the trim, orderly streets of Charlie's girlfriend's neighborhood.

The spatial disconnection of the Mizrahi neighborhood is backed up by the disengagement of authorities, since the filmic Mizrahi neighborhood is a place in which the authorities rarely appear. Although school-age children live in most of the neighborhoods, no schools are ever visible in the films, and although the residents are obviously impoverished, social workers or welfare agencies are seldom seen.[22] No one in the neighborhood is employed by the government or municipality.[23] Under the ministrations of the cinematic authors, Bourekas neighborhoods are worlds unto themselves, ignored by the authorities and alienated from society at large.[24]

The absence of law enforcement in the neighborhood is especially stark, considering the amount of crime depicted. Under the circumstances, it would make sense for the police to patrol the neighborhoods day and night. However, this is not what the films represent. In *Charlie and a Half*, although the criminal activity of the residents is obvious, the police are not around.

Salomonico also depicts a scene in which the police are absent—despite circumstances demanding their presence. Even when the wife of the protagonist, Salomonico (Reuven Yotam), explains that the escalating level of crime is their reason for wanting to leave the neighborhood, there are still no policemen in sight. Salomonico, who stands up to the crooks and felons who threaten his family, considers his solitary struggle against them to be natural, and the police don't enter the equation.

When the authorities' agents finally do appear in the Mizrahi neighborhoods of the Bourekas, their alienation and estrangement is very apparent. For instance, in *Sallah*, the social worker causes a big disturbance when she appears in the ma'abara. In *Kazablan*, when the lone municipal clerk comes to the neighborhood to prepare the papers for the destruction of the residents' homes, they unite against him.

The hostility between the Mizrahim and the authorities leads to an implicit contest between the two sectors, in which the members of the community usually have the last word. Time and again, the authority's officials, who are portrayed as incompetent, are tricked by the Mizrahi residents. In *Sallah*, the housing ministry's clerk is dumbfounded when facing the bogus strike that Sallah organizes as if they are against the evacuation of the transit camp's residents ("No housing complex! We want the ma'abara!").

In *Katz and Carasso*, Carasso's son manages to fool Mr. Yisraeli, a corrupt government official with an excessive sexual appetite: Carasso's son gets the contract from him by taking advantage of his weaknesses and making the most of his dubious character.

Maybe as a result of its disengagement from authorities, the Mizrahi neighborhood of the Bourekas suffers from neglect and a low level of configuration; "configuration" here indicates the amount of energy invested in the surroundings beyond the most basic level necessary for functioning. From the caustic remarks of previous critics, it seems that they are not satisfied with the way Bourekas show the space of the Mizrahi neighborhood. Ne'eman (1979, 20) blames the Bourekas, saying that in their reels, "reality is captured in its crudest form." Shohat (1989, 135) remarks that the shooting locations in the Bourekas films were, in fact, poverty-stricken neighborhoods, and Dayan (1976, 56) says that the Mizrahi neighborhood looks like an exilic Jewish "ghetto." But since the manipulation of space is a fundamental feature of the cinematic language, it can be difficult to distinguish between set construction in situ and the cinematic treatment of the set by the author. Previous critics have disregarded the difference between the neighborhood as is (as a shooting location) and its metonymic presentation by the cinematic sequence; they respond only to the low level of structure of the chosen Bourekas locations. However, authors of Bourekas also stress the empowering effects of low configurations throughout their cinematic rhetoric and style.

Indeed, the residential locations that were chosen for the Mizrahi communities in Bourekas are a mess. The streets of the ma'abara in *Sallah* are unpaved, and the inhabitants live in wooden huts or sheds.[25] In this atmosphere of neglect, animals roam the streets; chickens, and even a white goat, can be seen wandering around. The neighborhood in *Charlie and a Half* also suffers from underdevelopment, neglect, and a lack of cultivation. The streets are unpaved, there are dirt roads and gravel, and chickens roam around and peck at the dust. The neighborhood has no greenery, vegetation, or trees—never mind a bench, an electric pole, fences, or any other street fixtures. The roads aren't paved in *Kazablan*, either, and municipal neglect is apparent everywhere, with the neighborhood about to be torn down.

However, in all the above-mentioned films, the cinematic authors take the neglect of their locations one step further by using cinematic strategies that stress the chaos in the neighborhood. Cinema is essentially a tool of rhetoric placed in the hands of the cinematic author, who reconstructs certain spaces through the cinematic sequence, in which signifiers (functioning as indexes and informants) function to locate the fictional space in "real" time and space, while indicating the particular, unique nature of this space.[26] So even if the location filmed is chaotic, ugly, neglected, and distorted, the rhetoric of cinema gives the author a way to make it appear harmonious and ordered. In the Bourekas, however, the cinematic authors do not make use of the cinematic apparatus for harmonizing and ordering the locations but, on the contrary, use it to make the locations appear worse than they actually are.

While the selection of shooting locations in Bourekas seems to be motivated by the choice of low-level configuration by cinematic authors, on the level of the smaller units of cinematic syntax, the same motivation leads to

Figure 2.1. *Kazablan* (1973). A semiruined neighborhood. All's well that ends well: Kazablan (Yoram Gaon, center) is honored with godparents. Photo: Assa Dovrat.

the specific use of cinematic apparatuses; composition, positioning of cameras and their movements, lighting, and editing all serve to complete the neglectful picture offered by the shooting locations.[27] In *Sallah*, the author accomplishes this by offering a contrasting analogy between the ma'abara and the nearby kibbutz's representation, stressing the former's low level of configuration. The kibbutz is filmed using extreme long shots,[28] and the structures in the composition are sparse, emphasizing the spaciousness and greenery of the rural area,[29] as well as the high level of configuration in this space. The ma'abara, on the other hand, is filmed with "closed," dense shots that leave no room for nature in the margins or the depth of the composition. This representation casts the ma'abara as a hybrid space that is half urban and half rural, and points to its underdevelopment, neglect, and low level of configuration. The rustic elements and the sheds' slanted roofs, à la eastern European architecture, cannot save the ma'abara from its presentation as a slum.[30]

In *Kazablan*, the cinematic author worsens the chaotic appearance of the location he uses for the Mizrahi neighborhood by opening the film with an establishing extreme long shot that shows the neighborhood as practically destroyed, exposing its severe state of cultural and material deterioration. Right at the beginning of the film, the viewer meets the image of an entity facing extinction so that one's first impression is molded by the neighborhood's impending destruction.

As in photography or painting,[31] a classic composition in cinema is one in which the various elements harmonize. Accordingly, the choice of the character's zone of action is not capricious but, in fact, the result of aesthetic considerations that are aimed at creating a harmonious balance between all the elements that compose the shot. The compositions created by the cinematic authors in the Bourekas, on the other hand, appear to be random and arbitrary. In these compositions, action is the only formulating criterion; all the other aesthetic elements in the design of the space are disregarded. The outcome is a variety of seemingly negligent compositions that are unflattering toward the space they portray; through this, Bourekas' cinematic sequences stress Mizrahi neighborhoods' less appealing aspects and emphasize their underdevelopment, impoverishment, and decline. This is done even when the reductive presentation opposes the dramatic requirements of the scene.

For example, *Charlie and a Half* includes a dramatic scene in which Charlie and his friend Miko (an eleven-year-old) bully a driver and try to take his money. The scene is filmed with a handheld camera that pans quickly from one character to the other, accentuating its own presence while at the same time defying the scene's dramatic requirements. Furthermore, the compositions produced by the handheld camera are arbitrary and unbalanced, bringing out the ugliness, disharmony, and neglect of the Mizrahi neighborhood. *Snooker*'s filming techniques are just as chaotic: to make the audience believe that the twins Azriel and Gabriel (played by the same actor, Yehuda Barkan) are really two different people, the cinematic author would ordinarily make careful use of his shooting technique.[32] Yet here he chooses the simpler, cruder option of cutting between shots of the actor dressed in the other character's costume, producing momentary disorientation for the viewer—thereby echoing the chaotic, indigent, decadent, and disoriented nature of the world in which the characters live.

The authors of Bourekas are not cinematically incompetent; they adopt this strategy because it serves their intentions. The production teams were able to turn even the prettiest shooting locations into unconfigured spaces of neglect and ugliness. In Golan's *Katz and Carasso*, for example, the Mizrahi neighborhood is not the shooting location of the film. Instead, Katz and Carasso, the film's main characters, who are relatively well off, have nice-looking homes and luxurious offices; another main location of the film is Eilat's beach, which is resplendent with natural beauty. But the language of decline, ugliness, and low-level configuration makes its way into the film through the muddled organization of the cinematic sequence; these camera and editing decisions turn the film into a typical Bourekas production. Even the most romantic scene—on the beach in Eilat, with its stunning mountains in the background—has a low level of configuration and an atmosphere of chaos and neglect. The frame immortalizing the first kiss between Carasso's son (Yehuda Barkan) and Katz's daughter (Efrat Lavi) includes an enormous rusty tanker in the background, and the extreme long shot of the entire bay moves quickly into a medium shot that zooms in on the kissing couple.[33] This camera movement is unnerving as well as stomach turning for the viewers.

The use of low-level configuration, as well as signifiers (indexes) that give the impression of ugliness and decline, is typical of all the Bourekas films. Even those that avoid the representation of the Mizrahi neighborhood (such as *Katz and Carasso* or *Aliza Mizrahi*) use aesthetic decisions to resonate metonymically with the chaos, disorientation, decline, and neglect that characterize the spatial aspects of the Mizrahi neighborhood. In other words, although the shooting locations do not naturally have a low level of configuration and are not neglected, they are fashioned to appear that way via the cinematic author's rhetoric.

Another characteristic of the neighborhood space represented in Bourekas is its representation as a "hybrid" entity—between rural and urban. In *Charlie and a Half* and *Snooker*, the cinematic presentation of the neighborhood as both rural and urban is especially apparent. In both, the small ground-floor houses and unpaved streets, as well as the chickens that roam around, give a rural impression, while the crowdedness and neglect indicate urban slums. A similar hybrid representation can be found in *Sallah*, where the ma'abara is presented through the same cinematic rhetoric. The authors of all three films also give a rustic, east European look to the Mizrahi neighborhood. In *Sallah*, the huts typically have sloping roofs, and even in the more urban *Charlie and a Half* and *Snooker*, both heroes live in east European-style stone houses with sloping red roofs. An amazingly relevant historical fact in this sense is that the film *Two Kuni Lemel* (1968),

Figure 2.2. *Sallah*. The transit camp as a hybrid entity between the rural and the urban. Children in a transit camp in the company of a goat. Photo: Asher Molet.

featuring a historical east European Jewish shtetl of the nineteenth century, was filmed on the set that was used for *Sallah*'s ma'abara four years earlier.

A competitive atmosphere is indeed an important feature of the Mizrahi community's representation in the Bourekas.[34] Although the competitiveness is not exclusively attributed to the Mizrahi characters, it is perceived to be one of the key characteristics of this sector and is a central theme in these films. As opposed to what earlier critics implied, competition in the Bourekas films isn't limited to a struggle over sources of income and socioeconomic status between sectors, classes, or collectives; it has a more profound meaning. Competitiveness is indeed a way of life.

The isolation of the Mizrahi neighborhood created a crowded and confining world that offers only limited sources of income. The struggle for survival forces the residents to take part in ruthless competitions over anything that represents or could produce affluence: money, power, women, billiards, cleverness, knowledge, beauty, masculinity, and a talent for manipulating

Figure 2.3. *The Tzanani Family* (1976). Romantic competition in the neighborhood. Margalit, the seductive neighbor (Geula Noni)—the object of the joint courtship of the men of the neighborhood. Photo: Yoni Hamenachem.

others. Vicious, endemic competition in the Bourekas films can surpass financial boundaries and is clearly much more than a business competition.

In *Katz and Carasso*, survival demands that the characters both insurance agents engage in ongoing and ruthless competitions that go against the rules and confuse the boundaries between the business and family spheres. In *The Tzanani Family*, the financial competition between the Tzananis' and Na'ims' shoe shops involves a sexual aspect that intensifies it. Both Yisrael Ben-Na'im (Yosef Shiloah) and Tzion Tzanani (Gabi Amrani) woo the attractive neighbor Margalit (Geula Noni), while the competitive atmosphere is reinforced by overcrowding, as the two family shops are positioned side by side. Financial and materialistic competition turns into a fierce obsession in *You Can Work It Out, Salomonico*—a story about greedy sons who want to sell their elderly father's apartment—poisoning Salomonico's family life. The sons are too preoccupied with the competition to notice their father's situation, that is, to see that he is wasting away in his loneliness; they don't pay attention to him, and he is left devoid of dignity.

In some of the films, conflicts regarding matchmaking and finding a mate are represented as a competitive urge, as when two characters

Figure 2.4. *Katz and Carasso* (1971). Business competition that flows into all areas of life. The owner of the Katz insurance agency (Shmuel Rudansky) and his daughter (Nitza Shaul). Photo: Assa Dovrat.

compete over the same potential mate or when one character attempts to improve his or her financial standing through marriage. In *Fortuna*, two men compete over Fortuna (Ahuva Goren), a beautiful young woman from Dimona, a town in the Israeli desert. The rivalry is between Simon, an old man from Marseille (to whom Fortuna was promised by her father), and Pierre, a French engineer who took a job at the Dead Sea Works and falls in love with Fortuna. However, this is not only a romantic competition but, as it seems, these two men are symbols—one of a Near Eastern culture and the other of a west European culture—Competition between them implies a competition for domination and affluence between the two cultures at large. In *Rabbi Gamliel*, an Ashkenazi engineer, Uzi (Dov Freedman), faces a dilemma when two women compete over his affections: Dina, the gentle, silent, sensual Mizrahi woman, and Ilana, the aggressive, vulgar, yet educated and wealthy Ashkenazi woman. In *Fortuna*, the competition between East and West is unresolved and ends in Fortuna's death, but *Rabbi Gamliel* has a classic, rosy Bourekas ending: the engineer chooses Dina, the Mizrahi woman.

Competing for a woman is layered over other spheres of competition in *Snooker*. For example, the fact that Gabriel and Azriel swap identities while courting the rabbi's daughter Yona (Nitza Shaul), turns a major part of the film into a dramatic sequence that has at its core a contest between the two brothers over courting skills and masculinity and of course there is the competition between Azriel and Moshon for Yona. Competition also penetrates the smaller units of *Snooker*'s cinematic sequence. One of the most famous scenes revolves around a competition between Moshon, the nephew of Salvador (the mighty gangster), and Gabriel, when they are tested on their knowledge of the Hebrew Bible by the neighborhood rabbi, Yona's father.[35]

Charlie and a Half seems to be the film in which the cinematic author (Davidson) brings the motif of out-and-out war to its peak. The strong competitive atmosphere is created by a blend of various kinds of competition that are combined on different levels of the film's discourse. First, there is the traditional competition over a woman, where Charlie—a charismatic, charming, and libidinous young man who is poor, Mizrahi, and involved in petty crime and gambling—competes with Robert, an overweight, unattractive, and asexual Ashkenazi American nerd who is cultured, rich, and musically educated. Their "prize" is a beautiful, wealthy Ashkenazi woman named Gila, the daughter of a wealthy merchant. However, as in other Bourekas films, the rivalry also has additional aspects. Their competition also centers on prestige and financial status. Since Charlie is so poor and ignorant, this aspect is especially crucial: it is the only way he can attach himself to affluence. As in other films, this competition is also metonymic for the implicit competition between the Ashkenazi (Robert) and Mizrahi (Charlie) sectors. At the same time, there is yet another sphere of competition in the Mizrahi neighborhood depicted in the film: the competition between Sasson, the neighborhood bully, and Charlie (the protagonist) over control of the petty crime in the neighborhood and a contest over manhood (a car race that puts their masculinity to the test). Additionally, there is a secret competition over Charlie's attention between Miko, his eleven-year-old friend and "business" partner, and Gila, Charlie's girlfriend. The competition ends with Gila's triumph over the child, as Miko leaves the country for America with tears rolling down his cheeks.

The inhabitants of the Bourekas' Mizrahi neighborhoods live in cramped quarters, a condition that encumbers any individual's attempt to

Figure 2.5. *Charlie and a Half.* Competition for controlling petty crime in the neighborhood—Charlie (Yehuda Barkan) and Miko (David Shoshan) are hiding from Sasson, the neighborhood bully. Photo: Yoni Hamenachem.

secure privacy.[36] The films give the feeling that this imposed togetherness is a limitation that pressurizes the residents and that it is often the source of conflict and individual discomfort.

The ambiguous delineation between private space (the house) and public (the street) is another characteristic of these slums. Inhabitants frequently communicate with each other publicly, either on the street or through open windows, and random onlookers often appear within the residents' private space at critical moments and react to personal affairs, blatantly disregarding their right to privacy.

In *Sallah*, for instance, when a social worker arrives to question him about his personal life, the two naturally look for a place where they can have some privacy. However, where they end up—Sallah's shed backyard—is instantly invaded by ma'abara residents. Although the conversation becomes more and more personal, and although Sallah is noticeably bothered by the onlookers' presence, the residents continue to eavesdrop. They overtly and shamelessly watch Sallah and even react with scornful laughter when Sallah's ignorance is exposed in the course of the conversation. This motif of imposed togetherness and voyeurism reaches its peak with the help of a goat; the presence of an animal among the nosy onlookers gives the whole scene a farcical tinge.

In *The Tzanani Family*, the blurred borders between private and public are particularly apparent. The neighborhood's residents regularly communicate through their open windows and spy on each other from their windows and balconies. Walking home, Yisrael watches Mrs. Tzanani (Levana Finkelstein) through the window while she works in her kitchen. The beautiful neighbor, Margalit (Geula Noni), spies on Tzion Tzanani (Gabi Amrani), the main character, as well as on Yisrael's house from her balcony, and they peep back into her house.[37]

The exhibitionism and the residents' tendency to take their personal conflicts into the street—thereby bringing them into the public realm of the neighborhood and inflicting them upon the whole community—complete the tendency to mix the private and public spheres in the Bourekas neighborhoods and solidify the atmosphere of imposed togetherness. In *The Tzanani Family*, for example, private conflicts invade the public sphere. When Yisrael's wife sees her husband excitedly flirting with Margalit, the pretty neighbor, her response is to call her husband angrily—at the top of her voice—to come home. This kind of situation, involving the whole neighborhood in personal matters—in this case, Yisrael's unfaithfulness and his wife's resentment of it—recurs throughout the film. The sheer number of witnesses to these scenes of jealousy is a preoccupation of the film: neighbors peek out of their windows and balconies and delight in doing so.

There is an almost identical incident in *Charlie and a Half*. In the opening sequence of the film, Sasson's wife scolds him from the open window after catching him looking at a younger woman's derrière; in this scene, too, the shouting and the scolding are in the presence of neighbors, among them Sasson's chief rivals.

In *Aliza Mizrahi*, the cinematic author (Golan) takes the phenomenon of bringing the conflicts into the public realm to a crescendo. While Aharon (Aliza's husband) sits idly on the street near his home, Aliza (Edna Fliedel)

Figure 2.6. *Charlie and a Half.* Tendency to live on the street. Gedaliah (Moshe from Kassit) and Sasson (Ze'ev Revach) along with Charlie (Yehuda Barkan) and Miko (David Shoshan) at the entrance to the neighborhood café.

shouts at him from the thirtieth floor of a tower in Tel Aviv, accusing him of slacking off and ordering him to get back to work. The preposterousness of Aharon sitting on the street, the distance between him and Aliza, and the busy commercial center in which the scene takes place intensifies the distorted behavior. Across the Bourekas cycle, the recurrence of this absurdist pattern—taking personal conflicts to the public—brings to mind the possibility that it fulfills a certain function. In the *Tzanani Family*, *Charlie and a Half*, and *Aliza Mizrahi*, sharing one's insults with the public does, in fact, tend to impel the community to put pressure on the partner who has gone astray.

With this mentality of no privacy, it may be no surprise that gossip flourishes. Everybody knows everything about everybody else in these neighborhoods, and many people use that information either to embarrass others or to advance their own interests. In *Charlie and a Half*, Charlie knows about Sasson's infertility problems because his mother, Flora, with whom Sasson is consulting on this problem, tells him about it. In *Snooker*, Halfon (Arieh Elias), the neighborhood drunk, knows about Salvador the American mobster; he is familiar with his extraordinary talent for snooker and his toughness in "business" matters. In *Sallah*, the cab driver knows about Sallah's financial difficulties and his daughter's romance with Ziggy, the kibbutz member; he also knows that Sallah disapproves of the relationship and exploits this information to try and secure his consent to a marriage proposal he himself would like to make to Sallah's daughter. In *Salomonico*, Allegra (Etti Grottes), Salomonico's wife, knows everything about the neighbors and the places they have moved to. She uses this information to fuel her husband's competitive instincts to encourage him to buy a new house in a different neighborhood.

The threat of using gossip for material success or for overtaking rivals in the financial competition is always imminent in these films. Knowing about Mr. Yisraeli's excessive sexual appetite serves both sides fighting over him in *Katz and Carasso*, when each offers him a kind of sexual fantasy in return for his services. Similarly, in *Salomonico*, the protagonist uses the information he has about the high salaries of the senior officials at the Ashdod port to help him obtain a loan for an apartment from the ports' authority.

In the Bourekas neighborhoods, idleness, laziness, and avoiding productive work are all manifestly presented as characteristics of the men and women in the Mizrahi community.[38] It is made quite clear, for instance, that Sallah Shabati does not like to work. The film depicts him as more willing to try to make something out of virtually nothing than to accept the forestry job offered him. Instead, he occupies himself with questionable pursuits—such as selling stray dogs[39]—or even pimping his daughter for a dowry.[40] To make some extra money, he takes advantage of his Ashkenazi neighbor's lack of expertise in backgammon and bamboozles him out of a large sum of money. Finally, Sallah shows himself to be a real panderer when he pledges his loyalty in return for money to each of the various parties running in the general election. Idleness is fundamental to his character and is not a result of the hardships of living in the ma'abara. We know this because Sallah is puzzled when the government clerk asks him what his occupation is, thereby giving the impression that he never, not even in his native land, had an occupation or a job.[41]

In later Bourekas films, the Mizrahi protagonists still don't have productive jobs or engage in occupations that benefit society. Instead, they just laze around and try to make something from nothing via questionable pursuits. An example is *Rabbi Gamliel*. There the eponymous rabbi (Yossi Banai) makes his living from some sort of "practical" kabbalah (fortune-telling based on mystical Jewish knowledge) while his adult daughter, Dina

(Aviva Ger), serves coffee to her father's clients and has no real paying job. Indeed, his son works as an engineer in a quarry, but he no longer lives in the neighborhood. By contrasting these family members, the cinematic author insinuates that the brother's outstanding diligence is the reason that he left the neighborhood.

Even when a neighborhood's Mizrahi residents do have official occupations, the Bourekas directors make it very clear that these folks are always happy to avoid doing their jobs; work is unnatural for them. Aliza Mizrahi works as a cleaning lady at the police station, but instead of keeping herself busy with her real job, she spends her time gossiping and investigating a mysterious murder case that is officially none of her business. The pattern is also evident in *Snooker*: Hanukkah, a waiter in a café, doesn't devote much of his time to his job; instead, he spends most of it with an idler, Gabriel, and collaborates with him on fraud schemes. Azriel, Gabriel's twin, supposedly has a job working at a greengrocer's, but his boss complains about his laziness, tardiness, absentmindedness, and inefficiency, and he is eventually fired.[42] In *Charlie and a Half*, although Ezra (Aryeh Moskona) works as a waiter at the Pe'er (Hebrew for "splendor") Restaurant in the upscale Dan Hotel in Tel Aviv, the film makes it clear that the job is not natural for him. He looks uncomfortable in his fancy waiter's uniform; on the other hand, the film emphasizes, through a contrasting analogy, the fact that Ezra is very much at home in his run-down neighborhood, and he is seen roaming contentedly around the neighborhood in his pajamas and spending time with Sasson, the loafer.

Nonetheless, the neighborhood's many underemployed inhabitants are depicted as having a range of options. Some live at the expense of others. One example is Zachi, Charlie's father in *Charlie and a Half*, who lives off his wife, or Halfon, the drunkard from *Snooker*, who lives on handouts from Gabriel and Hanukkah. But many others make a living from occupations that are on the verge of fraud: fortune-telling (Gamliel in *Rabbi Gamliel* and Flora in *Charlie and a Half*), professional begging (Charlie and Miko in *Charlie and a Half*), petty fraud and borderline-criminal mediating businesses (Sallah in *Sallah*, Charlie in *Charlie and a Half*, and Gabriel and Hanukkah in *Snooker*), and petty crime (Sasson and Gedalia in *Charlie and a Half*).

As portrayed in Bourekas films, the crime and fraud in the fictional Mizrahi neighborhoods do not appear to be very dangerous or sophisticated; it is all mostly very naive criminal activity. Serious crime, such as mob activity, simply doesn't exist in these neighborhoods. The only criminal in the

Figure 2.7. *Charlie and a Half* (1974). Marginalists, idlers, and petty criminals: Charlie (Yehuda Barkan) and his half—the child Miko (David Shoshan). Photo: Yoni Hamenachem.

Bourekas films worthy of his title is Salvador (Yosef Shiloah), from *Snooker*. He has the reputation of a serious and dangerous criminal, and he gains the respect of the protagonists and the police. However, Salvador doesn't live in the neighborhood any longer but in the United States—the country that Shohat identifies as "the biggest dream" of the Mizrahi neighborhood's inhabitants in Bourekas films (Shohat 1989, 135).

The Bourekas depict a Jewish community in which religion has ceased to master the residents' consciousness and remains as an empty superficial shield. Although some Jewish practices, such as kissing the mezuzah (*Charlie and a Half* and *Snooker*), making kiddush on the Sabbath (*Charlie and a Half, Salomonico, The Zanani Family*), and holding a ritual circumcision (*Kazablan*) still persist, and there are talks about God that are integrated into the dialogue of the residents, nobody seems to seriously pray in the neighborhood or visit the synagogue regularly.[43] However, it seems that the most revealing feature of the reduction of religion within the Mizrahi neighborhood is the grotesque in the representation of the neighborhood rabbis and the irony that is directed toward them. In *Snooker*, the rabbi is shown as a fool who is completely clueless about the deception that is all around him. In *Rabbi Gamliel*, the rabbi is presented as poor and backhanded, who practices some kind of witchcraft to make a living.

As happens when there is a reduction of true religious feelings, superstitions crawl in. A layer of general superstition covers the trope of idle, fraudulent, and beggarly neighborhood folk in Bourekas films. Sallah, for instance, says a blessing over his backgammon dice out of the superstitious belief that it will help him get the numbers he wants. He also spits on the ground from time to time, a habit sure to have some sort of mystical significance in warding off the evil eye. *Rabbi Gamliel* is a film that is devoted—at least somewhat—to superstitious issues. The rabbi practices practical kabbalah, counseling that is based on a mystical interpretation of the holy scriptures. At the beginning of the film, we see him predicting the future of a client by reading a certain part of the Old Testament. In *Charlie and a Half*, Flora tells people's fortunes with the help of a cup of coffee and cards; Sasson, the neighborhood gangster, is very superstitious and is one of her regular clients; Charlie's father, Zachi, interprets the healing instructions his wife gives the clients as a sort of "shaman pharmacist"; and finally, the scene in which Sasson goes to the zoo to pluck a single hair from the giraffe's whiskers—to serve as a talisman for sexual potency—is one of the funniest in all the Bourekas movies.

Although Bourekas films represent a non-Orthodox Jewish community, the traditional Jewish way of bringing a man and woman together—the *shidduch* (matchmaking)—is very prominent in some of them. In *Rabbi Gamliel* (whose subtitle can be translated as "Marriage Games"), the narrative revolves around a shidduch for the daughter, which the provincial rabbi, the protagonist, tries to impose on a handsome, well-off engineer. In *Snooker*, the neighborhood rabbi's daughter is offered as a bride through

Figure 2.8. *Charlie and a Half*. Reductive religiosity and superstitions. Charlie's parents, Flora (Edna Fliedel) and Zaki (Arie Elias). Photo: Yoni Hamenachem.

a shidduch. Hence, although in many Bourekas films the relationship between a young man and young woman is at the center of the narrative, an instrumental and very practical view of this bond seems to rule. Most Bourekas films show a community that has not assimilated in terms of romantic ethos and for whom romance is seen as secondary to more basic material needs. *Snooker*'s love affair is partly the outcome of the successful realization of a secret plan by Gabriel, Azriel's twin brother, who, hoping to make money, secretly works behind the scenes to rouse the couple's emotions for one another. Gabriel pairs the two and maintains their romance in order to win eligibility to collect his father's inheritance money. In *Katz and Carasso*, romance is subordinated to business affairs. The romantic relationships between Katz's two daughters and Carasso's two sons begin because of their fathers' business competition; they receive the fathers' blessings only when they realize that the shidduch will benefit business. In the same way, Sallah at first sees his daughter's marriage as a promising business opportunity, and he tries to manipulate both her suitors to pay the highest dowry possible. For him, the romantic needs of his daughter come—if at all—only in second place.

This kind of instrumental view of the male-female bond is such a part of Bourekas communities that individuals who treasure romance are sometimes denounced and punished. In *Sallah*, Habuba, the daughter, is punished by Sallah because of her love for Ziggy, and Ziggy becomes the laughingstock of the kibbutz because of his love for her. In *Fortuna*, the heroine's punishment comes in the form of her tragic death, owing to her love for the French engineer.

The practical approach to romance in the Bourekas is not exclusive to the Mizrahi community. Ashkenazi families in the films live by a similar ethos. In *Kazablan*, the handsome young Kaza (Yehoram Gaon) must compete for the hand of Rachel, a pretty Ashkenazi woman, against the older and much less attractive Yanosh, whose material advantages—a solid profession, being Ashkenazi, and therefore belonging to a higher class—make him more desirable to Rachel's father as a son-in-law. In what is probably the most romantic of the Bourekas films, *Charlie and a Half*, the hero competes for the heart of Gila, a beautiful, young Ashkenazi woman. However, her parents clearly favor over him a shidduch with Robert, the wealthy schlemiel (unlucky bungler).

In Bourekas films that focus on a romance between two young people, the cinematic author prefers to present the courting plot through scenes that carry an inherent conflict between a romantic and an instrumental

Figure 2.9. *Snooker* (1975). Rejection of the romantic ethos. Matchmaking as a preferred option for establishing a relationship. Hacham (Rabbi) Chanukah—the matchmaker (Ze'ev Revach). Photo: Yoni Hamenachem.

Figure 2.10. *Snooker*. A comic reduction to scenes with romantic potential. Azriel (Yehuda Barkan) and Yona (Nitza Shaul) in a courtship that turns into a comedy of errors. Photo: Yoni Hamenachem.

view of the male-female bond. In *Charlie and a Half*, for example, most of the meetings between Charlie and Gila take place in the presence of people who represent an instrumental view of such a bond: their first encounter in the restaurant is in the presence of Robert, Gila's Ashkenazi shidduch; their meeting at the Caesarea golf course is in the presence of Gila's mother and father; and a gathering at Charlie's house is with both families present. In *Kazablan*, even the scene in which Kaza proposes to Rachel is in the presence of her reluctant parents.

Furthermore, when Bourekas films display scenes with romantic potential, they are sometimes constructed in a way that distorts the potentially romantic moments, making them grotesque. In *Snooker*, the potentially romantic setting (Jaffa's ancient port) and scene of Gabriel's proposal to the lovely Yona (Nitza Shaul) are warped beyond repair when Hanukkah, who sits next to the couple pretending to be a fisherman, gives Gabriel loud instructions on what to do during the proposal scene. In *Katz and Carasso*, as seen, the cinematic author highlights the rhetoric of the low-level configuration of the space when the two young lovers kiss for the first time on a beach in Eilat.

Conclusions

As analyzed here, the Bourekas films presented share a particular paradigmatic representation of Mizrahi community, neighborhood, and family. These common features confirm that the films do indeed belong to a distinct cinematic cycle and point to the paradigmatic representation of the Mizrahi community as their central thematic characteristic. The fundamental characteristic of the community representation in Bourekas films is the isolation of the neighborhood; the inhabitants live in a closed, detached cosmos whose connection with local authorities can only be called "estranged." Neglect characterizes the material culture of the Mizrahi neighborhood in the Bourekas corpus. The typical neighborhood is depicted as a poor-looking hybrid place that shares the worst aspects of a city slum and a rural village. This reduction of the material culture is also emphasized by the cinematic rhetoric. Instead of using the cinematic apparatus to elevate the various shooting locations and present them as harmonious, as dictated by film convention, the authors of Bourekas films utilize a low level of configuration on the cinematic sequence, using their cinematic apparatus to reduce the appearance of their sets and characters.

The neglect and seclusion leave the neighborhood with insufficient means of subsistence. This creates, in turn, a social and cultural space with perpetual drawbacks. The Mizrahi community's world, as portrayed in the films, revolves around one central element: competition. This wild contestation for survival and physical subsistence forces the inhabitants to fight over limited sources of material comfort, which means fighting over almost everything. Competition is such a central element of the paradigmatic representation of Mizrahim in this corpus of films that it becomes a significant part of the films' rhetoric. The cinematic authors construct each Bourekas film as a dramatic unit that turns on conflicts of competition on a different level of the cinematic sequence.

The constant dog-eat-dog struggle for survival turns into a reduction of the emotional and spiritual qualities of certain sociological behaviors. Interpersonal human actions that have significance beyond pragmatics—courting, marriage, falling in love, neighborly and work relations—are normally reduced solely to their instrumental functions. Loving or amorous relationships are typically transformed into pairings that have an apparent financial purpose.

Typically, neighborly relations within the Mizrahi neighborhood turn into imposed togetherness, spying, and the mutual violation of each other's private spaces. On the other hand of the blurred borders between the private and the public, an opposing exhibitionistic tendency is presented as a creative, popular way of dealing with the absence of such authorities as police, social workers, and the courts. Residents who expose their private matters can augur the community's sympathies or stir up condemnation for another party, thereby providing solutions for conflicts.

The Bourekas also present a world in which Jewish religion was emptied of its essence and superstitions took over. Rabbis are normally represented as fools (*Charlie and a Half*) or backward (*Rabbi Gamliel*).

In this atmosphere of reduced existence, the value of work is reduced to its instrumental aspects. Productive work is a nonexistent feature in the neighborhood; instead, the residents are middlemen; occupied with begging, fraud, and petty crime; or in deceitful occupations, such as fortune-telling. But the cinematic authors' position is that some of these "occupations" are not reprehensible; as long as people make enough money to live on, they should be applauded, and do-nothings, beggars, and crooks are often the protagonists (e.g., *Sallah, Charlie and a Half, Snooker, Rabbi Gamliel, Aliza Mizrahi,* and *Kazablan*).

Under these circumstances, romantic love is also reduced to its practical instrumental elements, since the Bourekas present a community that did not assimilate the romantic ethos; mates are still found through matchmaking that seems to be motivated by financial needs or at least held in the presence of people with an instrumental view on pairing.

Apart from the described particular and original representation of Mizrahim, there is one more feature common to all films in the Bourekas corpus: they were all made by Ashkenazi directors and producers. In the next chapter, I examine whether this characteristic is essential to a Bourekas film.

3

MIZRAHI SELF-REPRESENTATION FILMS

The Question of Self-Representation

Postcolonial studies indicate that there are various ways in which representation[1] is implicated in power inequalities and the subordination of the subaltern. The representation of subordinated groups, they argue, is biased by ideology (Said 1979, 21) and is unrealistic (Spivak 1990a, 90, 98, 1990b, 63).

Writing about Israeli film, Ella Shohat (1995) addresses what she terms the "power of representation," through which she implies that in a society, the ability of a certain group to represent and be represented is connected to its political power. The problem, she claims, does not rest solely on the fact that marginalized subaltern groups often do not hold the power over representation; rather, it exists also because representations of these underprivileged groups are both flawed and few in number—a difficulty that makes every representation of a subaltern group member highly influential and metonymically representative of the whole group (Shohat 1995, 171). The few representations of subaltern people, she continues, also increase the importance of agency and of the attendant question of who will produce the images of the subalterns—escalating the value of self-representation, a representation of a subaltern group by a subaltern individual.[2]

Shohat regards Mizrahim as an Israeli subaltern group. Discussing their representation in Israeli cinema, she highlights the importance of the fact that Mizrahim are represented in Israeli films through the agency of Zionist ideology and Eurocentric "myths which are prevalent in Israel"—about those whom the Zionist discourse regarded as "Levantines" (Shohat 1989, 119).

Specifically discussing the Bourekas in this context, Shohat underscores the fact that most of the Bourekas films were made by Ashkenazi filmmakers and that Ashkenazi actors played the roles of Mizrahi figures. She regards this denial of the Mizrahi right to aesthetic self-representation in Bourekas as homologous to the denial of Mizrahi rights for self-representation in other areas where the establishment took upon itself to speak in their name—very much like colonial anthropologists, who believe that only they can speak, as a sort of in loco parentis for the "primitives" and the "natives" of the societies they studied. Shohat (1989, 139) highlights the fact that like Ashkenazi politicians, sociologists, scientists, and writers, Ashkenazi filmmakers gave themselves the right to represent Mizrahim, something she views as one of the causes of the stereotypical and distorted presentation of Mizrahim in the Bourekas film cycle.

Orly Lubin (1999) also points to a possible homology between the nature of Mizrahi representation in the Bourekas and the denial of the Mizrahi right to self-representation. She compares their representation in three films by the Mizrahi director Moshe Mizrahi[3] with their representation in Bourekas films by Ashkenazi directors and finds that each group presents Mizrahim quite differently. As opposed to the culturally detached, unrealistic "Mizrahi" culture that is seen in Bourekas films, Lubin claims, Mizrahi life in Moshe Mizrahi's films shows an awareness of a Sephardic cultural past. His films represent a Sephardic folk culture that finds its expression in the characters' intensive use of expressions and sayings. In contrast to their representation in Bourekas films, the community in Moshe Mizrahi's films is shown to be culturally and ideologically cut off from the Zionist history and experience (Lubin 1999, 121).

One more important illustration of the significance of agency in Bourekas films lies in the inner hierarchy of these films as presented by previous critics. Their writings reveal that they label movies that deny Mizrahim self-representation as the archetypal models for the entire film group. Both in *Sallah*, which all critics agree is the "Father of the Bourekas," and *Fortuna*, considered archetypical (at least by Shohat), the Mizrahi protagonists and families at the narratives' center are presented through the agency of Ashkenazi directors, and principal Mizrahi figures are played by Ashkenazi actors. Looking at our Bourekas corpus, one cannot avoid noting the fact that the directors of all the films are Ashkenazim, even though the protagonists and communities depicted are Mizrahim. Taking into account both the fundamental hypothesis of this study—that the director is in effect the author of the film and, as such, the carrier of the film's cultural agency—and the significance of agency to the textual representations of subaltern groups, Ashkenazi subjectivity and agency can be said to typify Bourekas films.

Adopting a postcolonial approach to the Bourekas,[4] I would like to suggest that Ashkenazi cultural agency is indeed a prerequisite for Bourekas films. Furthermore, a Bourekas film is fundamentally characterized by specific paradigmatic representations of Mizrahi neighborhoods, communities, and families, focalized through the subjectivity of a director from an Ashkenazi cultural background. Although the director's identity plays a significant part in it, this is by no means an essentialist definition[5]; it does not relate to the director's race or ethnic origins but rather to his cultural identity. For this study, an Ashkenazi director is one who has a central or east European Jewish cultural background, especially as signaled by a familiarity with or ties to Yiddish language or culture. Often called the "Godfather of Multiculturalism," Stuart Hall suggested that cultural identity supplies the context from which one speaks.[6] That identification stems, on the one hand, from the fact that one was born to a certain family with a certain history and, on the other, from a process of production that never ends, in which one adapts to the knowledge, norms, and representations of a dominant discourse. Adopting these concepts to construct the meaning of the phrase "Ashkenazi cultural agency," I leave open the theoretical option that a Bourekas film could be made by a director born to a Mizrahi family, whose cultural identity was reconstructed through adopting the knowledge, norms, and representations of the Ashkenazi culture that is dominant in Israeli discourse.

In due course, I show that Ashkenazi agency was crucial to the Bourekas in more ways than one. It has not simply caused a distortion in the presentation of Mizrahim through a stereotypical portrayal, or an "othering" of them as an object of knowledge, as Shohat claims. In truth, Ashkenazi agency was responsible for the construction of the metanarratives, main conflicts, figures, ethos, and nature of the universe presented in the Bourekas films. Looking at Israeli popular (or "folk") films that were made during the Bourekas era (1964–1977), we examine the representation of Mizrahim in films that were directed by directors coming from Mizrahi cultural surroundings through the same prism of thematic analysis that we previously used to examine the Bourekas (chapter 2) and underscore their different representation of the Mizrahi neighborhood, hoping to stress the instrumentality and consequences of Ashkenazi cultural agency in making the Mizrahi neighborhood representational paradigm in Bourekas films.

But first, to be able to distinguish between Ashkenazi and Mizrahi Israeli cultures, we must answer the question, What is a Mizrahi culture?

The Evolution of the Cultural Content of the Mizrahi Category in Israeli Academic Discourse

Since my approach to Bourekas involves the effects of Ashkenazi cultural agency on them, this study benefits from distinguishing between Israeli Ashkenazi and Mizrahi cultural attributes. While all Israeli sociological research is, in fact, a study of Israeli Ashkenazi culture—being Israeli hegemonic culture and therefore the "default" one—this is hardly the case with Mizrahi culture. If so, what is Mizrahi culture anyway, and how does it differ from the hegemonic Israeli Ashkenazi culture?

The recent flourishing of Mizrahi poetry from the group that calls itself Ars Poetica,[7] together with a Mizrahi poet, Erez Biton, who won the Israel Prize[8] in poetry, disguises the fact that Mizrahi culture—like the category to which it apparently gives a stage, the Mizrahim—has yet to be defined in Israeli academic discourse. Here I review its evolution, characterizing the cultural content it has absorbed throughout the years.[9]

Before delving into Mizrahi culture or even the term *Mizrahim*, it would be helpful to discuss the more outdated category by which non-Ashkenazi Jews were known: "Sephardic" Jews. Sephardim was originally the name given to members of the Jewish community living in Spain until the end of the fifteenth century. Between the ninth and fifteenth centuries, Spanish Jewry was the largest of all Jewish Diaspora communities, commanding enormous influence over the rest of Jewry.[10] This came to an end after 1492, when Spanish Jews were given an ultimatum by King Ferdinand and Queen Isabella: convert to Catholicism, or leave Spain. Those Jews who chose not to convert to Christianity left Spain and settled in western Europe (Italy, France, the Netherlands, England, Germany), in areas of Europe under the rule of the Ottoman Empire, and in North Africa and the Middle East. While in western Europe they typically assimilated into local Jewry, in many parts of the Ottoman Empire and to a certain extent in Italy—they gradually imposed their traditions and prayer style on the communities they joined, eventually creating the "category" that, by the beginning of the nineteenth century, was known as Sephardic Jewry.[11] This was mainly a religious content category that pointed to certain religious traditions that were different in some ways from the Ashkenazi rituals that prevailed in the Jewish communities of eastern and central Europe and the New World.

In modern Israel, because of the identity politics played by Ashkenazi Zionist elites as colonial rulers of the Israeli sphere, the Sephardim category gradually expanded to include more non-Ashkenazi communities that immigrated to Israel; eventually a category was created that encompassed all Israeli non-Ashkenazi Jews, who were then referred to as Mizrahim. Having at best Jewish religious rituals in common, it was, at first, hardly a cultural or ethnic category—which implies a shared history or culture. But, as suggested here, due to the socioeconomic situation in Israel and the identity needs of the Zionist Ashkenazi elites and of Mizrahim themselves, the category became gradually more and more so with time.

Since Mizrahim are presented in Israeli academic discourse mainly dichotomously—with and against Ashkenazim—some academics have argued that the former is an abstract category artificially formed as a foil (Ben Sasson 1986). This view was supported by anthropological research conducted in the 1980s that found that no Jewish Israelis define themselves as Mizrahim and led sociologists to claim that Mizrahim are "nonexistent" and a "phantom ethnicity" (Avruch 1987, 333).[12]

Setting aside this radical postulation, however, mainstream Israeli academic discourse has shown, over time, a growing tendency toward accepting Mizrahim as a unified ethnic group with particular cultural content. In the early 1950s, Mizrahim were officially perceived through what Shlomo Swirski (1981, 3–75) later called the modernization approach, within which "ethnicness" figured as a premodern form of collective expression, a traditional concept that faded when exposed to modernity.[13] Accordingly, sociologists who shared this approach, such as Shmuel Eisenshtadt, Yossef Ben David, and Karl Frankenstein, viewed Mizrahim as a class collective, defined by the socioeconomic gap they maintained with the Israeli Ashkenazi elites (Ben David 1952; Eisenshtadt 1948; Frankenstein 1957). The Israeli reality in that era supported this perspective, reflecting as it did a complete match between class and ethnic categories, where the sociopolitical elite was composed almost exclusively of Ashkenazim and the working class primarily of Mizrahim (Swirski 1981, 3–75).

Sociologists who advocated the modernization approach typically ascribed no cultural content to the category of Mizrahim, which they referred to as "Edot Hamizrah" (lit. "communities of the East"),[14] a signifier they used to mark what this class collective lacked: modernity, economic means, and effective education and knowledge. In the early 1970s, sociologists who criticized the attitude of the modernization approach awarded Mizrahim de facto recognition as an ethnic group. In his analysis of Israeli society's structure, Sami Smooha (1970, 9) refers to Mizrahim and Ashkenazim explicitly as "ethnic groups"[15]; however, his "pluralistic model approach"[16] basically views Mizrahim through a dichotomy, with Ashkenazim at the other extremity, thereby naturally emphasizing Mizrahi social subordination and the group's apparent deficiencies, which included discrimination directly against them in the distribution of labor. This position still looks at Mizrahim vis-à-vis what they lack, that is, as an "underprivileged group," rather than with respect to any cultural substance they might have in common (Smooha 1970, 2).

The earliest study to attach some kind of cultural content to the Mizrahi category began in the 1950s and was carried out by anthropologists and historians whose attitudes toward Mizrahim Shohat (2001, 148–49) dubbed the "Love of Israel" approach.[17] According to her, these mostly Ashkenazi scholars saw Mizrahim as their lost Jewish brothers or ancient ancestors, and they heaped brotherhood and empathy on them. However, they tended to see Mizrahim through what they have in common with Orthodox Ashkenazim, for example, attributing to them mainly Jewish traditionalist characteristics.

The first Israeli scholar to point out that Mizrahim might indeed have a culture of their own that is not particularly Jewish was Shlomo Swirski. He does not yet attribute a particular nonobservant cultural essence to Mizrahim but anticipates and hopes for the development of such in the future, one that will draw from both the Mizrahi communal diasporic past and their "shared pattern of livinghood and economic activity in Israel" (Swirski 1981, 73).

Shohat's own study looks at Mizrahim through postcolonial discourse and suggests, for the first time, that the Mizrahi category might already have a particularly cohesive, relevant, cultural, nonreligiously observant substance. Referring to them as "Arab-Jews," she calls on the Mizrahim to reestablish the fading Arab aspects of their culture that disappeared in Israel under the duress of the Zionist Eurocentric hegemony. She does not elaborate on the specific content of Mizrahi culture, but it seems that, at this point, the entity later to be known as "Mizrahi culture" begins to be imagined (Shohat 2001, 142–43).[18]

The first to elaborate on the specific cultural content of the Mizrahi category was Ammiel Alcalay, who, from a postcolonial perspective, assigned to Mizrahim a Levantine culture—the natural culture of the Middle East[19]—which, in his eyes is not Arab culture but, by nature, a multilayered culture, with remnants of the cultures of ancient Egypt, Canaan, and Greece, as well as Christianity, Judaism, and Islam.

Alcalay's 1996 anthology *Keys to the Garden* appears to be the first serious study of Mizrahi literature in Israel. While trying to uncover the essence of this literature and what differentiates it from the official hegemonic Hebrew literature, he suggests some characteristics of what was beginning to emerge as the particular cultural substance of Mizrahi culture.[20] These characteristics include belonging to a Third World context more than to the local Hebrew culture, fragmentation and marginalization, a feeling of exile in the homeland (Israel), aesthetic innovation, multiculturalism, and a passion to unite with the great space of the Middle East and to relinquish the current political borders (Alcalay 1996, ix).

Hannan Hever (2002) further investigates Mizrahi cultural identity and broadens it. Hever highlights the tension between Mizrahi literature and Zionist concepts of homeland and exile as expressed by Hebrew hegemonic literature.[21] One of the fixed features of Mizrahi literature, Hever claims, is a description of emigration to Israel, which does not dwell on the hardships of crossing between two different worlds that is typical of hegemonic Hebrew literature. In contrast to such a dichotomy, in Mizrahi literature, the Land of Israel and the land of origin exist in the same world.

Homologous, in a way, to Ammiel Alcalay's and Hannan Hever's research on Mizrahi literature is Yaron Shemer's (2013) study of Mizrahi cinema. Shemer further develops what can already be called "Mizrahi culture," aiming to reveal the essence of Mizrahi cinema and what sets it apart from hegemonic Israeli cinema. However, like Alcalay, Shemer makes an effort to unplug the category of Mizrahim from its initial binary surroundings (with the Ashkenazi category) and relocate it to a global discourse on art. He analyzes a large corpus of films on Mizrahi subjects (almost exclusively by Mizrahi filmmakers) produced between 1990 and 2010, in light of Hamid Naficy's (2001) theory on "accented cinema"—films made in First World countries by filmmakers from Third World countries who are in exile or by first-, second-, or third-generation immigrants from Third World countries. Shemer, who sees accented cinema in films of second- and third-generation Mizrahi filmmakers, discovers that a relatively substantial number of contemporary Mizrahi films share the motif of a voyage that is at once physical, psychological, and symbolic and that sometimes takes the form of an actual journey in space and at other times of an abstract metaphorical voyage into the past. This voyage, adds Shemer (2013, 253), is fundamental to the films' structure and form.[22]

Shemer's findings on the characteristics of Mizrahi cinema maintain a curious homology with Alcalay's description of Mizrahi literature. Shared attributes—such as the feeling of exile in one's homeland, the desire to cross geopolitical borders, and an inclination toward multiculturalism—seem to come from the same source, indicating cultural and social unease, resistance, and protest as a characteristic of Mizrahi cultural identity. Films by Mizrahi filmmakers reflect ideas, ideologies, and feelings of resistance, protest, and identification with Third World anticolonial discourse that are similar to those expressed in Mizrahi literature but are given a particular cinematic form. However, more than Mizrahi literature, Mizrahi cinema is, according to Shemer, still a national *Israeli* cinema, and in it Israeli patriotism is evident.[23] Here it also departs from Hamid Naficy's (2001) Third World "accented cinema" (Shemer 2013, 254).[24]

A different approach to Mizrahi culture was taken by Hannan Hever, Yehouda Shenhav, and Pnina Motzafi-Haller (2002) in their joint study. Unlike the previously mentioned critics who made an effort to attach a fixed, essentialist, historical-cultural substance to the Mizrahi category, these scholars, following the findings of Stuart Hall (1994), transform the focus of Mizrahi discourse from essential cultural attributes to the shifting identity of the individuals who constitute the Mizrahi category. Mizrahi identity, they say, first, carries a substance that is not essential but is in a constant state of construction. Second, they strongly emphasize that the roots of Mizrahi identity are to be found fully within the sphere of Israeli discourse. Third, being inspired here by theories of Homi Bhabha (1994) on the relationships between the colonial ruler and the colonized subject, their outlook follows the idea that Mizrahi identity is not the opposite of but rather *contains* Ashkenazi identity—a connection that, they claim, can be visualized through two concentric circles, as a manifestation of relationships of inclusion and exclusion (Shenhav, Hever, and Mutsafi 2002, 17).

Following the findings of Hannan Hever, Yehouda Shenhav, and Pnina Motzafi-Haller, Merav Alush-Levron, in her research on Mizrahi autobiographical documentary cinema, is the first to have focused on the practice of Mizrahi self-identification through cinema. She analyzes the practices of Mizrahi filmmakers in constructing Mizrahi identity, which is free of hegemonic preconceptions and prejudices about Mizrahim, using universal theories on gender and identity construction, such as in the work of Leigh Gilmore. Her findings further stress the resistance mode of Mizrahi cultural identity, reaching the conclusion that autobiographical Mizrahi identity is constructed in the films that she examined as "an interference in the hegemonic discourse" (Alush-Levron 2007, 166–67).

Another variation on this tendency to look inside the consciousness of the Mizrahi subject can be found in the chapter that Raz Yossef (2010) devotes to Mizrahi cinema in his book on the representation of manhood in Israeli cinema. Using Freud's theory of melancholy, Yossef characterizes first-generation Mizrahi immigrants as suffering from a melancholy that results, on the one hand, from the loss of Arab culture (their original primary culture) and, on the other, from the fact that the Israeli hegemonic discourse never made it possible for this generation to openly mourn its loss. Yossef offers melancholia as a characteristic of the first-generation Mizrahi subjects and identification with the melancholia of the parents as a main characteristic of second-generation Mizrahi filmmakers and their films.[25]

To summarize, it seems that the evolution of the cultural content of the Mizrahi category is characterized by several processes that take place concurrently. The first is the change from attributing to it only Jewish traditional folklorist content to realizing its non-Jewish content; the second is the transformation from a cultural category in which content is defined through a diasporic history into a category based mainly on the experiences of immigration and oppression in Israel; the third is the move from an effort to convey fixed essential features of Mizrahi culture to stressing its mobility and constant change; and the fourth is the adoption of the identity discourse as a vehicle for exploring Mizrahi authentic culture.

The cultural content of the Mizrahi category at that time seems to be the product of an active resistance of Mizrahi authors to the stereotyping practices of the Zionist elites. Mizrahi authors protest via texts whose features affiliate them with Third World phenomena and a global Third World discourse more than with the local Hebrew hegemonic culture. Mizrahi culture criticizes the hegemonic culture in Israel while assimilating global postmodern discourses, such as neo-Marxism, postcolonialism, and gender discourses; fragmentation and artistic expressions of marginalization, aesthetic renovation, multiculturalism, a feeling of exile in the homeland, and a desire to unite with the Middle East region and to relinquish the current borders are all part of Mizrahi culture. But, on the other hand, Mizrahi cultural products also reveal strong nationalistic feelings about Israel.

Chetrit (2004) suggests that Mizrahi culture is a byproduct of what he calls "the Mizrahi struggle" and was developed in two main phases as a complementary response to Mizrahi political protest activities. This study adopts his model and proposes that the 1970s, after the Black Panthers (Ha'panterim Ha'shkhorim) protest of 1970–1973, was a period during which the Mizrahi category already contained some kind of cultural substance. Comparing the representation of Mizrahim in Bourekas films made by culture-oriented Ashkenazi directors mainly in the 1970s with their representation in films made by Mizrahi directors (assuming that they had a Mizrahi cultural identity by that time) shows what kind of culture is really reflected by the Bourekas and further clarifies what Mizrahi cultural identity is—and is not.

Representations of Mizrahi Neighborhoods in Ovadia and Revach Films

Looking specifically at Moshe Mizrahi's *Habayit B'rechov Shlush* (*The House on Shlush Street*, 1973) and Nissim Dayan's *Or Min Ha'efker* (*Light Out of Nowhere*, 1973), Lubin and Shohat have indicated that Mizrahi-directed projects differ from Bourekas films in many respects, particularly in their representations of the Mizrahi community, neighborhood, and family. Adding to that observation, I would like to point out that films by the Mizrahi directors Ze'ev Revach and George Ovadia—seen by all previous critics, including Shohat and Lubin, as *typical* Bourekas directors[26]— also represent the Mizrahi community in a way that challenges the paradigmatic representation of the Mizrahi community in the Bourekas cycle as a whole.

Ovadia's and Revach's earliest films,[27] *Ariana* (1971) and *Only Today* (*Rak Hayom*, 1976), respectively, are of particular interest. Both were made between 1964 and 1977, which have been already identified as the Bourekas cycle period; *Only Today* is Revach's only film made within this period, at the start of his directorial career.[28] In her discussion of the Bourekas films, Shohat (1989, 132–36) explicitly calls *Only Today* and *Ariana* "Bourekas films"; she does not mention other films by these directors.

The main criterion for comparison between the two groups of films that I employ involves the nature of the cinematic representation of the Mizrahi community. The rest of this chapter examines the extent to which the paradigmatic representation of Mizrahim in Bourekas films appears also in these Mizrahi-directed titles. The films discussed are not of any importance to this study on Bourekas for themselves and function here mainly as a control group to strengthen the hypothesis that the Bourekas are films employing Ashkenazi agency while denying the Mizrahi right to self-representation. At this point, I disregard the specifics of previous critiques since, up until now, none of them, in their loose and imprecise discussion on Bourekas, have noted the paradigmatic representation of the Mizrahi community in what they thought of as classical Bourekas films—and none whatsoever noted its crucial significance to the definition of this film cycle.

Solitude of Mizrahi Neighborhoods and Neglect by Authorities

There is no solitude in *Ariana*. First, unlike in Bourekas films, Ariana's neighborhood is identified as corresponding to a real location in the extratextual world.[29] A close-up of a sign hanging on the entrance to the local employment bureau identifies Ariana's dwelling place as a Tel Avivian neighborhood, Givat Aliya. Second, while Bourekas films achieve an atmosphere of seclusion by distinguishing between the architecture of the Mizrahi neighborhood and its surroundings, the architecture of Ariana is uniform; the Mizrahi neighborhood and the surrounding area do not differ. Third, while the Bourekas films emphasize the detachment of the neighborhood, documenting the long distance between it and other locations, in *Ariana*, the filmgoer is unaware of any distance separating the sewing workshop in which Ariana works from the neighborhood. The connection between the neighborhood and the city is accentuated rather than ruled out.

In the Bourekas, the spaces that belong to wealthy Ashkenazim are marked as distinct from the Mizrahi neighborhood. The expensive restaurant in *Charlie and a Half* is not within walking distance from the neighborhood; Sallah must make a long trip to reach the house of the middle-class Ashkenazi couple to whom he is trying to sell a stray dog. In *Ariana*, the spaces of the wealthy are not only close by; they lack any spatial distinctness. There is no indication, for example, that the spacious home of the wealthy Arthur Danieli (Avraham Ronai) is located outside the neighborhood. On the contrary, the fact that Abud (Arieh Elias), Ariana's father, serves as his private greengrocer attests to the proximity of his house and the Mizrahi neighborhood. Furthermore, *Ariana* points to a certain cultural alliance between the neighborhood and the well-to-do Danieli family: Danieli celebrates his son's release from the army with a band that plays Arabic music organized by Abud.

The sense of the neighborhood's exclusion in the Bourekas is emphasized by the absence of public institutions and the fact that the inhabitants have virtually no contact with the state or municipal government. In *Ariana*, conversely, we are given the impression that there are government bureaus located within the neighborhood.[30] One institution that appears early in the film as an integral part of the neighborhood is the employment bureau. In one of the first scenes, when Kochava is seen walking out of the bureau, the camera pauses on a sign that reads "Tel Aviv Employment Bureau, Givat Aliya Beit." Since Kochava is on foot, it is only reasonable to assume that the bureau is in the neighborhood. Nor is there evidence suggesting that the School for Fashion Trades, where Ariana studies, is outside of the neighborhood, because the school building and the street it is located on share the neighborhood's architectural style.

Furthermore, the community in *Ariana* maintains ongoing, even positive relations with public agencies and institutions—governmental or not. For example, the spectators witness a functional relationship with the government health system when a public ambulance rushes down the street to save Kochava after Abud calls emergency services. Even the Israeli military (IDF) appears to operate in harmony with *Ariana*'s community. Gadi, Ariana's wealthy suitor, serves as an officer in the army; the completion of his service is celebrated at a party organized by Ariana's father. In a conversation with Danieli, Abud affirms his appreciation of the IDF and national sentiment by calling out, "Hooray [*kolha' kavod*] for the IDF!" However, it seems that the institution that maintains the most positive relation with Ariana and her family is the court. When Ariana sues the Danieli family for breach of the marital contract, it is revealed that the lawyer defending the Danielis is, in fact, Ariana's biological father. In the end, the judge rules in favor of Ariana and her family.

Similar characteristics can be seen in Ze'ev Revach's *Only Today* (1976), another film where Mizrahi living space is not presented as detached or isolated. There are two Mizrahi living spaces presented in this film: the neighborhood of the protagonist's friend, Cohen (Jack Cohen), and the market where all the Mizrahi characters of the film work, and the extratextual location of both spaces is clearly identified. The opening shot is a long shot that captures the mostly flat roofs of the houses in Cohen's neighborhood; at the front of the frame and in the background, on the opposite ridge, the Old City of Jerusalem can be seen. This composition positions Cohen's neighborhood within that metropolis. As for the second represented space, the fact that Cohen goes to his job in the market by foot also identifies the market as located in Jerusalem. Anyone having even a basic familiarity with the area would identify the market as the Machane Yehuda—a famous outdoor market in the center of Jerusalem. By pointing out the Mizrahi location in extratextual space, and by emphasizing the proximity of the Mizrahi residential spaces to the center of Jerusalem, *Only Today* shows the Mizrahi quarter as being anything but isolated. On the contrary, it resides at the very center of the urban area of the nation's capital.

This film also features such state institutions as hospitals and universities as clearly involved in the life of the Mizrahi community. Two events point to a good working relationship between the community and the hospital: an ambulance that comes to the neighborhood to take a pregnant woman to give birth and the successful operation Cohen undergoes at the hospital, which, according to the establishing shot, is Jerusalem's renowned Hadassah Hospital.

However, the neighborhood's relationship with the Hebrew University of Jerusalem appears to be more complex. Sasson (Ze'ev Revach), the greengrocer protagonist of the film, comes to the university in search of a romantic conquest, Dahlia (Efrat Lavi), and appears to get quite lost on campus. He carries a large pile of books, which he believes will help him blend into the surroundings and make him seem more like a student. In actuality, they only single him out and make him appear out of place. His disorientation attests to a certain ignorance of the accepted social conventions on campus. Nonetheless, Dahlia is a good student; the fact that she is the daughter of Cohen, Sasson's close friend from the market, and the fact that she eventually becomes Sasson's girlfriend suggest a fundamentally positive association between the university and the Mizrahi community.

One apparent similarity to the Bourekas in *Only Today* is that no Mizrahi works for the establishment, since everyone is a "freelancer." But this can easily be explained by the fact that the film has chosen an open market as the Mizrahi community's living space. Despite this state of affairs, there is one conspicuous character who does receive his paycheck from the government—Shmaryahu (Ya'akov Bodo), the municipal inspector. Yet he is neither a foreign element in the market nor a representative of "others" or Ashkenazim[31] and seems to be an organic part of the community's social fabric. Like everyone else, he rushes to congratulate Hayun on the birth of his son, and like others, he joins his neighbors in visiting Cohen after his surgery, even bringing a gift. The community seems to accept him as an integral, and not entirely negative, part of its reality.

The Material Culture of the Mizrahi Neighborhood

At first sight, Ariana's neighborhood could be reminiscent of the space characterization of the neighborhoods portrayed in the Bourekas films. The streets of her neighborhood are unpaved, and the hybrid character of the neighborhood (rural as well as urban) is emphasized by shots that focus on chickens, a donkey, and even two sheep that live in Abud's backyard. Apparently here, too, the neighborhood suffers from a lack of development and cultivation. As in the streets of Sallah's ma'abara, no trees or greenery are in sight, and of course there are no street fixtures—benches, power lines, or fences—visible.

However, there are some important differences between the neighborhood's status here and in the Bourekas films. In many of the latter (*Kazablan, Charlie and a Half, Snooker, Rabbi Gamliel*), the neighborhood—the Mizrahi living space—is the space that opens the cinematic sequence of the films as an establishing shot, but *Ariana* opens on a highway, where her biological mother and father are riding in a car. The second location is the neighborhood in which Ariana's mother grew up, not the neighborhood that is the film's primary space. Only in the third scene do we see the neighborhood in which the Mizrahi family lives. This type of sequence raises doubts about the metonymical connection between the nature of space and the community represented, a vagueness that is not typical of a Bourekas film.

One might claim that while the authors of the Bourekas films use the neighborhood space as an instrument to metonymically characterize the community at the center of the film, *Ariana* presents a functional use of the Mizrahi neighborhood space that undermines any metonymic significance. Instead of utilizing the neighborhood space to characterize the heroine, the film uses the inner space of the house she lives in to shape her character. Thus, in *Ariana*, the metonymic presentation of the family or community shifts from the shared neighborhood space to the private indoor space. Unlike in the Bourekas films, where the protagonists are depicted mostly on the neighborhood streets and in cafés[32]—most of the scenes in *Ariana* take place indoors, filmed within the house. Hence the neighborhood representation of *Ariana* might have some resemblance to the Mizrahi neighborhood in the Bourekas, but in *Ariana* this is of marginal importance to the characterization of the Mizrahi community in the film, since it lacks any metonymic aspect. Moreover, in *Ariana*, space is neither crowded nor cinematically dense. On the contrary, the space gives a sparse impression; the streets are depicted as empty, and the houses have large yards that separate them from the street. For example, when Kochava reaches Ariana's house and knocks on the outer gate, the lady of the house comes out of the building, crosses an inner door, crosses a big yard, and only then opens the gate.

In *Only Today*, two spaces are at the center of the film: the neighborhood in which Cohen, Dalya's father, lives and the outdoor market, both in Jerusalem's city center. *Only Today*'s manifestly urban character contrasts with the hybrid character of Bourekas neighborhoods. The film's urban spaces have a relatively high level of configuration, quite the contrast to the neglect that dominates the Bourekas settings. The opening shot in *Only Today* depicts the neighborhood in which Cohen, Sasson's best friend, resides—a typical central Jerusalem neighborhood. The shot reveals stone houses with flat or domed roofs, and the Old City can be seen in the distance. The cinematic sequence escorts Cohen and his employee while they walk on paved or cobblestone streets on their way to the market (as we later discover). Unlike the depiction in the Bourekas films, the streets of the neighborhood do not show any neglect; furthermore, as in *Ariana*, the streets are not jam-packed with people. They are filmed in the early morning, when no one is around, in a way that emphasizes the sparseness.

However, the most evident difference between *Only Today* and the Bourekas films has to do with cinematic rhetoric. In clear contrast to the Bourekas films, *Only Today* makes an effort to beautify the space, to depict Mizrahim within a pattern of a positive, signifying cinematic sequence. By presenting the signified space through indexes that imply beauty, the author adorns the Mizrahi living space with aesthetic urban values. Although the marketplace, the primary Mizrahi location in the film, is essentially a chaotic space with inherently little aesthetic organization, the author endeavors to portray it in the most beautiful way possible—by producing a careful and highly configured cinematic sequence. The long shots of the market are filmed either at sunrise or sunset; the light at these times of day colors the objects either blue or gold, creating a romantic atmosphere, and the shots are, if anything, underexposed, which conceals the dirty surroundings and other imperfections.

Only Today's opening shot features a cinematic rhetoric of great virtuosity. This shot, which lasts four minutes with no cuts, opens with a beautiful framing of the domed roofs in Cohen's neighborhood, while on the horizon we see Jerusalem's historic Old City. The balanced composition and the perspective that gives a sense of depth together with the soft morning light combine to create a breathtaking composition. After a few seconds, the camera pans 180 degrees to show Cohen's beautiful stone house. He and his employee leave the house, and the camera follows them (using a crane), as they walk through a gate with a striking stone arch, take in the awe-inspiring view, and descend the stairs to the street. Both the slow pace of the shot and its compositions attest to the respect and appreciation the film directs toward this Mizrahi living space and to Jerusalem, Israel's capital—a respect that entirely contradicts the attitude that is fundamental to the Bourekas films' cinematic rhetoric.

Competition in the Mizrahi Neighborhood

The neighborhood boundaries in *Ariana* are not clearly delineated; indeed, a great spatial indistinctness characterizes its representation. Since the focus of attention here is not the neighborhood but the house in which Ariana lives with her mother and father, the Mizrahi community depicted in the film consists of Ariana's immediate family—the members of which do not compete financially. Even when other neighborhood residents are presented, there is no evidence of financial competition between them and Ariana's family or even among themselves. For example, Abud seems to be the only greengrocer in the area.

Competing with the Ashkenazim is yet another main characteristic of the Mizrahi neighborhood in the Bourekas films that is absent from this film. Unlike in the Bourekas, the wealthy in *Ariana* are not categorized as unquestionably Ashkenazi. Although one might initially assume that the well-to-do Arthur Danieli is of Ashkenazi descent, there are a number of hints that preclude ethnically classifying the character: his name is ethnically indistinct and certainly not classically Ashkenazi; he does not seem to be especially taken aback by a band playing Arab music at a party that Abud organizes for him; his son, Gadi, takes his date to a belly dancer performing to Arab music; and the Moroccan background of the actor-singer Avi Toledano, who plays the part of Gadi, his son, was common knowledge at the time of the film's release. As indicated, it is also far from clear that the affluent Danieli family lives in a space that is detached from the neighborhood in which the poor Abud resides. The fact that Abud is Mizrahi, that he is a stall-owning greengrocer, and that he serves as Danieli's personal food supplier all suggest that the Danieli family lives near Abud, perhaps even in the same neighborhood.

Because of this ambiguity among key characters of vastly different means, it is difficult to discuss any form of competition or conflict between the Ashkenazim and the Mizrahim in *Ariana*. It may be possible to discuss the conflicts between the rich and the poor, but these, too, should be examined as exploitive rather than competitive. It is unclear, for instance, whether Abud is paid to arrange Gadi's party; it is more likely that he organizes it because he fears that Danieli might terminate their financial relationship if he refuses to do so. Similarly, Ariana, who works as a seamstress, is fired without notice because it was decided that she had not been pulling her weight in terms of workload. Another exploitive financial relationship is presented through the affair portrayed in the film's prologue: Ariana's biological mother has an affair with a respectable attorney. After she becomes pregnant, she suggests that it might be time to tie the knot, but the attorney refuses and pulls out a stack of bills that he offers her as compensation.

Sexual competition does exist in *Ariana*, but here, unlike that depicted in most Bourekas films, the competition is between two women over a man. Ariana competes with the Polish heiress that Danieli had chosen for his son Gadi and, in the end, manages to win Gadi over. Again, in contrast to the Bourekas films, here the marriage between Gadi and Ariana does not allegorically echo reconciliation between the Mizrahim and the Ashkenazim; this is not only due to the fact that the groom's ethnic identity is ambiguous but also because the bride is of mixed Mizrahi-Ashkenazi descent. Ariana was born to a Mizrahi mother and raised in a Mizrahi family, but as the viewers are well aware, and as Ariana herself discovers at the end of the film, her father is actually Ashkenazi.

In *Only Today*, the central Mizrahi space is the outdoor market—by definition a competitive place. But surprisingly enough, there does not seem to be any rivalry among the merchants. Unlike the recurring paradigm in a number of Bourekas films, each of the merchants has a unique commercial enterprise and therefore has no apparent reason to compete with others. So, for example, Cohen sells cleaning supplies, Hayun is a tailor, Dabach (Gabi Amrani) is a carpenter, and Sasson, the protagonist, is a greengrocer. There is some tension between Sasson and the carpenter, which is apparent

Figure 3.1. *Only Today* (1976). A cheerful bunch. Harmony in the market space. Mr. Dabah (Yaakov Banai), Dr. Hershkovitz (Rafael Klachkin), Dalia (Efrat Lavie), and Mr. Cohen (Jacques Cohen). Photo: Yoni Hamenachem.

in their mutual teasing, but that, too, ends quickly enough, with the two clinking glasses and exchanging compliments.

Since there is no basis for competition, the stall owners in the market collaborate. They help each other steer clear of Shmaryahu, the inspector, and share each other's joys and pleasures. When Sasson has had enough of his Ashkenazi lover, he essentially hands her over to the owner of the market's café. "Tell her," Sasson says to him, insinuating their different levels of masculinity, "that the tomato season is over and it's now time for the cucumber season!" [The Hebrew word for "tomato," *agvania*, stems from a word meaning "to tempt someone for sex."] The lack of competition and the physical closeness unite the merchants, making them a cheerful bunch. They spend time together outside working hours; they meet every lunch break to chat and come up with answers to questions on quiz shows; they rush to assist a neighbor when his wife goes into labor; and they all come to visit Cohen in the hospital when he is recovering from surgery.

Unlike the Bourekas films, *Only Today*'s plot is not built around competition; its narrative is instead built around the process of coming of age of the male hero of the film. Sasson, who at the beginning is involved in juvenile love affairs with women not from his class, age, and ethnic group, at the end gets engaged to a girl from the same background as his, whom he will probably marry. However, his journey to this point of adulthood passes through sexual competition, a competition that is apparently—as it is in *Kazablan, Charlie and a Half, Fortuna,* and *Rabbi Gamliel*—a sexual competition with an allegorical aspect, since it involves two male figures, each of whom represents either the Mizrahi sector or the Ashkenazi sector. The two examples of the sexual competition in *Only Today* are between Sasson (the Mizrahi) and the Ashkenazi doctor, over Stella, the latter's wife, and between the Mizrahi Sasson and Alex, an Ashkenazi, over Dalya's affections.

Sasson meets Stella, the Ashkenazi wife of an Ashkenazi doctor, when she comes to the market to buy tomatoes. She invites Sasson to her house, where her husband also has his clinic, and she lures him into her bed. Their affair continues for quite a long time—long enough for Sasson to arrange for Cohen, who has a kidney problem, to get a free appointment with Stella's husband, followed by an operation performed by the husband. There is an apparent sexual competition in this film between Sasson and the doctor that is underscored by the fact that the husband is in the house when the couple meets for their intimate trysts. One scene even depicts an encounter between Sasson and the cuckolded husband: the doctor reaches the entrance to his wife's room just as Sasson comes out. He sees Sasson but suspects nothing, even greeting him absentmindedly.

Nonetheless, *Only Today* presents a subtler version of sexual competition. This is not the vulgar and visible competition between Robert, an Ashkenazi, and Charlie, a Mizrahi, in *Charlie and a Half*; nor is it the almost violent competition between the uncle from Marseille and the French engineer in *Fortuna* or the crude competition between Kazablan (the Mizrahi) and Yanosh (the Ashkenazi) in *Kazablan*. First and foremost, it is a competition of which one party (the husband) is completely unaware. And the competition seems less weighty, since the husband is depicted as being uninterested in his wife and, in fact, completely ignores her sexuality. Preoccupied with his work, the husband does not even notice that he does not satisfy his wife's great sexual appetite; actually, he doesn't even seem to think that she has any sexual appetite whatsoever. The husband is depicted as an asexual, dry character motivated mainly by money, which he prefers to any sexual pleasure—to the extent that when Stella phones him and asks him to join her in the bedroom, he lies and says that he is in the middle of a medical examination when he is actually in the middle of counting the money he gained form the day's work.

The interethnic competition between Sasson and Alex over Dalya's affections is, again, a competition of which one side is mostly unaware—a competition that dismisses Alex as a genuine competitor. Additionally, Alex is not really interested in winning the competition; he doesn't seriously want Dalya for a girlfriend, and he uses various excuses to avoid her. In fact, the relationship between Sasson and Dalya begins when Sasson courts Dalya in Alex's name, to cover for Alex's lack of interest in her.

Juxtaposing the sexual competition presented in *Only Today* with the sexual competition presented in the Bourekas films suggests that the allegorical message varies, in each case, according to the actual situations depicted. The films that deny Mizrahim self-representation (Bourekas) depict a *real* competition between men of Mizrahi and Ashkenazi origins over a woman, which ends with the triumph of the Mizrahi. In doing so, the Bourekas suggest that Mizrahi men have an advantage over Ashkenazi men in this respect. In *Only Today*, the unreal—or unequal, since it is not apparent to the Ashkenazi, or else he doesn't care—suggests the opposite. The Ashkenazi men have a clear advantage over the Mizrahi men, a situation in which the Mizrahim don't stand a chance unless their Ashkenazi competitors are unaware of the competition itself (the doctor) or are not interested in the woman for one reason or another (Alex).

While the sexual behavior in *Only Today* differs from the portrayal in films that deny self-representation, it is somewhat reminiscent of the sexual behavior presented in other Mizrahi self-representation films. In both *Only Today* and in *Father of the Girls* (1973), by Moshe Mizrahi, the narrative follows the coming-of-age conflict of two grown men and highlights certain oedipal elements of their behavior. From Sasson's point of view, it seems significant that, like the main character in *Father of the Girls*, he gets engaged to the daughter of his best friend, who is a father figure to him. The fact that Cohen is trying to manipulate the romantic behavior of his daughter is homological to the attitude of the father in *Father of the Girls* toward his daughter's love life. Both have oedipal aspects and significance.

The Nature of Togetherness and Community Life

The neighborhood in *Ariana* is not crowded, and there is no imposed togetherness or peeping. On the contrary, Ariana and her family live in relative seclusion with no close neighbors. Often, when the streets of the neighborhood are filmed, they are deserted or show little movement. In clear distinction from the situations depicted in the Bourekas films, in *Ariana* the private and public spaces are absolutely disassociated, symbolized by the large yard and high wall that separate her house from the street. This separation makes the transition from one space to the other very difficult; for example, when Abud first arrives with Kochava, Ariana's biological mother, and wants to speak to his wife, he must knock on the gate and wait for her to come out of the house through the interior door, cross the yard, and open the exterior gate separating the yard from the street. When the perimeters between the private and public spheres are so clearly defined and protected, there is no flow of information and no gossip. Ariana, for instance, constantly misses vital pieces of information; she does not know until the end of the film that Abud and his wife, who raised her, are not her real parents, and she does not know who her biological mother is. She is also unaware of the existence of an Ashkenazi contender for her affections. Personal business is personal, even to the extent that key players have major gaps in their information.

As discussed, the main space of the Mizrahi community in *Only Today* is the outdoor market. In this categorically crowded place, an atmosphere of togetherness prevails; indeed, the merchants lead the kind of life that could easily be defined as "communal." The ambiguous differentiation between the private and public spheres is also characteristic of the atmosphere of life in the market. An example of this is when Sasson, the main character, plays backgammon with his merchant friend outside his stand, and the merchants invite each other to have coffee at their stands. However, despite this apparent resemblance to the Bourekas films, a closer comparison of the settings uncovers some fundamental differences.

In the Bourekas films, togetherness characterizes the private living space, the home; in *Only Today*, it characterizes the workplace, which is public by nature. It would not be accurate, therefore, to talk about an ambiguous differentiation between the private and the public in *Only Today*; at most, we see a mixing of the professional and the personal. Correspondingly, it does seem as though the privacy is kept in the merchants' own homes; for example, Cohen's house, the only merchant's home seen in the movie, isn't characterized by free access to the surrounding space—rather quite the opposite. As in *Ariana*, the separation between the private and public spheres is emphasized by a yard and a wall that separate the house from the street.

The imposed togetherness in the Bourekas films is the result of competition, and this helps the neighborhood's inhabitants in their "espionage." In *Only Today*, the positive elements of togetherness and communal life come through; for example, when a woman goes into labor and the ambulance is delayed, many people storm into her house, but their invasion, which does indeed express an ambiguous separation between the public and private spaces, is presented as a positive event, an incident in which the market people offer to help a friend in need. On the whole, the togetherness in the market seems voluntary and serves social goals concerning responsibility and mutual support; these people also warn each other when Inspector Shmaryahu shows up, and they help each other get through the quiet hours—for instance, by playing backgammon at lunchtime. They support each other when in need and even share their pleasures, as when Sasson gives his mistress over to another man.

Proximity even helps moderate the interpersonal conflicts in the community. The imposed togetherness of the Bourekas film is the source of gossip, and it supports the unhindered flow of information from the individual to the public, but in *Only Today* this phenomenon has no place. In view of that, Sasson does not know that Dalya, his girlfriend-to-be, is Cohen's daughter, although they have been working together for years, and no one knows that Sasson has a lover, even though his trysts take place during work hours.

Work and Making a Living in the Neighborhood

There are no sordid or criminal elements in *Ariana*. The film depicts a working neighborhood: Abud is a greengrocer; Ariana works in a dress shop; Gadi is an army officer; and Danieli, his father, is presumably a businessman. In one of the scenes, a prostitute appears and tries to persuade Kochava, Ariana's biological mother, to join her, while two men who are probably her pimps stand in the background. However, the aggressiveness with which Abud deals with them is a device to persuade the viewers that they are not wanted in the neighborhood, and that their presence is not tolerated. In *Only Today* as well, we are confronted with a working community. The characters in the market all work, of course, and although they are seen playing board games, it is not the kind of "professional" backgammon that serves as a source of income in *Sallah*; instead, it is an amusement that helps reduce the tensions of work and pass the quiet hours of the day.

In fact, the only "idler" in the film, who is also an alcoholic, is Cohen's friend Hershkovitz, who works as his assistant—the only Ashkenazi in the market. The rumors are that he used to be a doctor but became a peddler once he began drinking. During one of the lunch breaks, he is seen taking a drunkard's snooze on the table, and, on another occasion, he asks Sasson to donate toward building a fence for a cemetery, but instead he uses the money to buy another bottle of vodka.

Although there is fraud in *Only Today*, it is restricted to the characters outside the community. Alex, for example, fools and misleads Dalya until the kindhearted Sasson saves her from him. But the primary type of fraud in the film is a particular kind of cunning. Sasson, for example, is a charming opportunist who knows how to exploit certain situations and weaknesses for his own benefit without seriously harming anyone else. He takes advantage of the carpenter's naïveté and manages to lead him on with a simple trick: making him mark the absolute value, before the mediating fee, of a chair that he wants to buy. Sasson also uses the doctor's wife's boredom to his own advantage, but this craftiness turns out for the best, since it gives Sasson a way of arranging free medical treatment for Cohen.

The neighborhood is represented in these two Mizrahi-directed films as completely secular, with no rabbis present and no superstitious practices or beliefs mentioned. In *Ariana*, the characters are in close contact with the concrete, visible, and practical world. When Gadi leaves Ariana, she does not go to a fortune-teller or an astrologer and does not search for mystical ways to get him back. Instead, she sues Gadi for breaking his promise of marriage. There are no superstitions in *Only Today*, either. When Cohen becomes ill, he doesn't go to a quack doctor but seeks modern medical treatment.

Noninstrumental Romantic Attitudes

Looking at the Mizrahi ethnic group through the melodramatic *Ariana*, one gets the impression that the romantic view of male-female relationships in it is obvious. The film presents two Mizrahi women, Kochava and Ariana (biological mother and daughter), who are willing to follow their hearts to the brink of self-destruction. Kochava, although abandoned by her lover, insists on giving birth to their love child; Ariana, who inherits her mother's destiny, becomes pregnant and is then abandoned by her fiancé but doesn't give up the love child or the fiancé. As opposed to the Bourekas, where this kind of impulsive, passionate, romantic behavior by youngsters draws criticism, and sometimes even sanctions from the family (for example in *Sallah*, in *Katz and Carasso*, and even in the melodramatic *Fortuna*), here the family stands firmly behind Ariana and proves that it shares her values and romantic worldview. And indeed the romantic ethos is so deeply ingrained in Ariana that she is even willing to go to court to sue the fiancé who left her. Officially, she charges him with breaking the marriage promise, but it is obvious that the fuel that feeds this lawsuit is her humiliation at the fact that he has spurned her.

In the Bourekas, we see the authors undermining the romantic feelings of the heroes through cinematic rhetoric, which forces a reductive presentation of scenes with romantic potential and adds a grotesque aspect to them. In *Ariana*, however, there is no ironic gap between the author and his romantic heroine, Ariana. On the contrary, the author identifies with Ariana and does his best to emphasize emotional and romantic aspects of film discourse. In Bourekas films that focus on affairs (such as *Charlie and a Half* and *Kazablan*), the romantic value of the film's courting plot is reduced by refracting it through characters who represent an instrumental view of the male-female bond. By contrast, *Ariana*'s cinematic sequence emphasizes romantic moments, first by constructing the courting plot from scenes in which the couple is alone—a strategy that gives the author a chance to linger on the couple's feelings for one another. Hence, Ariana and Gadi, her fiancé-to-be, are alone when they meet for the first time,[33] when riding in his car, and in the hotel when they first make love. Apart from this, the cinematic author creates a romantic atmosphere in the film by constructing scenes that naturally support the romance—such as when Ariana goes to the nightclub with Gadi. The film also stresses the romantic aspects of other scenes, such as the lovers' romantic car ride, during which the beautiful, forested landscape, the hour (sunset), and the music that accompanies everything all serve to create a dreamlike atmosphere.

Ariana's melodramatic narrative naturally supports its romantic ethos. The plot in which, after being abandoned by her fiancé for a shidduch (arranged match) with a rich girl, Ariana sues him and wins the case allegorically suggests that a bond formed through a natural, mutual attraction is both stronger and more honorable than one artificially produced that reflects an instrumental and materialistic view of marriage. *Ariana* supports and approves a romantic ethos not only through the heroine's triumph in court but also through the reunion of Ariana with her biological father.

Figure 3.2. *Only Today*. Romantic atmosphere: Sasson (Ze'ev Revach) and Dalia (Efrat Lavie). Photo: Yoni Hamenachem.

By means of this moving reunion, the film retrospectively approves and supports her mother Kochava's decision to follow her heart. It also shows that at the end of the day, there were no terrible consequences from her passionate decision, and that all ended well.

In *Only Today*, as a comedy with melodramatic features, a romantic atmosphere is also stressed—both through the narrative and the author's cinematic rhetoric. There is no matchmaking in the film. All the meetings between Sasson (the hero) and the women in his life are incidental, and mutual attraction is always involved. Sasson meets Stella, who will soon become his lover, when she comes to pick out tomatoes at his vegetable stand; he meets Dalya, the girl he will fall in love with, when she comes to visit her father, Cohen, who works at the stand next to his. In a way that is reminiscent of Ariana's insistence on the triumph of romance in her private life, Sasson, the protagonist, demands a revelation of romance in Dalya's relationships with Alex, her boyfriend. Sasson challenges Dalya to confront Alex's belittling, insulting, and instrumental attitude and tries to force romance back into their relationship. When it doesn't work and when Alex doesn't accept the challenge, Sasson replaces him, not only because of his love for Dalya but also for the sake of bringing romance back into Dalya's life. As in *Ariana*, scenes with romantic potential are integrated into the film's narrative: the long moments in which Sasson stands under Dalya's window waiting for her to appear and the meeting between Sasson and Dalya on the beach come to mind.

Representation of the Mizrahi Community in the Films of Ovadia and Revach

It is obvious that the films examined here, by the Mizrahi directors George Ovadia and Ze'ev Revach, have little to do with the Bourekas films, and the Bourekas' paradigmatic representation of Mizrahim does not exist in their cinematic discourses. The immediate conclusion would be that Ashkenazi agency is responsible for the paradigmatic representations of Mizrahim in Bourekas and therefore essential to them. However, if this is so, what is the correct context through which to perceive Ovadia's and Revach's films?

It would be easy to prove that both—with correspondence to a central trait of what was presented before as Mizrahi self-representation cultural products—are inspired by a specific tradition of one of the largest national movie industries of the Third World. In a way that hints at their authors' secret passion to unite with the great space of the Middle East and its dominant Arab culture, both films seem to draw paradigms from the classic Egyptian melodrama, about which Shafik (2007, 321) remarks that it "negotiates questions of modernity, gender roles, and the bourgeois family ideal of love-marriage," and in which "romantic love develops against the backgrounds of allegorical cross-class rape or seduction narratives." Although clearer in *Ariana*—focalized, like many Egyptian melodramas, through a female character and constructing an Israeli sphere as if it were an Egyptian one, integrating belly dances and Arab music, blaring the ethnicity of its main characters—both films, as seen earlier in this chapter, seem to favor the ideal of romantic love as the starting point of legitimate and lawful bourgeois marriages and put the pursuit of its realization at the center of their narratives. Moreover, the main character in both films seems to be motivated by the urge to subordinate any other aspect of the bond between the sexes to romantic love. In addition, both films present cross-class seduction narratives.[34] In *Ariana*, it is evident in the story of both Kochava, the heroine's biological mother, being seduced by a much older, wealthy attorney, and Ariana, who repeats her mother's fate when she is seduced by Gadi, a young man from a well-to-do family who has already been promised to another. In *Only Today*, although focalized through a deprived Mizrahi male figure, there are two cross-class seduction narratives as well: that of Sasson, the greengrocer, who is seduced by Stella, the rich Ashkenazi surgeon's wife, and that of Dalya, the poor Mizrahi, who is seduced by Alex, the wealthy Ashkenazi, who has no intention to marry her. In both films the seduction plots help "to express and ventilate class injustice" (Shafik 2007, 321) since they end with the deprived Mizrahi film's hero winning against all odds.

Early Egyptian melodramas, says Shafik (2007, 256), were concerned with moral distinctions as much as with social status. Indeed, moral distinctions are at stake in both films. *Ariana* is framed around the distinctions between the honesty and integrity of the lead character and the fraud and intrigues of the wealthy Danieli, while *Only Today* hinges on the differences between the integrity of Sasson and the decisiveness of Alex while courting Dalya.

In general, *Ariana* is closer to Egyptian melodrama than is *Only Today*. Its plot is more obviously "based on love rendered impossible by insurmountable class differences," putting "individual happiness and love . . . on one side, while tradition and family . . . on the other" (Shafik 2007, 249). In the film, the lovers are more obviously confronted "with an authority's father" (Danieli) and with "a figure related to him . . . a wicked person who helps impose the father's law [Amrani] . . . as their major opponent" (Shafik 2007, 249). Arab music and Arab belly dancers are incorporated into the film sequence, and the nightclub scene is typical of Egyptian melodrama; that is, it presents the club as a place of sensuality, crime, and sin (Shafik 2007, 164).

To conclude, *Ariana* is a classic melodrama that portrays the relationships between the wealthy and the poor, while realizing the principles of universal justice. Its source would not be Bourekas films but a cinematic genre of the Third World: the Egyptian melodrama, the film formula that was prevalent throughout the Middle East beginning in the 1930s, in which, "it is always love that is in first place, spiced with mean seductions, rapes, adultery, prisons, death, suicide, and mental illness" (Shafik 1998,

28). This formula is typical also of other famous films made by Ovadia, such as *Nurit* (1972), *Sarit* (1973), *Midnight Entertainer* (*Badranit B'hazot*, 1977), and *Nurit 2* (1983), which were all focalized through a female main character. *Ariana* is linked to a Mizrahi culture also through its apparent Israeli patriotism; in it, the Israeli army (IDF) seems to have a favorable representation through Gadi, Ariana's charismatic lover, who is an IDF officer, and through the obvious admiration of Abud, Ariana's father, for the IDF.

Although it has, as shown, a close linkage to Egyptian melodrama, and because it presents a Mizrahi living space reminiscent of the neighborhoods in the Bourekas, Revach's *Only Today* seems closer to Bourekas films than does *Ariana*. However, the market setting of *Only Today* could also be influenced by Egyptian "realistic" films that are characterized by melodramatic narratives imbued and installed into seemingly authentic common sets (Shafik 2007, 255). Second, the environment of the Mizrahi living space in the film, the sociology and culture of the Mizrahi community, and the rhetoric employed by the cinematic author to characterize the two are completely distinguishable from those of Bourekas films. In *Only Today*—apparently more so than in *Ariana*—the cinematic author acts to associate the Mizrahi living space with the surrounding spaces. As a result, he discards the source of the reduction of human values to instrumental aspects, which is fundamental to the reductive representation of the Mizrahi community in the Bourekas. Accordingly, the representation of the Mizrahi community in the film is quite different: the film presents a community in which the ethos includes good neighborly relations, mutual help, friendship, loyalty, and love.[35] *Only Today* also ignores the Zionist discourse dichotomy of modern/premodern, which forms the representation of Mizrahim vis-à-vis Ashkenazim in Bourekas films. Sasson, the romantic Mizrahi, for example, is much more modern in this respect than his Ashkenazi competitors. The film also displays national pride, shown earlier to be a feature of a Mizrahi cultural product. Nationalism and patriotism come to mind due to the added aesthetic value that the film attaches to Jerusalem, the Jewish and Israeli capital.

Although its cross-class seduction narrative, borrowed from Egyptian classical melodrama (which also has metaphorical interpretations of class conflict between Ashkenazim and Mizrahim[36]) and its melodramatic focus on romantic love, features such as an accommodating representation of the Mizrahi community and neighborhood, a narrative that focuses on the coming-of-age process of the male hero, the cinematic author's elevated rhetoric and style, and the eradication of Zionist ideology and narratives alongside Israeli Jewish national pride make *Only Today* reminiscent of other Mizrahi self-representation films of its time, specifically those made by Moshe Mizrahi.³⁷

4

BOUREKAS AND CLASSICAL YIDDISH LITERATURE

The Definition of Bourekas Movies—and a New Challenge

It seems that both the differences between Bourekas films and Mizrahi self-representation films—pertaining to the space and social-cultural character of the Mizrahi neighborhood, community, and family—and the homology within the Bourekas films concerning the presentation of Mizrahim point to the uniqueness and inner uniformity of the Bourekas cycle, as described in chapter 2.[1] Indicating the exclusive features of the representation of the Mizrahi community, neighborhood, and family that are common to all Bourekas, a comparative study shows that the essence of the Bourekas as a distinguishable group of films lies in its unique themes about Mizrahim, expressed through a paradigmatic representation of a particular nature within them. The Bourekas do bear features of a more rhetorical and poetic nature: a distinctive competition-structured mode of narrative construction and a reductive representation of space that is supported by specific cinematic strategies; these include choice of location and set design as well as cinematic techniques, such as camera handling, composition, and editing.

Juxtaposing the Bourekas with the films that embody Mizrahi self-representation emphasizes the fact that the cinematic authors of Bourekas films uniquely organized their narratives to revolve around an axis of conflict based on competition.[2] The authors then arranged the smaller units of the film (sequences and scenes) to accentuate elements of scarcity and rivalry. This can be seen in *Snooker*, where the competition between Azriel (Yehuda Barkan) and Mushon (Tuvia Tzafir) over Yona (Nitza Shaul) is the central conflict, while the scenes are structured around competitive situations between the characters, such as the game of snooker between Salvador (Yosef Shiloah) and Gabriel (also Yehuda Barkan) or the competition between Azriel and Mushon over their knowledge of scripture.

Comparative analysis also reveals that the rhetoric in the Bourekas revolves around low levels of aesthetic organization. The cinematic sequences of Bourekas films are reduced to documenting the characters' dramatic actions, thereby presenting a chaotic cinematic space that signifies a torn, cutoff society in a constant war of all against all, one defined by a fierce struggle for survival. The choices to degrade the aesthetic organization and spatial continuity of cinematic sequence create a disorienting effect that can even oppose the nature of the situation depicted. For example, in *Katz and Carasso*, when Carasso's son (once again, Yehuda Barkan) and Katz's daughter (Efrat Lavi) kiss on the beach in Eilat, the cinematic author includes in the sequence features that turn this potentially romantic scene into a grotesque one.

New Explanations, New Phenomena, and a Definition

In the previous chapters, I have identified, cataloged, described, explained, and showed "in action" all the characteristics that contribute to the paradigmatic representation of Mizrahim in the Bourekas. These are the thematic traits of the cycle, inherent in the Bourekas' cinematic rhetoric, and part of a recurring pattern in the films. A comprehensive and rational array of reasons may exist for this pattern. The chronic neglect of the Mizrahi community by local authorities and its insulation are ready intratextual explanations.

One can describe the logic behind the recurring pattern in the Bourekas' representation of Mizrahim as follows: the Bourekas depict the Mizrahim as a premodern Jewish society that is ignored by the authorities and is financially and socially isolated. This results in severely restricted resources and in overwhelming crowding (the result of imposed isolation), which leads to a society hell-bent on a ruthless struggle for survival, and whose members live in an atmosphere of chaos, anarchy, and decadence. Consequentially, social values within this communal sphere are reduced to their instrumental aspects.

Ella Shohat and other critics of the postcolonial school have argued that Mizrahim are *mis*represented in Bourekas films. The findings of this research strongly support her claims (Shohat 1989, 124). The differences regarding the mode of Mizrahi representation found in the two groups compared in the study—the films that embody Mizrahi self-representation on one end and the Bourekas films on the other—are crucial in this respect. These differences, which can be described somewhat reductively as pointing to Mizrahi self-representation films as having more favorable representations of Mizrahim, and which prove that Mizrahim see themselves differently (and in a more "positive" way) than presented in Bourekas films, support the critics of the postcolonial school in their objections to the misrepresentation of Mizrahim in the Bourekas. On the other hand, the match between some of the features of the Mizrahi self-representation films and what was described in the previous chapter as Mizrahi culture cannot be disregarded.

While such modern critics as Yehuda Ne'eman attribute the reductive cinematic sequence in Bourekas to the incompetence or greed of directors, I offer a different explanation. The rather poor cinematic language and use of cinematic conventions are conscious choices constituting a *rhetoric* that I describe as a "reduction of the cinematic sequence" used by the cinematic authors. This reduction to mere documentation of the character's dramatic action, the low aesthetic organization of the films' compositions, and the breaching of spatial continuity through pockets of disorientation are all, in fact, rhetorical tactics used by the authors to present the Mizrahi community and its neighborhood as constituting a chaotic sphere that suffers deterioration and is characterized by corrupt values.

Although we are only halfway through this study, a definition of the Bourekas can already be articulated: the Bourekas are a distinguishable cycle of eleven films produced between 1964 and 1977 that share a particular, paradigmatic representation of the Mizrahi neighborhood, community, and family as a premodern Jewish community, focalized through the agency of a director with an Ashkenazi cultural background. In a Bourekas film, the narrative is developed around the focal conflict of competition, and the cinematic sequence uses a rhetoric of low configuration.

Answering fundamental questions seems to encourage the emergence of new ones. Previous critics explained the misrepresentation of Mizrahim in the Bourekas as influenced by the Eurocentric ideology of the authors (Shohat 1989), as a reflection of Zionist modernization theory (Shenhav, Hever, and Mutsafi 2002), or as a means to anesthetize the citizenry's social criticism of Mizrahi viewers (Ne'eman 1979). As we explore these explanations, we see that they are all based on the assumption that representation of Mizrahim in the Bourekas is built upon two elements: an essentially authentic Mizrahi reality (that these critics assume actually exists) and an ideology of the cinematic authors of Bourekas films that pragmatically distorts this authentic reality.

However, after sustained analysis of the films in question, these explanations no longer fit. The significant difference that was found between the representation of Mizrahim in the self-representation films and their representation in the Bourekas hints at the fact that the Bourekas offer neither a twisted nor biased Mizrahi reality but a totally different one. In light of the commonsensical structure of the Bourekas paradigmatic representation of Mizrahi community and the harmony that the study finds between its recurring patterns, it makes little sense to claim that it is composed of two clashing elements: authentic Mizrahi reality and a twisted ideology. Instead, this paradigmatic representation apparently has only one source—a harmonized one. A new answer, then, is needed for the question of where this representation begins. Since Ashkenazi cultural background has been proven essential in the production of this paradigmatic representation, Jewish Ashkenazi culture could be the place to look for its origins.

At this point, a quotation from Amos Eilon's 1988 book *The Israelis*, in which he talks about the culture of the founding fathers of Israel, is fitting. It gives a clue as to where the origins of the Mizrahi representation in Bourekas films can be found: "The deterioration of the [Jewish] shtetl had drawn the attention of a well-known author who said, 'This is an ugly life.' It was Shalom Yaakov Abramovitz a.k.a. Mendele Mocher Sforim. . . . In his bitter novels, which are based on [Jewish] life in Eastern Europe, *pathetic, horrific products of a deteriorating society are huddled together: scroungers, beggars, consumed by fleas, vagrants, fools, idlers, witch doctors, and charlatan rabbis*" (Eilon 1988, 50–51; emphasis added).

Since Mendele Mocher Sforim was the pioneer of what was later called "classical Yiddish literature," in the next section, I try to determine whether this literature was a source of the paradigmatic representation of Mizrahim in the Bourekas.

Cultural Roots of the Bourekas in Classical Yiddish Literature

Through the paradigm of Mizrahi representation and the cinematic rhetoric applied by their authors/directors, Bourekas films clearly tapped into deep cultural currents. Considering the Ashkenazi agency inherent in them all and the fact that they depict a traditional Jewish community in isolation, it comes to mind that the origins of the representation paradigms used in the Bourekas' depiction of Mizrahi neighborhoods might be found in the shtetl representations of classical Yiddish writers,[3] such as Mendele Mocher

Sforim, Sholem Aleichem, and Y. L. Peretz. In fact, I find it quite reasonable that at the time that Hollywood took notice of shtetl culture from *Tevye the Dairyman* in *Fiddler on the Roof* (1972)—an adaptation of Sholem Aleichem's story—Israeli cinema showed the same curiosity, making effective use of it in Bourekas films, even though this usage was disguised owing to a hostility toward Yiddish culture in Israeli discourse at the time.[4]

This chapter analyzes a prominent work featuring relatively rich descriptions of the shtetl community and space by each Yiddish writer mentioned above: Mendele's *B'emek Habacha* (*In the Valley of Tears*),[5] Sholem Aleichem's *Motl Ben Peysi Hahazan* (*Motl, Peysi the Cantor's Son*), and Peretz's short story "Bein Shnei Harim" ("Between Two Mountains").

I have read the three works in their Hebrew translation, for two reasons. Some of these are no less "original" than the Yiddish version. The Hebrew translation of *In the Valley of Tears* was done by the author himself, and "Between Two Mountains" was written in Hebrew to begin with. The Hebrew translations were also the most common and widespread versions of these works in Israel during the 1960s and 1970s when Bourekas films were produced.[6]

The main purpose of this thematic analysis is to trace the homology between the various features of the representation paradigm of the shtetl in the works selected and the representation of the Mizrahi neighborhood in the Bourekas, as illustrated in chapter 2. I only focus here on the internal structure and logic of that paradigm in the work selected and its homology to that found in Bourekas films, not on any literal, historical, or anthropological meaning that might be attached to it.

Of the three works discussed here, only *In the Valley of Tears* is of an epic nature, and thus the only one that supplies the reader with what Barthes calls "informants" whose density is adequate for this research, a limited number of other works by Sholem Aleichem (particularly *Tevye the Dairyman*) and Peretz (one short story from his *Hassidism* collection and a few short stories from the *Mipi Am* collection) are used as additional sources.

Thematic Analysis of Shtetl Representation in Yiddish Classical Literature

What we notice immediately in the Mendele, Sholem Aleichem, and Peretz stories is that, like the neighborhoods of the Bourekas, their shtetls are fundamentally set apart from the broader society of the hosting country. The isolation of Kabtziel (a fictional shtetl in Ukraine) in Mendele's *In the Valley of Tears* is even deeper than that of the Bourekas' Mizrahi neighborhoods; the Bourekas neighborhoods' residents, while cut off from and neglected by the establishment, have some connection with their surroundings and a motivation to assimilate into the broader society by pairing with individuals from outside, but the isolation of Kabtziel is almost absolute. The most powerful indication of its total isolation, detachment, and lack of interaction with its surroundings comes right at the beginning of the story: "Now when Hershel [the protagonist] looks at the map searching for Kabtziel, he doesn't find it. In his childhood, he thought that it was the center of the universe and outside its borders there was only desolation" (158).[7]

The nature of isolation of Kasrilevke (another fictional shtetl in Ukraine) in Sholem Aleichem's *Motl Ben Peysi Hahazan* bears a greater resemblance to that of the Bourekas neighborhoods. Its residents are presented (like Sallah Shabati and his family in *Sallah*) as culturally and economically detached from the world around them; the fact that they do not speak any language other than Yiddish seems to be the major reason for their cultural detachment.[8] Even when very close to their shtetl, for example, at the nearby railway station, the family already encounters people with whom they cannot communicate since they don't speak their language. As for the economic aspect, it is obvious that like in the Bourekas neighborhoods, no member of the community is employed by the authorities and all are self-employed.

Generally, relations with authorities are bad, and people of Kasrilevke, just like those of the Mizrahi neighborhoods in the Bourekas, are hostile to authorities and sometimes gather to interrupt their work, for example, rescuing Motl from the policeman who wants to jail him. Normally, government officials have little control over the town. No one in the shtetl thinks about turning to the police to settle differences or quarrels, and, like in the Bourekas neighborhoods, the Jewish residents of the shtetl have developed the habit of settling conflicts by themselves.

Those features reoccur in the representations of Biala—the shtetl of Peretz's "Between Two Mountains" (unlike Kasrilevke and Kabtziel, this was a real place in Poland), where economic, cultural, and institutional isolation of the Jewish community from its surroundings can be observed. Similar to the author of *In the Valley of Tears*, Peretz hints at its residents' sense of being alone in the universe. In the story's only description of the town, it appears as if the Jewish community lives alone on this land, surrounded only by nature, which also happens to be Jewish. The earth and the heavens appear to be simply extensions or projections of this separated Jewish world: nature and the heavens are also happy when the Hassidim dance for their rabbi.

Indeed, most of the shtetl representations of the three writers suggest a greater degree of isolation than that depicted in the Mizrahi neighborhoods in the Bourekas. However, while the authors of the Bourekas tend to stress only the negative aspects of isolation, some of the Yiddish stories present also some positive ones. In the Kabtziel of *In the Valley of Tears*, Mendele shows how isolation leads to the establishment of strong community organizations and to the founding of institutions for mutual aid that help the poor to survive. In all three stories, the residents share a strong sense of community, of togetherness, of a collective destiny that seems to stem from this isolation.

Is the reduction of material culture evident in the description of Bourekas neighborhoods also found in the shtetls of Yiddish literature? When talking about the representation of material culture in this context, one has to note that an important difference between cinematic and literary representation lies in the primacy of physical description to the mimetic sequence. For the cinema, physical description and the formalization of space embody the main linguistic structures of representation. In contrast, for a book, the space where the action takes place is not often directly described by the author; information about it must be gleaned from textual units that have other primary functions. In *In the Valley of Tears*, Mendele does not bother to describe Kabtziel. Therefore, the site must be traced and interpreted within the framework of the units with other functions in the literary text. In doing so, the reader recognizes a considerable similarity between the presentation of the Mizrahi neighborhood in the Bourekas and that of Kabtziel.

As in the Mizrahi neighborhood of the Bourekas, in Kabtziel the streets are unpaved ("God creates wind to dry the earth so the Jewish women would not have trouble walking to the markets" [158]), the earthen streets are filled with puddles ("God brings water to the streets for the goats to drink" [158]), and livestock roam freely in the mud. In *Motl* also the information about the space, which can be read between the lines, presents a gloomy scene: the houses are wooden (even the houses of the rich—Yossi's house, for example, is built of logs); the streets are unpaved and are full of garbage and building materials; the shtetl, like the Bourekas neighborhoods, is a hybrid space, the worst of rural and urban; on one hand, animals wander freely in the streets, but at the same time, the houses are so close together that it is possible for one to move from house to house via the windows. The houses are also dirty and poorly maintained, their interior walls covered with stains.

As mentioned earlier, Peretz's lyrical short story does not describe a dense and detailed space. Transparent space is typical of other stories by Peretz.[9] A description of the shtetl's space that is close in spirit to the presentation of neighborhood space in the Bourekas is evident in another of Peretz's stories, "Impressions of a Journey through the Tomaszow Region." Here the narrator visits the shtetls of this region in Poland to specifically describe their living conditions. When he arrives at Tishevitz, he begins to tour the town, which is populated by both Jews and Christians, as historically most of the shtetls were.[10] At one point, the narrator reflects on the differences between the Jewish and Christian neighborhoods, hinting that the neglect of dwelling places is especially Jewish: "I do not need to be told where the Jews and where the non-Jews live. All I have to do is look at the windows. Unwashed windows are a sign of the Chosen People, especially where gaps left by missing panes have been filled by pillows or sacking. On the other hand, flowerpots and curtains strongly suggest that the inhabitants don't have the same inherent right to poverty" (i.e., they are not Jews; 24).

However, in this aspect, too, there is a difference between Bourekas films and Yiddish stories. Its concern is the authors' attitude toward the ugliness and neglect. Bourekas cinematic authors seem detached from the neighborhood reality, at best, and hostile to it at worst. Such a disparaging sentiment is evident in the "look" of the Bourekas films: the style of the shooting increases the effect of the ugliness, shabbiness, and chaos of the neighborhood, and in fact this physical aspect of neighborhood representation is being used as further evidence of its general decadence (see chapter 2). However, Yiddish literature authors seem at peace with the shtetl setting and even nostalgic for it. Nostalgia is evident in the descriptions of the Shtetl by night in "the valley of tears" and in the fact that Motl from "Motl Son of Peysi the Cantor " seems to miss the shtetl's chaos and neglect while visiting the more cultured locations of western Europe (48).

* * *

Like the Mizrahi neighborhood of the Bourekas, the shtetls of classical Yiddish writers experience the same kind of ruthless struggle and competition, originating in conditions of limited economic means and isolation.

For Mendele, in *In the Valley of Tears*, this tendency toward struggle is the Kabtziel residents' main characteristic. Accordingly, Mendele opens the novel with a metaphoric description of the competition and its sources: "The people of Kabtziel are beggars. In Kabtziel there is no livelihood for them [*parnussa*] but this, that they beg one from each other, *maintaining their families by invading their neighbors' territory*" (145; emphasis added). The struggle described in Kabtziel has no particular object and no limitations; it penetrates every aspect of life. People are struggling all the time—Leizer, Hershel's father, and Ben Zion, his neighbor, "fight and make peace and then fight again" (157)—and about everything. They quarrel about knowledge, about the myth of the shtetl's foundation, about food, about astrology, and more. Struggle is the norm in Kabtziel.

As in the Bourekas, women are another subject to fight over. Gedalia-Hirsh and Leizer fight over Hershel's mother until Leizer wins to become Hershel's father.

In *Motl* the appears most reductive form of competition: quarreling over food. At the home of Pesia, one of Motl's neighbors, this kind of competition is a part of everyday life. Fourteen people, mostly children, sit around Pesia's dinner table. All grab food, competing with each other when food is set out. However, a major aspect of competition in the novel is commercial. In the first chapter, the narrator presents the bitter commercial competition in the shtetl by describing the auctioning off of Motl's dying father's belongings. While the father lies dying in his bedroom, Michel, the book peddler, takes advantage of the family's helplessness by purchasing the father's books for "pennies," and he "grabs them very fast and hastily escapes the house" (13). This behavior seems to reflect a norm of abusive behavior in Kasrilevke since the scene repeats itself when Yossel, the goldsmith, comes to buy Motl's mother's jewelry; when Nachman, the carpenter, comes to buy the furniture; and when Chana, the Yiddene,[11] negotiates the purchase of a bed and a sofa.

Here too competition between residents spreads to every aspect of life. As in the Bourekas, residents of Kasrilevke also compete over knowledge, such as the accuracy of their knowledge of geography (e.g., the actual size of cities in Europe and the United States) and even about their understanding of border police routines. Being highly competitive in nature, Pini seems to be most anxious that his position as "Mister Know-It-All" might be in jeopardy. He cannot stand it that someone other than him can show mastery of knowledge in such fields as history, geography, philosophy, and political trivia, and he fights those people heatedly, using some questionable methods.

As in the Bourekas, the shtetl's ruthless commercial competition gives rise to deception. The residents of Kasrilevke mislead one another, using deception as a legitimate tactic of commercial competition. For example, the pulp author deceives Eli about the number of inkbottles he uses in a year.

Women in Kasrilevke are also something to compete for. Everyone in Motl's world, especially his mother (and Pesia the neighbor), are impressed when Eli marries Bracha, thus becoming the son-in-law of Yona, the wealthy baker. Talking about it, the women make it sound as though Eli won a competitive sporting victory.

Competition is the kernel of the story in "Between Two Mountains." Although it is an ideological difference that apparently causes the rivalry between the two main characters, the *rov* of Brisk (believed to be Brest in modern-day Belarus) and the rebbe of Biala, it seems that it is the competitive nature of each that fuels it. This trait in the rov of Brisk is obvious and manifests itself through his unnecessary cruelty when dealing with all opposition and rivalries, his generosity to his allies, and through his rude attitude toward his former student, the Biala rebbe, whom he accuses of running away from his yeshiva.

However, the competitive nature of the Biala rebbe is harder to observe. This is partly because he is introduced to the reader by the narrator, his follower, who adores him and presents him as a great humanist. However, after examining the rebbe's actions in the story, one can dismiss this as mythology. As a small man with a small voice, the rebbe of Biala is portrayed by the author (behind the back of his unreliable narrator) as a highly competitive man and full of bitterness. The rebbe refuses to give a blessing to the daughter-in-law of the rov of Brisk, his opponent, when she is about to die,[12] and actually hints that the dying young wife is none of his business but is rather the concern of his opponent (the rov of Brisk). The rebbe is not going to make it easier for his adversary: "Perhaps the Brisker Rov will come," (to help the woman) is his answer (16).

The view of the competitive nature of the rebbe is strengthened by his behavior during the meeting with the rov of Brisk. Upon greeting him, the rov of Brisk asks him callously, "Why did you run away from my yeshiva?" (22). Instead of calming the offended rabbi with kind words, the rebbe chooses first to tease the rov and further humiliate him: "What I lacked was air. I could never catch my breath" (194); he then proceeds to attack him:

"Your Torah is nothing but law. . . . It is nothing but steel and iron commandments, copper laws" (22). The competitive nature of these two leaders of the shtetl's community metonymically stands for the nature of their communities as a whole and indicates their essential competitiveness.

This story, which focuses on a conflict within patriarchal Jewish orthodoxy, does not deal with sexual competition. But in other stories by Peretz, one can find it. This is certainly the case of "A Virgin Gets Married,"[13] where Lea, the protagonist, is being courted by two men: Rabbi Zeinwilli, her father's old but wealthy employer, and the local doctor's young assistant. As in some of the Bourekas films, such as *Sallah* and *Fortuna*, here the competition over the girl occurs between two characters who symbolize different generations and different worldviews. While the doctor's assistant represents modernity—he dresses in modern clothes, his mustache is curled, he sings secular songs, and he speaks with a Polish accent—Rabbi Zeinwilli, an elderly merchant, represents Jewish tradition in both his habits and his appearance.

Nevertheless, in this aspect too there are differences between the Bourekas and classical Yiddish stories. Unlike the Bourekas, where the only explanation for the residents' extreme competitiveness is their isolation, here at least one work points to a more stable source. *In the Valley of Tears* points to a mythological source of this competitive behavior, suggesting that it is inherent in the soul of Jews and is essential and unchangeable.

As in the Bourekas, the existential spirit of survival and the struggle and antagonism presented in these stories result in the deterioration of social and interpersonal relationships that, by their nature, include emotional and spiritual aspects. It seems that in Yiddish classical writings' representations of the shtetl, too, human actions, capable of extrainstrumental value, devolve through a process of reduction to their basic and instrumental functions in the daily struggle for survival.

First, it seems that also in Yiddish literature, neighborly relations are reduced to frictional conflicts and blurred boundaries between the private and public domains. The social behavior of the residents of Kabtziel in *In the Valley of Tears* is characterized by such blurring of boundaries between private and public and intrusion into their neighbors' affairs. Mendele hints that this behavior results from the limited livelihood that Kabtziel provides. At the beginning of the story, he describes how every resident who opens a successful shop pushes other residents to immediately open similar shops in the same location. However, it seems that the phenomenon that begins as a survival impulse becomes habitual, gradually expanding to all aspects of life—until Kabtziel becomes a place in which "everyone goes into their friend's private domain and pushes them around. In a place where two Jews are standing, a third and then a fourth come, and thus they come and grow into a group of ten to fulfill the biblical saying: 'and you had joined us together'" (145).

Predating the Bourekas, here gossip is another means by which borders between private and public space become blurred. In Kabtziel, gossip is described as one of the main activities among the men. In the *beit midrash* (house of religious studies), the men "tell each other stories and gossip about the rich people of Kissalon" (156).

The extreme crowding that is typical in Motl's Kasrilevke makes the blurred borders between private and public seem unavoidable. Life in Kasrilevke brings people together. The women do their laundry together in the town's only river, and the wagon drivers and water deliverers also use the same small river. As in the Bourekas films, here, too, people live much of their lives outdoors, on the streets. People gather in particular public places and on certain occasions. For the people of Kasrilevke, the marketplace and the streets serve as gathering places, as do such special occasions as weddings, funerals, and the departure of residents.[14]

Moreover, one cannot do anything in private in Kasrilevke, since "in every spot and corner," as Motl complains, "people suddenly pop up" (83). The novel portrays this habit of togetherness as being so deeply rooted in the residents' lives that they export it to the places they travel to. Throughout the family's journey to the United States, there is crowding wherever there are emigrants from any shtetl. It is crowded near the emigration committee bureau in Lemberg, at the emigrant's inn in Antwerp, on the walk leading to the ship that takes emigrants to the United States, and on the deck of the ship itself.

As in the Bourekas, this blurring of the private and public cuts two ways. Not only is the private domain being intruded upon by the public but also vice versa: shtetl residents share their most private moments with others in the community, thereby exposing their intimacy in the public sphere. When Motl's father dies, his mother is in a hurry to share her deep sorrow and trauma with neighbors and those who have gathered around the house. Motl describes a conversation between his mother and Yossi the Gvir (wealthy man) that takes place in the public sphere, outside the house, in front of everyone, right after his father's death but before the funeral.

Motl's mother cries and wails loudly that she did everything she could to save her husband's life, while Yossi loudly blames her for hiding the illness from the community.

As for Peretz's story, it seems that nothing is private in the shtetl of Biala either; the habit of gossip prevails, and everybody knows almost everything about everyone else. Here, the narrator, although only a witness and a character within the story—and thus lacking the ability to freely penetrate the consciousness of those he describes—is nevertheless well versed in the details of shtetl life, probably through alternative sources of information, such as gossip. The narrator knows a great deal about his rebbe, the Brisker rov's cruelty toward Hassidim, and even the exact amount of money (one thousand gold pieces) his employer gave his daughter for a dowry.

An opportunity to see how this network of information works within the shtetl arises after the rov of Brisk arrives in Biala. When he sits around the table with his hosts after dinner and enquires about the Bialer rebbe, a conversation develops in which he learns that there is a "certain Noah" who is a rebbe in Biala and who has performed miracles. The rov adds some new gossip of his own about the rebbe, telling them about when he studied with him.

However unlike Bourekas films, Yiddish shtetl stories portray some positive neighborly behaviors. Within the borders of Kasrilevke, the value of neighborliness has not been totally eliminated. There is one major example of this in *Motl*: Pesia, although described as aggressive and pushy, habitually intruding into other people's business, is also described as a responsible and helpful neighbor. She takes Motl into her family and adopts him right after his father's death; she helps promote Eli's business; she lets Motl's mother wear one of her dresses to Eli's wedding; she stands clearly on the side of the family in arguments with others and protects them. She also quarrels with Eli's future father-in-law when he suspects that Eli has gambled away the watch he was given.

At times, Motl admits that he enjoys the positive aspects of this togetherness. When he talks about the hostel the family was sent to by the emigration aid committee of Lemberg, he says, "It was cheerful. Getting to know new emigrants, sitting together, eating together, telling stories. Oh, what beautiful stories, miracles, miracles from the pogrom, miracles from the recruitment bureau, miracles from the border" (82).

Peretz's story also stresses the positive aspects of togetherness. Through the story about Noah's becoming a rebbe, the narrator presents the togetherness, the sharing, as the most significant value of Hassidism. According to the rebbe, this togetherness has its mythological source at Mount Sinai, where the Torah was given to and shared by all the people of Israel at the time and to all the Jewish souls that had not yet been born.

In a way that resembles the situation in the Mizrahi communities of the Bourekas, the residents of the literary shtetls provide for themselves through nonprofessional, marginal work. In *In the Valley of Tears*, with the exception of Gedalia-Hirsh, the tailor, and a few women who darn socks, none of the occupations mentioned by the narrator are productive. In both the Bourekas neighborhoods and in Kabtziel, idleness prevails, and only a few people seem to have steady jobs.

In both, people have to beg for a living.[15] The narrator of Mendele also seems to characterize Kabtziel in general through this quality: "The people of Kabtziel are total beggars. There is never a dime in their pockets and they provide for themselves by begging one from the other" (145).[16] Residents of Kabtziel prove extremely creative in inventing new forms of begging. The list of the villagers' "occupations" hides some creative forms of begging: "Jews who receive (money from somebody), Jews who own documents and letters of recommendation that say that they are honest and needy (to help them beg), Jews who have hemorrhoids (and other illnesses that help them to beg)" (145). In the Bourekas neighborhoods, people sometimes make their living from occupations that border on petty crime, or else they are outright criminals.[17] Although these occupations are not represented in Kabtziel, they are found among the Jews of Kissalon, the nearest large city.[18]

People of the Mizrahi community in the Bourekas are presented mainly as idlers; they are not work oriented and prefer easy money. Residents of *Motl*'s Kasrilevke seem to have the same attitude toward work; physically easy, nonmanufacturing work has a higher status than productive labor. Occupations that have the greatest status are religious or communal in nature. Motl explains his brother Eli's marrying a rich girl while still having no position as a result of his father's pedigree as a cantor. Pesia remarks that "Peysi, the cantor, doesn't deserve for his son to be a craftsman" (41), and Motl's mother says, "All my enemies won't accomplish making Motl, the son of Peysi the cantor, a craftsman" (43).

Peretz's short story "Between Two Mountains" offers no real description of shtetl society and its everyday life. Nevertheless, in other stories by Peretz, begging is a major source of income. In *The Dead Town*, the narrator meets a Jew who tells him about his home, the eponymous "dead town."

When the narrator wonders what the townspeople do for a living, the man reveals that it is a town of idlers: "We all live quite respectably, I assure you. But from what, from what? From the same things everyone else does! Our poor folks live on hope, our merchants live on air, and our gravediggers live from the soil" (163).

Other stories by Peretz reveal more realistically the idleness and economic depression caused by the isolation of the shtetl. "Impressions of a Journey through the Tomaszow Region"—in a scene reminiscent of that of the social worker scene in Sallah (see chapter 2)—presents the shtetl of Tishevitz as a place of many idlers and forced togetherness. When the narrator goes on his tour with the shtetl's only *maskil* (learned man), a "handful of idlers" (31) tag along and listen to his conversation with the maskil, trailing them curiously and peering through the windows whenever they enter a house (32).[19]

* * *

As in the Bourekas, relationships with romantic potential are reduced in the literary shtetls to pairings that merely fulfill a financial function. In *In the Valley of Tears*, Kabtziel is described as a community in which the concept of romantic love is not prevalent. Instead, the community holds a more materialistic view of marriage; romantic love is subordinated to more basic needs. The story of the arranged marriage of Leizer, Hershel's father, and his mother is a perfect example of these kinds of marriage priorities. Leizer won his wife since he was thought of by her family to be a better provider than the fellow she was in love with.

In *Motl*'s Kasrilevke, it seems that a romantic attitude toward a bond is even less common: there are no love affairs in the novel—only marriages. Here too,[20] the raisons d'être of the marriages (e.g., the marriages of Eli and Bracha and of Pini and Teible) are not romantic but socioeconomic. Bracha, the daughter of Yona the Baker, is rich. However, Eli, the son of the shtetl's cantor, has a higher status. Both gain materially from their marriage. Eli is in a hurry to marry Bracha, since the economic condition of the family declines dramatically with the death of the father, its sole provider.

Biala's community in Peretz's story also devalues romantic love. The paragraph that shows this most effectively is the one in which the narrator talks about the harmony and love between his employer's daughter and her husband, along with his astonishing remark that "they tried to conceal from others this harmony and love that prevailed between them" (15). The fact that love and harmony between the married couple has to be concealed shows that this kind of relationship can be considered either inappropriate or childish—something that should be hidden.

Biala's community prefers functional relationships between men and women: women work and make money, while the men must pray for them. Romantic love, or sensuality, is not part of their worldview. A woman is expected to create the connection between her father and "the great religious figures of Israel through a successful match" and to bring her husband a "thousand gold pieces" (14).

* * *

In Yiddish literature, as in Bourekas films, the value of religion is reduced, and superstitions take over. Although Jewish religion is still quite strong in the community of Kabtziel, superstitions are interwoven through the fabric of daily life. For example, when Hershel's mother wants her husband to agree to name the child after her former fiancé, she tells him about a dream she had in which the dead Gedalia-Hirsh appears to ask that she call the child by this name. It is the tale that ultimately convinces him. The villagers incorporate not only dreams but also astrology into their belief systems (158). Moreover, like in the Bourekas, many villagers make their living from occupations based on superstitions. For example, one main occupation for women is to "whisper against illnesses and injuries and children's sicknesses" (148). The extent to which the superstitions become a part of the community discourse and replace some aspects of religion can be seen in the earliest Jewish education that Hershel receives as a grown-up, which corresponds to de facto superstitions. The adults tell him about "reincarnation" and dead people who wander the universe and also about ghosts, spooks, and demons (153).

In *Motl*, Sholem Aleichem describes a community less engaged with religious life and ceremonies than in Mendele's *In the Valley of Tears*,[21] and thus it resembles the communities of the Bourekas. People still fulfill the religious commandments and use "God-related" expressions, but more by force of habit and without too much thinking. This resembles what can be seen in the Bourekas, for example, the common but unconscious habit of kissing the mezuzah (a small box containing a scroll that is affixed to the doorposts of Jewish houses) when entering or leaving a Jewish home.[22]

Motl is not concerned with God; from his perspective, Kasrilevke is a place in which God and his commandments are no longer a part of life, and the villagers do not fear God anymore. Gedalia, the butcher, "fattens the whole town with unkosher meat" (chap. 8a). Eli's wife, Bracha, is another example of the materialistic, nonreligious spirit of Kasrilevke: "Honesty for her is a hot oven and God himself is nothing but the money you have in your pocket" (71). Although religious occupations still hold a high status in the shtetl, as in the Bourekas, *Motl* also reductively presents religiously important characters, such as a Jewish scholar who turns Judaism into paganism and cannibalism.[23] The ambivalent status of religious characters in Kasrilevke is also underscored by the fact that Pesia's sons call their fat cat "Feige Leah, the synagogue administrator" (26) and Pini writes satirical poems about the corruptness of another synagogue's administrator (76).

Superstitions provide the spiritual core that fills the vacuum created by the retreating religious observance. And, indeed, there are many superstitions in Kasrilevke: Motl's friend from the *heder*[24] believes that holding a cat damages one's memory, and Motl's mother thinks that Yona's bankruptcy was due to the evil eye. When Berel, the tailor, spreads a rumor that Eli drove the rats out of his house using a magic whisper, the villagers' response is to ask Eli to perform the same magic on their rats.

A lessening in the community's religious observance is at the core of "Between Two Mountains." The story describes the two central branches of Judaism in eastern Europe—Lithuanians and Hassidim—by presenting the ideological conflict between their two worldviews as if it were a personal conflict driven by the respective religious leaders' desire for power. Focusing on this desire for power hints at the deterioration of true Jewish belief within the shtetl (see section on competition above). As in the Bourekas, we can find here reductive portraits of religious figures. The portrayal of the rov of Brisk hardly shows him to be a "holy man"; he is described as crass, almost animallike. He "curses" (11), and his voice "thunders" when he is "furious" and sometimes even "roars like a lion" (18). His appearance is so intimidating that the narrator does not trust him to help the woman who has difficulties giving birth; on the contrary, he is afraid that the rov's rudeness will kill her.

There are people in Biala who believe in superstitions: the women believe that the rebbe performs miracles, and the narrator believes that "demons are flying in every direction at once" around his cart and that the rov is able to control the weather. However, how the status of Judaism is represented in Biala is much more refined and ambiguous than it is in Kasrilevke or Kabtziel. Although irony is directed toward important religious figures by the author, God is still very much alive in Biala; his presence seems to fill the consciousness of the characters, who lead lives in which faith and Jewish rituals are essential. This ambiguous and ambivalent approach toward the presentation of Hassidic life in the shtetl is at the core of Peretz's stories. On the one hand, he describes characters who are in total agreement with their Jewish religion, who love God and Jewish ritual; on the other, Peretz uses modern irony in his presentation to mock their beliefs and rituals and present them as premodern superstitions.[25]

In this aspect also, there is a difference between Bourekas neighborhoods and shtetl representations. Yiddish literature's representations of shtetls as places of superstition are basically different from that of the Mizrahi neighborhoods of the Bourekas, since while the Mizrahi residents almost totally replace religious ceremonies and belief with superstitious practices, in the shtetls religion is still more (Kabtziel, Biala) or less (Kasrilevke) alive side by side with superstitions. In the representation of the former, descriptions of the daily practice of the Jewish commandments, rituals, and visits to the synagogue attest to this. Moreover, the status of God's servants in The Jewish shtetls of Yiddish Classical Literature is not so low. Sometimes as we have seen in the stories they are respected. In contrast, in most of the Bourekas, religious figures are either irrelevant or the butt of many jokes.

Summary and Conclusions

Differences obviously exist between the representation paradigms of the shtetl in the various literary works discussed. *In the Valley of Tears* and "Between Two Mountains" portray the shtetl as a premodern community where life leads away from any progress. *Motl* Shalom Aleichem's story describes a community already struggling with its assimilation into the contemporary world of modernism.[26] But the foundational features of the shtetl common to the three works form a constant representation paradigm that resembles that of the Mizrahi communities in Bourekas films.

All the features that form the paradigmatic representation of the Mizrahi neighborhoods in the Bourekas—and which are, as I have shown, essential to any Bourekas film—likewise appear in the representation of the shtetls in the literary works examined. These recurring features are the isolation of the community, an unflattering description of its dwellings, competition and a ruthless struggle over physical subsistence, and a reduction of values. The singularity of this set of definitive features justifies the assertion that there is a shared paradigm of representation of Jewish communities between the Bourekas films and classical Yiddish literature.

However, there are differences in the presentations of the two communities, which should be analyzed and evaluated. An important difference is the dissimilarity in the degree of isolation of each community. The isolation of the shtetls of Kabtziel, Kasrilevke, and Biala appears more stark and deprived than any of the Bourekas neighborhoods. This is primarily due to the fact that in each case, the authors reflect different opportunities and potentials for shattering this isolation. Among the classical Yiddish works, it seems that the authors of *In the Valley of Tears* and *Motl* presume an *inability* to shatter the isolation, while the author of "Between Two Mountains" indicates only a *faint motivation* of the community to do so. However, the authors of the Bourekas describe communities that have the motivation, as well as the ability, to shatter their isolation, primarily through pairing with those outside the community—that is, Ashkenazim—which is a key feature of many of the films.

Another difference lies in the dissimilarity in the nature of the explanations that justify the characteristics of the respective communities. The Bourekas explain these characteristics only as a reaction of the community to certain circumstances and pressures. In contrast, *In the Valley of Tears* and "Between Two Mountains" make an effort to elevate some of these characteristics; the former offers mythological explanations to pushiness, competition, and forced togetherness, while the latter explains forced togetherness and isolation in both religious and mythological terms. Although ironically presented, these explanations contribute positive attributes to the community represented, highlighting shared values and traditions.

Another major difference is that while the Bourekas present only the negative aspects of community characteristics, classic Yiddish literature shows positive ones as well. In *In the Valley of Tears* and "Between Two Mountains," the authors usually show positive aspects of the main characteristics, such as isolation and togetherness. Some of the positive aspects of togetherness are also stressed in *Motl*; however, the relatively positive tone of the community's representation in *Motl* is achieved mainly because Motl, the child and narrator of the story, is a nine-year-old boy who is enthusiastic, naive, cheerful, and full of life. His consciousness serves as a metonym for the inner consciousness of the shtetl's residents.

In Bourekas films, the decline in religious observance, religious education, and neighborliness, as well as the abundance of superstitions and sexual competition are emphasized more strongly than in the literary Yiddish works and seem indicative of a more severely critical tone by the authors. Critics such as Miron (2000, 1–49) have shown that representations of the shtetl in classical Yiddish literature are ahistorical in nature. If this is indeed so, the differences in representational paradigms between the Bourekas and classical Yiddish literature can be better explained not as flowing from the nature of the various objects represented (the shtetl or the Mizrahi neighborhood) but as the result of either the different authors' ideologies or different relationships that the authors have with their objects. In part, this difference is probably an outcome of the totally different identification patterns and emotional bonds that the authors have with their object. While the classical Yiddish writers described their own ethnic group, and thus bear both an emotional investment in and essential knowledge of their object, the authors of the Bourekas (Ashkenazi Israelis) were emotionally detached from the Mizrahi neighborhoods they described and had little real knowledge of the Mizrahi community. This dissimilarity, rooted in a fundamental and preexisting disposition of the authors toward their objects, partially explains the differences in representations. Setting aside Peretz's irony, Yiddish classical writers appear more positively attached to their objects than Bourekas authors.

Differences in the levels of the community's isolation in both groups can also be explained by the background of the different ideologies of the authors and the dissimilar raisons d'être of each group of texts. One of the functions of the Bourekas (discussed in chapter 2) was *to persuade* the Mizrahim that the gaps between them and the Ashkenazim, although justified, would be closed in the coming generations, upon the assimilation of the Mizrahim into modernity—a mission that could be achieved also by marrying "modern" Ashkenazim.[27] Bourekas narratives, therefore, emphasize these options. However, classical Yiddish literature had different raisons d'être, one of which was *to encourage* the assimilation of traditional Jewish communities into European culture. Tactics adopted by authors to promote this change included criticizing the provinciality of shtetl life (Frieden 1995, 1–9). It seems that accentuating the isolation of the Jewish traditional communities in the shtetl and the deficiencies it brought upon them is part of this tactic (Miron 2000).

How this paradigm of representation from classical Yiddish literature found its way into the Bourekas remains to be determined. The next chapter outlines the possibilities.

5

THE DYNAMICS OF CONTINUITY BETWEEN TWO DISPARATE CULTURES

IT SEEMS THAT THE PATTERN OF COMMUNITY REPRESENTATION appearing in the Bourekas has no previous or parallel cinematic source.[1] The shtetl-like depiction of the Mizrahi neighborhood is unique and particular to that film cycle. Even the group of films that are thematically and aesthetically closest—the aforementioned comedies and melodramas representing the Mizrahi community, created during the same period by Mizrahi directors—do not rely on this specific paradigmatic representation of life in an ethnic enclave.

Despite the homology seen in Yiddish classical literature and the Bourekas patterns of representing Mizrahim, it is not the intention of this book to prove a direct, determining influence of this literature on Bourekas films. Instead, my aim is to show that there is a reasonable probability that Bourekas films correspond with classical Yiddish literature through the agency of their Ashkenazi directors, thereby facilitating an intersection of content and form. To demonstrate the likelihood of such a development, it is necessary to verify that classical Yiddish literature was present in Israeli cultural discourse and accessible to educated Israelis around the time the Bourekas films were produced and that the directors of the Bourekas had good reason to adopt some of its themes and forms—especially its paradigmatic representation of the Jewish community—into their films. Accordingly, this chapter shows that despite what seems unfavorable ideological ground, in general, classical Yiddish literature did achieve an equitable reception in Israel, maintaining a considerable presence in Israeli cultural discourse of the time.[2]

In due course, I show that classical Yiddish literature's presence in Israeli discourse was a fair one—being but one element of a larger trend that, during the 1960s and 1970s, allowed the survival of Yiddish cultural elements "under the surface" of an official institutional and cultural discourse that was officially oppressive toward Yiddish—and that Bourekas directors had more than one reason to adopt classical Yiddish literature's paradigmatic representation of the Jewish shtetl community and to present the Mizrahi community and neighborhood through it.

First, I survey the factors that affected the reception of classical Yiddish literature in the second half of the twentieth century—a period characterized by ambivalence toward Yiddish culture and one in which the clash between forces suppressing and preserving Yiddish culture reached its peak. I look at the differences between the modes of reception of the various writers and show how they were the result of different relationships with ideologies that prevailed at that time in Israeli discourse.

Classical Yiddish Literature within Israeli Zionist Discourse

All in all, several factors seem to have affected the reception of classical Yiddish literature in Israel: Zionist ideology, especially the phenomenon known as the "negation of exile"; the historical "inferiority" of Yiddish vis-à-vis Hebrew and the triumph of Hebrew over Yiddish in the Israeli sphere as the national language; and the demand by mainstream critics of Hebrew literature that the national literature serve as *hatzofe l'beit Yisrael* (the Israeli nation watcher); that is, it should foresee threatening events and offer solutions to the nation's cultural, sociological, and political conflicts while reflecting a Zionist ethos and narrative (Miron 1987b, 17).

While all of the above had a negative effect on its reception, what really saved classical Yiddish literature in the end was the secret but vital role that Yiddish language and culture played in the creation of the Hebrew identity within the Zionist Ashkenazi elites in Israel (Kimchi 2011; Miron 2004, 9–13; Pinsker 2014), the attitude of Israeli Ashkenazi elites that were not part of the Zionist elite and their very pronounced emphasis on cultural continuity over time, which drove them to try to keep Yiddish alive—as a vernacular as well as a culture.

According to Amnon Raz-Krakotskin (1993, 23), Israeli Jews' consciousness revolves around a central axis of *shlilat ha'galut*—the negation of exile. This concept shapes both their view of history and their collective memory, reflecting a belief in a natural sequence—a continuity—between the present state of Israel and Jewish sovereignty of the Hasmonean kingdom in the days of the Second Temple (140-63 BC). According to this notion, the centuries of exile that separated these two periods of Jewish sovereignty—the Hasmonean kingdom and the modern state of Israel—were an era in which the Jewish people lived under abnormal conditions, in a partial and flawed existence, where the nation's spirit could not survive due to external limitations. The absorption of this idea led Israeli discourse to reject all that was considered "exilic," including Jewish cultural creations of the period of "exile."[3]

Israeli negation of exile is also the result of the efforts taken by Zionist Ashkenazi elites to ratify what Sara Chinski (2002, 64-65) sees as their "fabricated" Western identity for which the metaphor she uses is "albinism"; for her, this project is concerned mainly with wiping away and repressing their Jewish diasporic subjectivity and replacing it with a new Hebrew Zionist one.

One can assume that the reception of classical Yiddish literature was seriously delayed by the negation-of-exile discourse. This literature, which portrays the premodern Jewish provincial and traditional shtetl of eastern Europe—typically from a critical and negative point of view—was more than just a decadent literature of the Jewish exilic period; it was a testimony to the "decaying" Zionist elites' ethnocultural sources.

As already implied, the historical "inferiority" of Yiddish vis-à-vis Hebrew also had an effect on the reception of classical Yiddish literature. Prior to Zionist discourse and the rise of Jewish nationality, Yiddish had already come to be seen as inferior to Hebrew and not worthy of serious literature. While Hebrew continued to be venerated by Jews and non-Jews alike, if not as a "holy tongue," then as a great classical language, yiddish, in contrast, was despised by both educated Jews and gentiles. Although it was a practical and highly expressive language, it came to be seen as an inferior dialect, a language unfit for modern education, and a grotesque hybrid form of German.

Zionist discourse inherited this attitude toward Yiddish and expanded it. For Zionism, Yiddish was even less than a hybrid language with no literary history; it was a part of the Jewish exilic-diasporic culture that "had to be forgotten" (Chaver 2004). This Zionist negation of Yiddish became significant in 1922, after Yiddish lost the "language war" in the Land of Israel (Palestine) to Hebrew. The result of the defeat was that Hebrew became the official teaching, speaking, and writing language of the Yishuv (the pre-independence, Zionist-organized population in Palestine), and the Land of Israel became the territory of Hebrew.[4] It seems that after Israel's independence in 1948, this history—which stresses the conflict between Yiddish and Hebrew—inevitably created a situation within Israeli Zionist discourse that was highly unfavorable and even hostile to Yiddish.[5]

In this atmosphere, the reception of any Yiddish text would have been inherently and immediately problematic.[6] But there is more to it. Elaborating on Hebrew literature's special status, that is, appearing as a national literature before the nation-state came into existence, Shimon Halkin (1950) called it "Hatzofeh L'beit Yisrael" (the Jewish nation watcher). Halkin, among others, expected Hebrew literature to act like a prophet, to be a pillar of fire that marches before the nation, foresees events, and offer solutions for the nation's cultural, sociological, and political conflicts (Miron 1987b, 418–29). This demand on Hebrew literature also influenced the reception of Yiddish writing; in fact, many Zionist critics have judged Yiddish literature mainly for its national message and the ways it reflected or avoided reflecting official Zionist ideology, sometimes completely disregarding its aesthetic and artistic aspects.

Given Israel's cultural history, the reception of classical Yiddish writers in Israeli discourse should have been outright catastrophic; however, the reality was more complex. While the marginalizing of various kinds of this literature occurred on many levels, the harmony between certain aspects of this literature and the demands of Zionist discourse gave other kinds of Yiddish classical writing a surprisingly central place in Israeli cultural discourse.

Each of the three classical Yiddish writers—Y. L. Peretz, Sholem Aleichem, and Mendele Mocher Sforim—holds a slightly different position within Israeli discourse. These positions are the outcome of different relationships between the author's work and the demands, ideas, and viewpoints of Israeli discourse described above.

Peretz's work was received quite poorly in Israel. While his contribution to the evolution of the national literature cannot be completely ignored,[7] the relative marginality of Peretz's works that had been translated from Yiddish to Hebrew was determined by the fact that throughout his writing, Peretz—not personally a Zionist—showed a lasting commitment to the Diaspora Jewish nationalism of Shimon Dubnov (Frieden 1995, 225–31) and strove to offer an alternative path for the Jewish people's nationality in exile, in Europe.[8] He struggled to provide his contemporary European Jews with the vocabulary of their collective experience and the modulation of their individual moods. Moreover, Peretz was no exile negator. Although he criticized the shtetl and Jewish diasporic life, his criticism is so well immersed in the literary fabric of his stories that it is hardly noticeable. The outcome was that Peretz's works had a very minor presence in Israeli literary discourse and have not been translated since 1962 (the Dvir edition).

The position of Sholem Aleichem within Israeli discourse is different. Although he is not part of the Hebrew literature narrative, his writings have been translated from Yiddish into Hebrew several times; a new edition of all his works[9] was published as late as 1997, and some of his novels and stories, such as "Tevye the Dairyman," have been adapted for the cinema in Israel.[10] Sholem Aleichem's more favorable reception is the result of a different correspondence with the relevant aspects of Zionist ideology.[11] First, although Frieden (1995, 119) notes that Sholem Aleichem never found his "voice" in Hebrew, his original Hebrew writings were never totally forgotten and won some recognition in Israel.[12] Second, his style of writing in Yiddish—consisting of monologues and dialogues—seems to lend itself to translation more easily than the sophisticated literary style of Peretz. Finally, Miron's appreciation of Sholem Aleichem's writings and his successful effort to present his main works as reflecting elements of Zionist ideology made palpable contributions to his legacy.[13] Miron finds that the heroes of some of Sholem Aleichem's key stories ("Tevye the Dairyman," *Motl*, and "Menachem Mendel") reject the shtetl and its values and thus proclaims Sholem Aleichem to be a writer who actually expresses the Zionist negation of exile.

Nevertheless, not all the Hebrew literature critics were as favorable as Miron toward Sholem Aleichem. Some of them could not forgive what they perceived as a lack of national ideology and nationalist message; that is, they could not bear the fact that Sholem Aleichem failed to take upon himself the role of the "Israeli nation watcher."[14]

Of the three classical Yiddish writers highlighted, Mendele Mocher Sforim has had the most successful reception within Israeli literary discourse. Mendele is a true bilingual writer. For some critics, his work in Hebrew is more important than what he wrote in Yiddish.[15] Research has been published about his work since it first appeared in the nineteenth century,[16] making him one of the most closely studied writers in Israel. In the past, his works were part of the Hebrew literature program required for matriculation, and nowadays they are commonly taught in Hebrew literature departments in universities throughout Israel. The latest translation from his novels took place as recently as 2012 (*The Little Fellow*, Carmel edition). Hebrew literature critics are usually favorable toward him, first and foremost due to the ideology reflected through his writings. Mendele, says Brenner, is the first real Jewish national writer because of his talent to truly analyze the national spirit and evaluate the truly horrible condition of the Jewish nation in exile.[17] In other words, for Brenner, Mendele was first the greatest exile negator of them all. In an essay he wrote for Mendele's seventieth birthday, he claims that Mendele knew that the Jewish people didn't create anything in exile and that all hopes for something good to happen in exile were nonsense (Brenner 1955, 58).

Mendele is also the only one of the three writers that critics considered to be "a watcher of the Jewish nation."[18] He was seen as a prophet, although not an entirely Zionist one.[19] It seems that the Zionist critics also appreciate Mendele's didactic tendency, which they saw as a sign of national responsibility.

Politics and ideology aside, Mendele is certainly considered to be an important part of the history of Hebrew literature. In an article on the collection of Mendele's stories,[20] Brenner (1955, 58) crowns him the number one Hebrew writer and the pioneer of Hebrew literature. When reviewing this history, Miron (1987b) not only mentions Mendele as being unsurpassed but also presents him as the "grandfather" of the new Hebrew literature.[21] While describing the Hebrew literary circle of Odessa, Miron (1987b, 357) recounts how the young writers behaved like pilgrims when coming to Mendele's house, treating him as though he were a holy man. Meanwhile, neither Sholem Aleichem nor Peretz receive a single mention in the book.[22] This seems to be the common outlook on Mendele among Hebrew literature critics today. To summarize, it seems that not only relative to the other Yiddish writers but in principle as well, Mendele's writings well withstood the suppression of Yiddish in Israeli Zionist discourse and have had more than a fair presence in Israeli literary discourse since its very beginning.

Yiddish Culture in Israeli Discourse of the 1960s and 1970s

The initial positive reception that Israeli literary discourse generally showed Mendele Mocher Sforim, and to a certain extent Sholem Aleichem, seems to improve further during the 1960s and 1970s. Due to a variety of specific circumstances, their Yiddish works in Hebrew translation, as well as their images of the shtetl, repeatedly turned up in Israeli discourse during this era.²³ Nevertheless, the writings of Mendele and Sholem Aleichem were not the only faces of Yiddish culture to survive the Zionist suppression in that period. Other elements of Yiddish culture, although officially rejected, continued to echo through the Israeli discourse of the time.²⁴

Joshua and David Fishman have described the curious ambivalence toward Yiddish throughout the 1960s and early 1970s. They maintain that although officially and institutionally suppressed, in Israel there was a very widespread yet low-key receptiveness toward Yiddish that functioned at the level of a vernacular, as entertainment, and as nostalgia, while Yiddish expressions were then "a part of almost everyone's stylistic repertoire" (Fishman and Fishman 1974, 140). Miron also describes the vividness of the Yiddish vernacular in the Zionist Israeli discourse of the 1960s and 1970s²⁵—a presence, he mentions, that does not exist any longer since Israeli acquaintance with the language has declined dramatically. Like the Fishmans, Miron stresses the penetration of Yiddish as a vernacular adjunct to the Zionist Hebrew environment during that period. There was consensus at the time, Miron claims (2004, 9–20), about Yiddish vernacular being amusing; as a result, entertainers and speakers used Yiddish to create comic relief and a feeling of partnership and solidarity with their Zionist Hebrew audience that their intimacy with Yiddish vernacular, on the one hand, and their readiness to mock the language and cooperate with its reductive representation, on the other, turn them, in their own eyes, into Hebrew human beings.²⁶ Thus it seems that in those years, an arbitrary use of Yiddish vernacular was a secret component in the construction of Hebrew subjectivity.

The precarious status of Yiddish and the relative receptiveness to its vernacular were also reflected in Israeli cinema of the time. Weitzner (2002) claims that while in the 1950s, Israeli cinema was indifferent and, at times, hostile to Yiddish, in the 1960s, after it was already clear that Zionism had been culturally "victorious" and the state of Israel was confident enough to make room for non-Zionist sensibilities, Yiddish made its entrance into Israeli films as a vernacular. This phenomenon was also connected, claims Weitzner (2002, 188), to the emergence of commercial cinema, which, beginning in the early 1960s, received less financing from the government and thus was less ideologically tied to the Zionist project.

Yet it seems that the reception of Yiddish and Yiddish culture throughout the 1960s and 1970s goes beyond this vernacular penetration into Israeli cinema and beyond its secret role in the construction of the Hebrew identity of the Zionist elites. During those years, the number of students in

Yiddish research centers at Israeli universities grew steadily (Fishman and Fishman 1974, 137), and original Yiddish literature was once again being written. Shachar Pinsker (2007, 47) claims that up until the mid-1960s, there was a group of young Yiddish writers and poets that went by the name Yung Yisroel; they published a periodical of Yiddish literary criticism and a series of original Yiddish literature and poetry books, maintaining a lively Yiddish literary discourse in Israel. Yung Yisroel, continues Pinsker (2014, 330), also took part in forming the modernist style of "statehood generation" (*dor ha'medina*) poetry in Israel through influencing central poets in this group, such as Nathan Zach, Yehuda Amichay, and David Avidan.

Moreover, a critical reading of Fishman and Fishman's articles (1973, 1974) reveals that not only the vernacular but also written Yiddish and Yiddish "high culture" had a considerable presence in the Israeli discourse of the time. This presence was, of course, not comparable to the place of then-contemporary Hebrew literature, nor was it as effective; nevertheless, the presence of this "underground" culture was quite meaningful, especially in Yiddish-speaking environments.

During those two decades, for example, the publication of Yiddish books flourished. Although the language was always firmly established as a vernacular and as an informal spoken medium, and although poetry, novels, dramas, short stories, essays, literary criticism, and science books written in Yiddish were always the privilege of a relatively small circle, Yiddish book publishing in Israel boomed in the early 1970s. In addition, Israeli publishers also served as a publishing vehicle for American and other non-Israeli Yiddish authors (Fishman and Fishman 1974, 131).[27] The publication of these books grew rapidly, while the number of books published in other European languages remained very small. In 1970, for example, fifty-four Yiddish books were published, as compared to only eight in French, six in German, four in Hungarian, and three in Romanian (Fishman and Fishman 1974, 132, table 17). This Yiddish achievement is especially impressive when taking into account the fact that not a single book was published in 1970 in the two other Jewish diasporic languages, Ladino and Judeo-Arabic.

But the Fishman's research offers two other even more interesting facts. The first is that the total number of Yiddish books published in Israel jumped from ten in 1955 to thirty-eight in 1960 and then to fifty-four in 1970—an increase of 360 percent at the end of the 1950s and of 65 percent during the 1960s. Indeed, the Fishmans do not distinguish between classical and nonclassical Yiddish literature, but one may assume that many of the published books were part of the classical Yiddish literature corpus.

Another interesting fact is that although many works in Yiddish were deemed valuable enough to warrant translation into Hebrew, and this particular branch of translation was thriving, these books' original language (Yiddish) was ignored in the new Hebrew publications and thus hidden from the reader. This may be concrete proof of the suppressive force of exile negation, on the one hand, and the vitality of Yiddish culture on the other, but it also indicates that the real scope of the underground infiltration of Yiddish literature into Israeli discourse was a lot deeper than it seems when analyzing conventional sources.

Also testifying to the relative popularity of classical Yiddish literature in this era was the fact that Israeli cinema adapted two Sholem Aleichem stories during the 1960s: *Nes Ba'ayara* (*Miracle in Our Shtetl*, 1966), an adaptation of *Motl Ben Peysi Hahazan* (*Motl, Son of Pessi the Cantor*), and *Tuvia Ve'sheva Benotav* (*Tuvia and His Seven Daughters*, 1968), an adaptation of *Tuvia Haholev* (*Tevye the Milkman*). Considering the small number of literary adaptations produced in the country's tiny film industry at the time, this embrace of Sholem Aleichem speaks volumes.[28]

So despite being institutionally oppressed, Yiddish culture succeeded in maintaining a considerable presence and vitality in the Israel of the 1960s and 1970s, the era in which Bourekas films were produced. One can assume that classic Yiddish works—loaded with their particular paradigmatic representation of the Jewish shtetl community—both in Hebrew translation and adapted into film, were disseminating Yiddish culture into Israeli discourse during that period.

Functions of the Appropriation of Yiddish Culture Elements into Hebrew Zionist Surroundings

Classical Yiddish shtetl stories have their own ideologies, of course. The defining ethos of classical Yiddish literature was formed during the Jewish Enlightenment (Haskalah) era[29] and assimilated some Haskalah and post-Haskalah sensibilities.[30] This ideological orientation is what separates the literary representation of the shtetl from historical reality. While some (mostly earlier) critics seem to think that classical Yiddish literature's representations of the shtetl possess a historical or anthropological value, Miron (2000), among other more recent critics, indicates that these representations are ahistorical and, indeed, ideologically biased. Karib (1950, 42) describes Mendele's stories as "the very ripe fruit of the Haskalah ideology."[31] He also claims that this ideology, which was absorbed into the stories, turns Mendele's shtetl representations into a twisted mirror that emphasizes and highlights all that is distorted and defective in the lives of the residents (Karib 1950, 12).

As for Sholem Aleichem, Miron—after dividing all Yiddish writers before World War I into two groups, the "marginal" maskilim (believers in Haskalah ideology) and the "radical" maskilim—places him (and Mendele) in the radical group who sought more aggressive modernization and assimilation.[32] Their radicalism affects both their choice of satire and parody as main literary genres and their choice of what Miron calls the "esthetic of ugliness" as a main literary tactic when describing the shtetl's space.[33] Early Peretz stories also reflect Haskalah ideology as indicated by Ruth Wisse (1991, xiii–3), since they fought Hassidic influence, championed the study of European languages by Jews, and promoted a positive emphasis on productive labor and providing Jews with production skills.[34]

Taking all this into account, it seems that through its writers-themselves members of the Ashkenazi diasporic elite—classical Yiddish literature served as an ideological apparatus for this elite, helping to spread Haskalah ideas among the Jewish masses and "educating them in the spirit of Haskalah" (Miron 2000, 10).[35] However, with its comic, sometimes critical and satiric representation of the shtetl, classical Yiddish literature had one more important sociopsychological role. This sort of Yiddish canon seems also to function to ease the oedipal guilt of Jewish elites for abandoning the shtetl and the traditional Jewish world.

One can claim that classical Yiddish literature, as an apparatus in the hands of the European Ashkenazi elites, plays a double role. It was a part of the general Eurocentric Jewish discourse that meant to turn the east European Jewish masses into "Europeans" in the spirit of the Haskalah, but at the same time, it was a part of the Ashkenazi elite's inner discourse, which helped its members who were already modern and European, to justify their abandoning of the shtetl and their original Jewish traditional subjectivity. If so, we should not be surprised to discover Yiddish serving the Israeli Zionist elites—the successors of the Ashkenazi elites of eastern Europe—as an ideological apparatus, in a somewhat similar manner.

The Fishmans claim that the vernacular form of the preservation of Yiddish in the Zionist sphere shows that Yiddish, for Ashkenazi Zionist

Hebrew speakers, was connected to an oedipal guilt—a guilt they felt for abandoning and rejecting their ancestors' language/culture. Those Hebrew speakers preferred to use Yiddish at the level of the vernacular, since, as opposed to high canonical Yiddish, the vernacular level would not elicit too much of this guilt. Taking a homological path, Miron (2004) seems to think that Yiddish survived as a comic vernacular in the Israeli sphere because this mode of preservation served two necessary functions, both connected to the ratification of Ashkenazi Israeli Zionists' desired Hebrew identity (subjectivity). For him, this mode of preservation first created a necessary differentiation between people who used Yiddish only in this reductive form from those who used Yiddish seriously in all its layers, as their cultural language. The former were tagged as acculturated, Hebrew Zionist Israelis, while the latter as exilic, traditional, diasporic Jews, who lacked either Zionist Hebrew or European acculturation (Miron 2004, 10). This differentiation, which served to strengthen the Hebrew subjectivity of users of the Yiddish vernacular, was extremely important, because at that time the Zionist Hebrew subjectivity was still unstable, and the exilic-diasporic self of these Ashkenazi Hebrew speakers was still strong, especially within family circles.

Miron's (2004) second argument is that this mode of preservation served to distinguish between Ashkenazi Israelis and the non-Ashkenazim—Near Eastern, North African, and Sephardic Jews (Mizrahim), who were not familiar with the Yiddish vernacular. This differentiation between Zionist Ashkenazi elites and Mizrahim was important. It proved that although negation of exile threatened to wipe away all pre-Zionist Jewish diasporic subjectivities, a diasporic Ashkenazi element in Hebrew subjectivity was still—although officially rejected—a "secret" element, needed as a final confirmation of such subjectivity and as an entry ticket into the Zionist Israeli elite.[36]

As a consequence of all the above, I would like to claim that from the beginning of the 1960s—a period in which the presence of Yiddish culture in the Zionist sphere reached its peak, but the ideology of the negation of exile and the institutional suppression of Yiddish were still quite strong (albeit weaker than during the 1950s)—Bourekas films joined Israeli discourse as a phenomenon using Yiddish culture "secretly" and in a manner that is reductive and narrowing, to achieve identical goals.

Bourekas films are comparable in their strategy and function to other textual phenomena of that period, such as the camouflaged Hebrew translations from Yiddish literature and the comic use of Yiddish vernacular. There is, indeed, considerable similarity between the Bourekas and these two textual phenomena. The camouflaged translation of Yiddish literature into Hebrew literature offers a literary parallel to Bourekas films. The two textual structures seem to share the function of "marinating" and preserving Yiddish culture, within the hostile environment of Israeli Zionist discourse. Both textual structures have their sources in Yiddish culture, and both veil these sources.

One can also see parallels between the comic use of Yiddish vernacular by entertainers and speakers throughout the 1960s and 1970s (in official speeches, theatrical and comic performances, and in Israeli cinema in general) and the use of Yiddish literature in the Bourekas films. First, both phenomena were created through the agency of the Israeli Ashkenazim, apparently somewhat familiar with Yiddish culture[37] but living in a Zionist world hostile to this traditional culture. Both phenomena also share a reductive use of aspects of Yiddish culture. The comic use of the Yiddish vernacular offers a simplistic rendering of Yiddish, while Bourekas films' use of the paradigmatic shtetl representation of classical Yiddish literature to describe Mizrahi neighborhoods and communities also offers a reductive, twisted use of Yiddish culture. Both phenomena also use projection—in the Freudian sense. The speaker who uses Yiddish comically, for laughs, projects the serious use of the Yiddish language on the other—the traditional pre-Hebrew Ashkenazim. Similarly, the Bourekas directors seem to project the traditional Jewish Ashkenazi culture onto their ethnic "others": the Mizrahim, residents of the Mizrahi neighborhood.

In light of the similarities between the two textual phenomena, I suggest here that the two also share a function: to ratify and reinforce the desired subjectivity of the Hebrew Zionist presenter and of his laughing audience. The adoption of the paradigm of shtetl representation in the Bourekas thus turned these films into an apparatus that served that function—both for their Ashkenazi directors, as part of Israel's elite, and for their Ashkenazi audiences.

Ephraim Kishon, the director of *Sallah*, writes in his autobiography that although he grew up in a family that had assimilated into Hungarian culture, Yiddish was still all around him. His grandparents spoke Yiddish, and the children in his family were aware of Yiddish (London 1993, 10, 17).

The Ashkenazi directors of the Bourekas, who were raised in a Yiddish-speaking environment or, at least, like Kishon, in a world where Yiddish culture was still evident, used the Bourekas to secretly reexperience their original, rejected Yiddish culture while reducing the oedipal guilt they felt for having abandoned it (since the presentation of Yiddish cultural elements in the Bourekas is reductive).[38] The films were also a way to sanction their (and their Ashkenazi audience's) desired identity as European Hebrew Zionist Israelis. At the same time, Bourekas films redefined the borders of Hebrew subjectivity, adding some Jewish Ashkenazi diasporic flavor to it. By presenting mythological or successful Zionist Hebrew figures as having some features of Ashkenazi subjectivity, the Bourekas promoted Hebrew subjectivity as an identity that required some ethnic Ashkenazi input.[39]

Recognizing the role that Bourekas films' paradigmatic representation of the shtetl had in the ratification of Ashkenazi Hebrew Zionist subjectivity would be sufficient for understanding its relevance to the needs of the Zionist Ashkenazi elites; however, the Bourekas met the needs of these elites in diverse ways. As emerges from the analysis of *Sallah* (chapter 1), one of the most important aspects of this relationship lies in the Bourekas films' reflection of the Zionist modernization approach, which supported the ethnic distribution of wealth and work that favored the Ashkenazim in Israel at the time, through condemning Mizrahim as premodern while indicating Ashkenazim as the role model of modernity (Avruch 1987, 229).[40]

Pursuant to the discussion of *Sallah*, I suggest here that the adaptation of the paradigmatic shtetl representation as a Jewish premodern community and projecting it on the Mizrahi neighborhood in the films—adding a denunciation to it through reductive representation—allowed Bourekas films to echo, reproduce, and distribute the Zionist demand from the Mizrahim to modernize. Moreover, by denouncing Mizrahim as premodern while tagging Ashkenazim in the films as ultramodern, the Bourekas also promoted the idea of the similarity between premodernity and Mizrahiness and modernity and Ashkenaziness, which underlies the Zionist modernization approach.

* * *

Nevertheless, the Bourekas also stress the option for Mizrahim to "become Ashkenazim," through intermarriage, as a preferable solution for their premodernity, blurring the path between becoming Ashkenazim and becoming modern.[41] The portrayal of the Mizrahim as historical shtetl Ashkenazim likewise allows the Bourekas films to realize—by way of an imaginative presentation—what Kevin Avruch (1987) sees as the ultimate goal of the modernization approach: the transformation of Mizrahim into Ashkenazim.[42]

To summarize, Bourekas films as cultural products using Yiddish culture reductively helped Zionist elites in reducing their oedipal guilt for abandoning Yiddish culture and language and ratifying their Zionist Hebrew subjectivity. Nevertheless, the Bourekas's reuse of classical Yiddish literature's paradigm of representation of the Jewish community and projection of this representation onto the Mizrahim—while presenting the Ashkenazim as ultramodern and reflecting the modernization approach—helped Zionist Ashkenazi elites to promote their ideology and status as the natural leaders of the Israeli sphere.

Bourekas Films as a Location for the Construction of Mizrahi Subjectivity by Ashkenazi Elites

It is interesting to look at the function of the Bourekas for the Ashkenazi elites through Homi Bhabha's (1994, 66–85) discussion of the intersection between the "colonizer" and the "colonized." Bhabha claims that this juncture is not only an event in which the colonizer constructs the identity of the colonized through the production of a colonized stereotype but also an interruption that eradicates the ethnic purity desired by the colonizer.[43] The colonizer wishes to return to the primeval fantasy of an idyllic ego. This ego—white and whole—that was violated by the difference reinforced through the appearance of the colonized "other" and would like to have his purity and wholeness back; this longing is similar to the child in the preoedipal stage, who desires the purity of a world without differences (since for him the outside world is perceived as something that is within the inner self). Bhabha criticizes Edward Said's theory of orientalism for ignoring this vulnerable aspect of the colonizer and alluding, therefore, to the ambivalent nature of the colonized stereotype produced by the colonizer. In contrast, Bhabha considers the production of the colonized "other" stereotype as one of the colonizer's ways of coping with this threatening interruption. As a strategy for coping with this threat to his identity, the colonist produces the colonized stereotype as a fixed reality that is, at the same time, both unfamiliar and well known. All originality is negated from the colonized, and, concurrently, all that is threatening in their otherness is incorporated within (assimilated into) the known aspect of this likeness, which constructs the colonized stereotype.

Bhabha's study of the ambivalence of the colonized stereotype offers a perspective on the Bourekas that illuminates the needs of Ashkenazi elites, which these films fulfill. We know that these movies were made by Ashkenazi directors representing Ashkenazi elites—whom postmodern critics see as the "colonizers" of the Zionist sphere—and that they forced a stereotype on the Mizrahi community that was constructed by a paradigm homologous to classical Yiddish literature's presentation of the shtetl Ashkenazi community. Through the use of this paradigm, the Bourekas present Mizrahim as if they were Ashkenazim of the nineteenth-century shtetls. This effort, made by Ashkenazi directors representing their own elites, negates all originality on the part of the Mizrahim while assimilating all that is strange and foreign (and therefore threatening) about the Mizrahim into a known entity—the premodern, pre-Westernized east European Jewish ancestors of Israeli Ashkenazi elites.

The colonizer's creation of the stereotype of the colonized "other" has three stages, according to Bhabha's schema: the recognition of differences between the colonizer and the colonized, the denial of these differences, and the subsequent obscuring of these differences by their formalization as a fetish. One can identify this mechanism in the Bourekas films' history and features. The fact that the Bourekas are the first films in Israeli cinema to focus on and describe a community defined as Mizrahi could be taken as the first stage—the recognition of differences between the Ashkenazim and the colonized Mizrahim. At the same time, the portrayal of Mizrahim in the Bourekas as premodern and pre-Westernized Ashkenazim of the shtetl can be seen as an effort to negate these differences.

The combination of these two aspects turns the Bourekas into texts that create a formalization of differences—a kind of fetish, an unthreatening object through which the otherness of the colonized Mizrahim is presented and perceived. The cinematic production and distribution of this fetish makes sense, since according to Bhabha (1994, 104–112), unlike the individual fetishist who is driven to hide his secret, the colonizer's motivation is to expose and disseminate his fetish to support his colonialist power.

The Bourekas, in which a Mizrahi community is masked by Ashkenazi tropes, can be seen also in light of Bhabha's (1994, 85–93) discussion of colonial mimicry—one of the most elusive and effective strategies of colonial power and knowledge. The effect of the colonized mimicking the colonizer is a camouflage, claims Bhabha (following Lacan). The colonized do not harmonize with the new identity (of the colonizer) that they mimic, nor do they totally become it; rather, they partially cover their original identity with it. It is not a situation of completely covering a certain background but of producing a "mottled entity" (1994, 85). The Bourekas—which define the community presented in them as Mizrahi but portray it as if it were an archaic Ashkenazi one—can be seen as texts through which colonial mimicry is implemented. The impulse of the colonized to mimic is realized through the fact that the Mizrahim's desire to "act like" Ashkenazim is presented in the films as a natural impulse of the Mizrahi characters. The Bourekas films' display of the grotesque aspects of the Mizrahim—a feature that colonial mimicry always attaches to its performers—seems to flatter Ashkenazi elites and thereby helps in the process of sanctioning their new status as colonizers.

Israeli Ashkenazi elites of the 1960s were not as confident as the British colonizers in India upon whom Bhabha bases his study. Only one generation earlier they had served as the internal "others" of Europe and suffered from discrimination, prejudice, and discourse that presented them as un-European and pre-Westernized (Chinski 2002, 63–68). Even after gaining control of Israel and ruling it for more than a decade, in the 1960s these elites were not yet sure that the colonized Mizrahim would follow them and mimic their identity. To ratify their status as colonizers and strengthen the confidence in their colonial control, these elites created—through the Bourekas and through the adoption of classical Yiddish literature's paradigmatic representation of the Ashkenazi Jewish community in the films—a fictional world in which Mizrahim mimic the archaic, premodern Ashkenazim and look ridiculous while doing so.

New Explanations for the Success of the Bourekas

Looking at the Bourekas through these various perspectives offers new explanations for their success among Ashkenazi as well as Mizrahi audiences. Understood in this way, one can conclude that the Bourekas films' success is due to the various ideological, sociological, political, and psychological needs that the films satisfy for Ashkenazi and Mizrahi spectators separately. Since the effect of colonial mimicry is a camouflage and only partly covers the mimicker's original identity with the aforementioned "mottled entity," the Ashkenazi characteristics of the Mizrahi neighborhood, community, and family in Bourekas films could be felt (however subconsciously) by both audiences. However, this cinematic mottled entity of "half and half" could be interpreted by each group of moviegoers differently, according to its collective psychological and sociological needs. Ashkenazi audiences might see these films as a fictional territory in which Mizrahim mimic Ashkenazim, whereas Mizrahi audiences might see a universe in which Ashkenazim mimic Mizrahim. Each group of spectators could at the same time accept or reject the fictional presentation of Mizrahim as Ashkenazim on-screen, according to its needs.

* * *

Given these initial assumptions, we are in a position to outline the reasons for the Bourekas films' success among each of its audiences. As for the success among Ashkenazi audiences, by echoing classical Yiddish literature's presentation of an Ashkenazi shtetl (and thus traditional Ashkenazi community and culture) and then projecting it onto Mizrahim, the Bourekas films confirmed both the Jewish Ashkenazi cultural origins and the contemporary Zionist Hebrew subjectivity of Ashkenazi audiences. At the same time, the films—displaying Yiddish culture using a comic reductive mode of representation—helped them cope with their oedipal guilt for abandoning these cultural origins to become Hebrew human beings. By reflecting the modernization approach, the Bourekas also ratified and distributed the desired identity of Ashkenazi moviegoers as Westernized, modern Europeans and lent moral support to the Ashkenazi audiences' privileges in the Zionist sphere relative to Mizrahim.

Conscious of Ashkenazi vulnerability as colonizers of the Zionist sphere, the Bourekas also helped Ashkenazi audiences (the colonizers) cope with the threat of the Mizrahi (the colonized other) by turning Mizrahi otherness into something familiar, something that was already well known, that is, Ashkenazi Jews of the shtetl. In addition, the fictional world of the Bourekas was perceived by Ashkenazi audiences as a world in which Mizrahi figures and communities mimic Ashkenazi ones. This flattered Ashkenazi moviegoers and, at the same time, confirmed their colonial power over Israelis of non-Ashkenazi descent.

Mizrahi audiences, on the other hand, recognized that they were being presented in Bourekas as traditional Jews and were themselves flattered,[44] since this portrayal—in contrast to the more common image of a group that had lost its Jewish identity and assimilated into "Arabness" (Shenhav 2003, 17–18)—signaled acceptance of the Mizrahim, not as colonized others (Shohat 1989, 119–79) but as an integral part of the Israeli nation. Beneath the modernization approach's official call for the Mizrahim to modernize, as a prerequisite to their assimilation into Israeli society, lay the demand that Mizrahim become culturally Ashkenazi. By constructing and characterizing the Mizrahi community as though it were an Ashkenazi premodern polity, the Bourekas encouraged Mizrahi audiences, presenting them as a group that was on its way to completing its assimilation into Ashkenaziness and, as a result, into Israeli society.[45]

The very fact that Mizrahim were presented as traditional archaic Ashkenazim in the Bourekas also encouraged Mizrahi moviegoers. Despite the negation of exile, Ashkenazi diasporic subjectivity was a necessary component of Hebrew subjectivity and the secret identity of the Israeli elites (Miron 2004, 9–13) and thus the favored cultural-ethnic subjectivity in Israel of the 1960s and 1970s.[46] Mizrahi audiences were also flattered because they saw in the Bourekas a fictional universe in which Ashkenazi figures and communities mimic Mizrahi ones.[47]

Conclusions

As we have seen, Bourekas directors, themselves part of the Zionist Ashkenazi elite, had more than one good reason to adopt in their films classical Yiddish literature paradigmatic representations of the shtetl. However, at the same time, this perspective on the Bourekas opens up a whole new range of explanations for the success of these films. The Bourekas films' secret reuse of elements of Yiddish culture can thus be seen as cultural invention in which the ambivalence of Israeli Zionist discourse toward Yiddish culture was internalized and became inherent to the esthetic object. As such, Bourekas were a cultural product designed to ease the tension that arose due to the vacillation of the Zionist Ashkenazi elites, who at the same time could neither completely give up Yiddish culture nor fully and openly embrace it.

However, Bourekas also served some of the Ashkenazi elite's more practical goals. The film cycle was a tool in the hands of elites to ratify and spread their desirable Western identity and as such was a part of their "Sisyphean Westernization project" (Chinski 2002). At the same time, the Bourekas films reflected the Zionist institutional modernization approach by presenting the Ashkenazim as ultramodern Europeans and the Mizrahim as premodern Jews. Thus the films were part of a larger effort by these elites to confirm the modern identity of the Ashkenazim, thereby justifying the ethnic distribution of wealth and work that favored the Ashkenazim in Israel at the time. Furthermore, the Bourekas gave the Ashkenazi colonizers of the Zionist sphere a symbolic vehicle for coping with the threat of the colonized Mizrahim, as well as for reestablishing their colonial authority.

These interethnic dynamics go a long way toward explaining the popularity of Bourekas films among Ashkenazi and Mizrahi audiences alike. Ashkenazi audiences felt a mixture of satisfaction and relief from their sense of the Bourekas as simultaneously reviving and projecting parts of their beloved, rejected, "forbidden" Yiddish culture onto the Mizrahi other and from the way that the Bourekas assisted them in endorsing both their Hebrew Zionist subjectivity and their colonial power over the Mizrahim. The popularity of the Bourekas among the Mizrahim, in contrast, is drawn from the complex relationships of inclusion and rejection between colonizer and colonized that they reflect. Despite presenting the Mizrahim in a demeaning light, Bourekas films do not totally denigrate Mizrahim. Rather, they offer the Mizrahi moviegoer a complex message, incorporating disparate motifs of inclusion.

I maintain that Mizrahi spectators strongly experienced the Jewishness in the presentation of the Mizrahi community in the Bourekas, and in light of the rejection they faced during the 1960s and 1970s, which cast doubt on their Jewishness (Shenhav 2003, 17–18), even this slight sign of recognition may explain the appeal of these films to that audience. However, there are more flattering aspects of Bourekas for Mizrahi viewers. The Bourekas can be interpreted (and *were* interpreted, by the Mizrahi moviegoers) as texts in which the Ashkenazim mimic the Mizrahim, an interpretation that no doubt flattered the Mizrahim. One can also see the Bourekas as films in which Mizrahim are presented as Ashkenazi Jews (however archaic)—that is, as people who are part of the Jewish Israeli nation—and are on their way to becoming Hebrew, even if they have not yet accomplished total social assimilation.

Although this book presents classical Yiddish literature as the source of the paradigmatic representation of the Mizrahi neighborhoods in the Bourekas, it does not unequivocally allege that Yiddish writers directly influenced the Bourekas filmmakers. It is clear, though, that to represent the Mizrahi neighborhood and community cinematically, the Ashkenazi directors of the Bourekas films used representational paradigms that bore a resemblance to those formerly used to described the shtetl in the Yiddish literary classics. The directors did so to reproduce an image of Jewish life that was part of their cultural heritage and to satisfy certain ideological, sociological, and psychological needs of the Zionist Ashkenazi elite of which they were a part. They did it naturally, since this was the most available apparatus they had to represent a community that they saw as a Jewish premodern one. Hence it seems that, in a way that recalls the process described by Barthes (1977, 142), these Ashkenazi authors-directors emptied themselves of their individual identity in the process of production and made way for content and forms that were part of their Ashkenazi culture to pass through into the films. Through this transmission of a representational paradigm, across both generations and genres, we can see a cultural continuity of Ashkenazi Jewish culture.

Nevertheless, one cannot rule out the possibility that the Bourekas authors were directly or indirectly influenced by classical Yiddish literature, since they had both the opportunity to integrate such an influence as well as a reason to do so. Despite being suppressed, and even in a way "invisible," Yiddish culture maintained its vitality in Zionist Israel, a popularity that, in fact, peaked in Israel in the early 1960s, just as the Bourekas films began to emerge. Considering the mode of reception of classical Yiddish writers into Israeli discourse, Bourekas directors could have been influenced by the writings of Mendele Mocher Sforim or Sholem Aleichem, whose integration into Israeli Hebrew literary discourse was fairly significant.

6

BOUREKAS LEGACY
Post-Bourekas and Neo-Bourekas

Toward the end of the first decade of the new millennium, I took part in a conference in Tel Aviv entitled Between Ashkenaziness and Israelism that was devoted to Jewish Ashkenazi ethnic identity in Israel. Among the papers presented was Shachar Pinsker's study of Yossl Birstein (1920–2003), a bilingual Israeli writer who wrote in both Hebrew and Yiddish. The paper claimed that some of Birstein's Hebrew stories use Israeli reality, such as the streets and sets of Jerusalem neighborhoods, to reconstruct the atmosphere of the east European Jewish shtetl. Nowadays, Ashkenazi Yiddish culture is more seriously and openly discussed in Israel.[1] In the process, rereading texts that use Ashkenazi cultural agency sometimes reveals hidden evidence of a hybrid Yiddish/Hebrew Israeli culture that produces a mottled contemporary Israeli reality that is also archaic and Ashkenazi.

This book has offered an interpretation focusing exactly on this hybrid cultural reality: a new reading of the Bourekas as Yiddish/Hebrew Israeli texts that create a mixed reality—contemporary and Mizrahi—while also archaic, east European, and Ashkenazi. My findings relocate Bourekas films as a phase in Israeli cinema's quest to openly reflect the true range of ethnicity and cultural diversity in Israel. The Bourekas represent a stage during which Israeli cinema was already prepared to reflect some kind of ethnic diversity while challenging the borders of the Zionist ethos of Israeli Jewish homogeneity (the melting pot ethos), but it was still a period when Ashkenazi filmmakers, pressured by the negation-of-exile ideology, had to express their exilic Jewish ethnic culture (Yiddish) by projecting it onto others, twisting it, and demeaning it.

As pseudo-ethnic films, the Bourekas did make way for a successful recent group of Israeli Mizrahi ethnic films of identity by second-generation immigrant filmmakers who inherited the Mizrahi self-representation films of the Mizrahi first-generation directors. Beginning in the mid-1990s, these young Israeli directors began to present openly their Jewish, exilic, pre-Zionist ethnic cultures in such films as *Late Marriage* (2001), representing Jewish Georgian culture; the Alkabetz Brothers' trilogy of *Take a Wife* (2005), *Shiva* (2008), and *Gett: The Trial of Vivian Amsalem* (2014), describing Jewish Moroccan culture; *Farewell Baghdad* (2013), echoing Jewish Iraqi culture; and *Baba Joon* (2015), with the flavor of Jewish Iranian culture.

If the Bourekas had opened the gates to the production of Israeli Ashkenazi ethnic fiction films of identity as well, it would have made sense. However, the time for that has not yet come. As far as Yiddish culture is concerned, the negation of exile still holds strong. There are indeed some films produced in the last few decades in Israel—some of which include Yiddish vernacular—that depict a Jewish Ashkenazi ethnicity,[2] among them *Kadosh* (2000),[3] *Ushpizin* (2006), and *To Fill the Void* (2011). However, these films are again projecting Ashkenazi ethnicity onto the ethnocultural "other" of the Israeli Ashkenazi Zionist elite—typically located in isolated, ultra-Orthodox communities, which stand out as worlds of their own in Israel and are still contaminated with sharp criticism toward Ashkenazi ethnic culture, which still seems to reflect the Zionist ideology of the negation of exile.

Hamid Naficy (2001) argues that a major element of any true ethnic film is the inner conflict of the hero who is torn between his original culture, usually represented by his family, and the culture of the host country, which he would like to adopt. Mizrahi ethnic Israeli films follow this precondition.[4] The protagonists of the Israeli Ashkenazi identity films mentioned, however, while indeed suffering from conflicts that the rigid religious norms of Ashkenazi ultraorthodox culture impose on them, are as a rule not torn between two worlds: assimilation into the surrounding secular Hebrew Israeli society doesn't cross their minds and is never an option. The heroine of *Kadosh* fights to keep her marriage against the firm Hassidic Jewish code that threatens it when she fails, she commits suicide. The heroine of *Fill the Void* rebels against her family's expectations—which are supported by Jewish law (*halacha*)—that she fills the void of her dead sister by marrying her brother-in-law, a much older widower; however, leaving her family or the ultra-Orthodox Ashkenazi community never occurs to

Figure 6.1. *To Fill the Void* (2010). A family photo. Rebellion against the family matriarchy. Photo: Karin Bar.

her. Indeed, one can see *Ushpizin* as a film in which the main character embodies an inner cultural conflict, but its direction is the opposite of what is typically exemplified in true ethnic films: the recently repented ultra-Orthodox hero struggles to forget his secular Israeli Hebrew context—the host country's culture—while trying to assimilate into the world of the Ashkenazi Hassidic culture.

Moreover, the Ashkenazi pseudo-ethnic films tend to condemn the ultra-Orthodox world of the Ashkenazi ethnicity as frozen, rigid, archaic, premodern, and exilic, reflecting the now-familiar negation-of-exile ideology. In *Kadosh*, the sympathy goes entirely to the suffering, childless heroine for whom the religious code has been unjust. The cruelty of this tough, rigid code is metonymically expressed through the character of the heroine's father-in-law, who heartlessly demands that his son divorce her—his beloved wife. Greater objection is raised through the brother-in-law—a fat, vulgar man who brutally rapes his wife on their wedding night. In *Fill the Void*, the empathy goes to the beautiful young, naive heroine who is being manipulated by the matriarchs of her family—heartlessly ignoring her feelings and needs—to marry her much older brother-in-law.

Figure 6.2. *Ushpizin* (2004). Moshe (Shuli Rand) and Mali (Michal Rand) and the Holy Citron. Criticism of Hassidic society. Photo: Yonatan Danino.

However, in *Ushpizin* the hero is not in conflict with the Ashkenazi ultra-Orthodox Hassidic society of his neighborhood; on the contrary, he adores it. The criticism of the Hassidic world takes on a more refined nature. It relies on irony directed toward the protagonist and his wife: while they see themselves as pious people for whom miracles happen, the author subtly hints at the fact that they are no more than fools who devalue God with their too friendly, too intimate attitude and for whom no miracles have happened; anything resembling the miraculous is simply a coincidence. In its subtle irony toward the Hassidic world, *Ushpizin* displays an interesting homology with the pseudo-Hassidic stories of Y. L. Peretz (see chapter 5).

If Jewish Ashkenazi culture is still being reduced and projected onto the ultraorthodox "other" in Israeli Ashkenazi pseudo-ethnic films, which present it openly, it is no wonder that mottled films depicting a hybrid Yiddish Israeli Mizrahi culture by projecting Ashkenazi culture onto Mizrahim are still being produced in Israel and that the Bourekas formula has not disappeared from current Israeli filmmaking. In mainstream Israeli cinema of recent years, one can find films that maintain some of the fundamental characteristics of Bourekas films; these can be defined as *post-Bourekas* or *neo-Bourekas*. I ascribe the *post-* label to films that describe Mizrahi communities using the Bourekas representation paradigm that deliberately and consciously exaggerate or twist one or more features of this paradigm. Taking an ironic stance, these films both reproduce and criticize the Bourekas and cast doubt on whether any such culturally hybrid communities really exist. Among these films are *Lovesick in Housing Complex C* (1995), the internationally successful *The Band's Visit* (2007),[5] and the local hit *This Is Sodom* (2010).

Lovesick in Housing Complex C focuses on a radical implementation of the yearning of the Mizrahi male hero for an Ashkenazi girl, the reduction of the romantic ethos in the Mizrahi neighborhood, and the unromantic stand taken by Bourekas films. The film focuses on a man who is not only unromantic but suffers from borderline personality disorder with sexual behavior disturbances. The film opens with a high-angled long shot of the hero, Victor, a young Mizrahi neighborhood's ne'er-do-well, speaking to one of the neighborhood's elderly residents. While the camera begins craning down, we learn from the dialogue that Victor is sharing with the old man a memoir with some pornographic elements; at a certain moment, the listener goes pale, but the hero does not spare any details, and when he starts enthusiastically performing a soft-porn scene imitating a woman's moaning, his pale companion has a heart attack.

Later, it turns out that Victor is the owner of the Mizrahi neighborhood's pirated cable TV network (such outfits were widespread in Israel's outlying areas in the 1980s and 1990s). He broadcasts both romantic melodramas and porno films. This bothersome proximity between romance and pornography symbolizes the reduction of the romantic ethos in the Mizrahi neighborhood of the film. However, a similar proximity is being mirrored through the hero's behavior. Victor "falls in love" with a nice, blond Ashkenazi girl who came to live in the neighborhood with her boyfriend and to work at the local community center. An obsessive and completely unrealistic suitor (since the girl is not single and in general finds him repulsive), Victor, in his lovesickness, stands outside the girl's balcony all night long, serenades her, and sends her flowers—essentially harassing her and her poor boyfriend—in the name of love.

This contrapuntal pseudo-romantic reality of the neighborhood that integrates tender love with pornography and courtship with madness receives support in the film in a way that shows that lunacy about love is a typical, widespread disease in the neighborhood rather than just the hero's affliction. In the government-run mental hospital that is near the neighborhood

Figure 6.3. *Lovesick on Nana Street* (1995). A violent fight over a pirate cable station that broadcasts porn. Elijah (Uri Gabriel) threatens Victor (Moshe Ivgi). Photo: Yoni Hamenachem.

is a patient, a man in his thirties, who has a lovesickness of his own. Every night at the same time, he goes out to the hospital's garden and cries out loud, "Evelyn, please don't leave me. . . . Evelyn, please don't go." His tormented cries to the love who has left him intermingle with the soundtracks of the porno films that emerge from the TV sets of the Mizrahi neighborhood's residents.

A different kind of radical implementation of the Bourekas films' paradigmatic representation of the reduction of a romantic ethos in the Mizrahi neighborhood can be seen in *This Is Sodom*. While the story takes place in the biblical city of Sodom, the residents have some of the characteristics of the Mizrahim in Bourekas. The reduction of romantic love is the most obvious. In short, the city is presented as a biblical Las Vegas, where the main businesses are gambling and sex. In Sodom's case, that sex includes bestiality and huge dildos sold by peddlers on the street.

Repeating, albeit ironically, the paradigmatic love affair in the Bourekas—between a Mizrahi boy, Nineveh, the son of the city's cruel ruler, and an Ashkenazi girl, Charlotte, the daughter of the pious Lot—the film presents a parody of a love affair seasoned with pornographic and vulgar flavors. As in *Snooker* (1975), the romance in the film begins as an instrumental plot: the ruler of the city's scheme to unite with Lot's family to be rescued from the destruction that God plans to bring on the city. Nineveh, his successful son, is ordered to court Charlotte and make her fall in love with him. Reduction of the romantic ethos seems to run in Charlotte's family, too. The first time seen, she is at home with her parents, eating dinner. The couple's relationship has obviously run into difficulties. The rude, mannish mother (in fact played by a man) loudly blames her useless husband, Lot, and calls him names. Showing an instrumental attitude toward marriage, she pushes Charlotte to marry as quickly as possible, claiming that if she doesn't, she will stay at the "bottom of the barrel"—a jab at her own unfortunate match with Lot. Toward the end of the scene, while Charlotte is busy singing an optimistic love song in the foreground, the mother is seen in the background, brutally beating poor Lot.

Searching for Charlotte at his father's command, Nineveh finds her at the local pub. A bizarre reductive courting scene takes place between them. Its witty dialogue has a major twist as a courting dialogue, involving the biblical word *nod*, which in Hebrew has a double meaning: either a biblical drinking bottle made of leather or an uncouth way of saying "fart." When Nineveh enters the pub, Charlotte is drinking out of her nod. The waiter comes to her with a new nod, points to Nineveh, and says that the man there sent her a nod (a bottle). Charlotte replies that she brought (in Hebrew slang also "made" or "did") her own nod and doesn't need his. "This is the first time that a girl has refused to receive my nod," replies Nineveh, approaching her table. "That's the problem with you men," says Charlotte. "You come, bring [make] a nod, and disappear." And so it continues—the witty courtship conversation "perfumed" with the odor of the grotesque.

A porno film atmosphere accompanies the scene of the marriage proposal to Charlotte. While Nineveh, who is by now in love with Charlotte, can't speak because he is too nervous, Charlotte feeds what is supposed to be a baby fox from a bottle. The sucking sounds and the way she inserts and takes the spout of the bottle out of the baby fox's mouth suggest oral sex. As is typical in a parody on romantic love, the couple does not marry in the end but instead has a wild sexual encounter in the presence of Lot, the father, in the cave where they find shelter from the coming disaster. "There is no love in the world," moralizes Sodom's ruler, while castigating his son, Nineveh, for falling in love with Charlotte. "Love is only a bad excuse for porn."

Figure 6.4. *This Is Sodom* (2010). Nineveh (Asi Cohen) and Charlotte (Alma Zack): reductive romance. Photo: Giora Bich.

The reduction of romantic love is also central to and exaggerated in *The Band's Visit* (2007). The film is about a classical Arab music band from Egypt that arrives at an Israeli Mizrahi town and intermingles with the locals. Within it, the agent of reduction of romantic love—the cupid of the instrumental unromantic relations—is the Egyptian Haled, a handsome young trumpet player. Haled flirts with every attractive woman around, trying to get them into his bed, using the same strategy again and again. When Taufik, the band's leader, sends him to the information counter at the airport to ask for a bus to their destination, he flirts with the young clerk, asking her whether she is familiar with Chet Baker and vocally performing "My Funny Valentine" for her. This repeats itself when Haled tries to lure Dina, his beautiful Mizrahi hostess, into his bed.

However, the Mizrahi town residents are no less instrumental in their attitude toward love. Dina is having an affair with a married man whom she thinks is "a son of a bitch." Confessing about her life, she never talks about love, only about a disappointing husband and flirtations that she has had over the years. Dina seems to fancy the cultured and genteel Taufik, but he is so conservative and restrained that he won't reciprocate. Dina's free, assertive behavior intimidates him. Disappointed, Dina finally ends up as she usually does, making perfunctory love—this time with Haled, the Casanova, who is at least ten years younger than her.

The married couples of the Mizrahi town are also not rousing romantic successes. The film presents two married couples; both seem to have serious relationship issues. However, the most grotesque lover of them all is Pafi, a young, off-putting Mizrahi who is still a virgin. A friend of his tries to fix him up with Yula, a lackluster girl from the neighborhood, but Pafi is not enthusiastic about her and does not know how to court a girl. In a very funny scene (that is similar in a way to the scene in *Snooker* where Hanuka helps Gavriel to court Yona in the old Jaffa port [see chapter2] but sharper in its criticism toward the lowly status of romantic love in the Mizrahi neighborhood), Haled hurries to help Pafi in his courting endeavors. Sitting beside Pafi, Haled hands him a handkerchief to wipe Yula's tears and then a small bottle of an alcoholic drink to raise Yula's spirit. Haled shows Pafi how to caress her thigh, hug her, and kiss her, while he is demonstrating everything on Pafi's body. With all of Haled's demonstrations and Pafi's implementations taking place simultaneously in front of the camera, which captures all three of them in a steady shot, the scene—which could have been romantic, showing two hesitant youngsters who have found each other—becomes a reductive, unromantic scene, one of the funniest in the movie, in which the male is presented as a robot and the girl as gullible.

But *The Band's Visit* also focuses on an extreme and exaggerated representation of two other central Bourekas themes: the isolation of the neighborhood community from its surroundings and forced togetherness—the blurring of boundaries between the private and the public domains within the Mizrahi neighborhood. The film's narrative is based on conflicts emerging from a forced encounter between the residents of the remote and isolated little Mizrahi town on the edge of the Israeli desert and members of the Egyptian band who, due to a planning error, are obliged to stay overnight in the small, stuffy housing project apartments of the Mizrahim.

The isolation is tied to the Mizrahi neighborhood of the film—an Israeli desert town called Beit Hatikva ("House of Hope," a nonexistent town)—right at the beginning. The bus that takes the band from the airport leaves them with their outlandish blue uniforms, large musical instruments, and identical suitcases at a desolate bus stop in the middle of the desert—that is, nowhere. As Israel is one of the most densely populated countries on earth, there is actually no "nowhere" in it. Even the most remote roads see some traffic activity. But where the band is left is totally desolate, with no cars and just yellow, empty desert all around. The town is seen through the dusty air from afar, small and gloomy—a row of modest gray housing projects. In due course it is revealed that the town not only *looks* but also *is* in fact isolated; there are no buses or other public transportation until the next day. No cars are seen in its main entrance. Wandering up and down the empty streets of the deserted town for the next twenty hours, following the interaction of the band members with the few Mizrahi locals that they do meet, the cinematic sequence thickens the atmosphere of desolation of its Mizrahi neighborhood right until the end.

One more aspect of the Bourekas neighborhood is the neglect by local authorities. Also in Beit Hatikva, as in other Bourekas neighborhoods, nobody is employed by the authorities; the residents who have jobs—like Pafi and Dina—work in the private sector (Dina runs a restaurant in which Pafi works) and don't seem too busy, and the main Mizrahi male character, Avi, is unemployed.

However, despite its severe isolation, and since in the forced togetherness is one of Bourekas most fundamental features, the community of Beit Hatikva also suffers badly from it; *The Band's Visit* cleverly uses this device not only to characterize the social code of the Mizrahi community but also to deepen the cultural conflict between the Jewish Israeli working-class Mizrahim and their uninvited guests—the Arab-cultured Levantine Egyptian musicians. With no hotel in town, the band members are spread out among a few apartments. In some of them, forced togetherness plays a major part in triggering the characters' behavior and encouraging exhibitionism. It is, as in the Bourekas films, only exaggerated and incredibly aware of itself.

Three of the band members find shelter in the stuffy housing project flat of Avi, the young, unemployed Mizrahi. That evening is Avi's wife's birthday. She had other plans for the evening, inviting her best friend and her husband for an intimate dinner for four, so she is quite unhappy with the three unexpected, non-Hebrew-speaking guests who are now crowded, silent and embarrassed, around her too small dinner table, eating her now too small delicacies. They seem to ruin both the splendor and the intimacy of her birthday dinner, forcing what is meant to be a cheerful, private dinner into the public domain, turning it into a worthless, silent, tense event. As an assertive Israeli woman, she won't tolerate this quietly. The stings that she directs, in Hebrew, to the embarrassed guests of her husband and the

Figure 6.5. *The Band's Visit* (2007). The Alexandrian Police Band in the gates of a rural Israeli town. An extremely deserted and lonely place. Photo: Shai Goldman.

blunt sarcasm that she directs, in English, toward Avi himself expose her uninvited guests to the family conflicts and to the fact that this house is in a way a matriarchal territory. The guests, being conservative and patriarchal, seem to feel lost in this troublesome, forced togetherness. To break the ice, the friend's husband tries to tell a "funny" story—the story of how he and his wife fell in love. But his bad English and the ironic interruptions, corrections, and stings of his wife, who seems to see their history in a much less glamorous way, turn this, too, into a humiliating, exhibitionist, grotesque scene. The Egyptians, in their performance suits and ties, watch in panic at how the wife publicly humiliates her husband.

Elsewhere, forced togetherness brings about more dramatic consequences. Beautiful Dina, the owner of the local restaurant, is the first of the town's residents to speak with the band members, and she feels responsible for them. She invites Taufik, the rigid commander of the band, and Haled, the band's "playboy," to sleep at her flat. Being single, alone, and a Mizrahi who adores Arab music, she fancies the cultured and genteel Taufik. As a free and independent Israeli woman, she would have liked to have realized this affection in an affair, but the patriarchal Taufik is intimidated by her assertive behavior; Dina then positively responds to Haled's obstinate courtship, and when Dina and Haled finally make love, it is Taufik—on the way to the toilet of the stuffy flat—who sees and hears it all.

The next interaction seems to realize metonymically the idea of blurring the borders between the private and the public in the town. The location is a public phone booth on one of Beit Hatikva's streets. In the early 1990s, in Israel, before smartphones came into being, public telephones were very important, especially in peripheral areas where some of the poorer residents did not have home phones, and there were no businesses with phones for public use. In this Mizrahi town, there is only one public phone—but it's actually private. It seems that it belongs to Tzachi, a young Mizrahi resident whose girlfriend left town. At any rate, he sees it as his personal phone, since he stands near it every evening waiting for her to call. One of the band's musicians finds Tzachi there when he goes to call the headquarters in Alexandria to report their location. The polite musician has to muster up all his nerve to make the call while the intimidating Tzachi hovers over him very closely, almost touching him and whistling in his ears, signaling to him that this is his public-private phone and that he should beat it as quickly as possible.

However, the courageous musician succeeds in giving the phone number to the headquarters and making an appointment with them to call back in an hour. When he comes at the right time to get the call, Tzachi is still there, waiting for a phone call that never comes. Soon the phone rings, and the musician of course wants to answer, but with a small, intimidating move of his arm, Tzachi prevents him from picking up the receiver. Tzachi counts the number of rings, and only when it exceeds what he apparently arranged with his girlfriend, he lets the musician take the call; of course, he stays very close by to listen, carefully watching his not-quite-private, not-quite-public telephone.

The second category that I would like to outline—the neo-Bourekas—includes films that, at least in part, naturally imitate and reproduce the paradigmatic representation of the Mizrahi community in Bourekas films, with some changes to adjust the representation to the period and place in which the story takes place. There is no ironic stance here on behalf of the cinematic author. The viewers are called upon to respond emotionally, to identify with the characters, and to believe that this is "real life." Such films include *Colombian Love* (2004), which describes its Mizrahi male character's weddings and the Mizrahi family of the hero, repeating the paradigmatic representation of Bourekas films; *Turn Left at the End of the World* (2004), in which the paradigmatic Bourekas representation of the community is used to describe the Mizrahi population of Dimona (a town in the Israeli desert) during the 1960s; and *Aviva, My Love* (2006), which transfers the Mizrahi neighborhood of Bourekas films to contemporary Tiberias.

I begin with *Colombian Love*, since of the three neo-Bourekas films that I analyze, it is closest to the post-Bourekas category. The film implements some features of Mizrahi representation in Bourekas in a very exaggerated manner (like post-Bourekas films) but fails to present any ironic stance. The viewers are called upon to believe that these are real people who lead real lives and to identify with them. The Bourekas inherited the tendency to devalue people of the Jewish religious establishment from classical Yiddish writings; the best example is the ludicrous representation of the neighborhood rabbi in *Snooker* as a fool (see chapter 2). *Colombian Love* repeats and exaggerates this tendency.

The film opens with a wedding scene. Omer, the Mizrahi, is marrying Ya'el, his longtime Ashkenazi girlfriend. Unfortunately, the young Mizrahi rabbi of the wedding is stoned. Like the nervous priest in *Four Weddings and a Funeral* (1994), he mixes up the names and confuses all the blessings at the wedding ceremony, inserting some remarks that bear witness to his fear of losing his lofty, well-paying job as a rabbi and going back to being a greengrocer. However, the scene ends with a disaster that wipes the smiles off the viewers' faces and erases its ironic aspects: the stoned rabbi puts the traditional glass vertically (instead of horizontally) under the groom's foot. As he crushes it, Omer's foot is seriously cut, and he is rushed to the hospital by ambulance.

The most obvious Bourekas feature used in the film is the minimization of romantic love. The two weddings that take place in the film are of Mizrahi men to Ashkenazi women. Throughout both, the romantic ethos is played down. Omer and Yael's wedding ends with his hospitalization. Soon after, he stops being sexually interested in his new wife, and in the end she leaves him for an Arab drug dealer.

But the greater homage to the Bourekas is concealed in the wedding and premarital interactions between Ori, the real hero of the film, and his love, Tali. Ori proposes to Tali only after she leaves him. He does this in the presence of two Russian immigrant musicians whom he has found on the street, an element that gives the otherwise romantic scene an outlandish edge. After Tali agrees, they seem to be in love, but then the families have to meet for the traditional prewedding dinner. Much like the famous meeting between Gila's and Charlie's parents in *Charlie and a Half* (1974), with two narcissists, one on each side—Tali's mother and Ori's father—this get-together of Ashkenazi and Mizrahi families feels like a conversation among deaf people. During the meal, Tali's mother (echoing Gila's mother thirty years earlier) swallows too big a portion of Ori's father's extremely spicy salad and almost chokes to death.

Surprisingly enough, the parents of both families agree on one thing: the wedding is for *them*. They see the youngsters who are about to get married, and who have some stupid ideas of an intimate romantic reception on the beach, as only supporting actors in the event, which they see as totally business oriented.

One of the most typical features of Bourekas romance lies in the fact that the older people, whether parents or other people of authority, are always interrupting the romance and interfering. In *Sallah* (1964), *Fortuna* (1966), *Kazablan* (1970), and *Katz and Carasso* (1971), these conflicts provide the central narrative axis. In *Colombian Love*, it is the father of the groom who demands that the newly married couple divorce or, rather, publicly apologize for their "inconsideration" toward him during the wedding ceremony, threatening to disown Ori. With this narrative move, the film seems to stretch the feature of the older generation's objection to the younger generation's romance to the limit. It could have been a grotesque situation involving an ironic viewpoint on behalf of the author, but the humiliating ceremony that Tali has to go through, apologizing to her father-in-law in front of everybody, in a second wedding ceremony, is not funny. The viewers are called upon to identify with the loving Ashkenazi Tali and to hate Ori's Mizrahi father for his despicable self-respect, which in Israel is considered a quality typical of Arabs and Mizrahim.

Turn Left at the End of the World, like the archetypical Bourekas film *Fortuna* (1966), takes place in the 1960s in the desert Mizrahi immigrant town of Dimona and, like *Fortuna*, weaves its narrative around a strike at the local factory that employs most of the men of the town. The film naturally adopts the now well-evidenced features of Bourekas films' representation of the Mizrahi community: isolation, forced togetherness, and the reduction of romantic love. As opposed to the post-Bourekas films, and in a way that is homologous to the approach of the original Bourekas cycle, this paradigmatic representation is presented as realistic.

The isolation motif is stressed from the opening scene, through the film's description of the arrival of Sarah—one of the two heroines of the film. Her family arrives in town in a truck via an empty road, surrounded by a yellow, desolate desert. Evidence of the town's isolation and remoteness from Israel's center, both geographically and culturally, is seen throughout the film. For example, several times road signs indicating the distance to Tel Aviv (187 km), on the one hand, and to Eilat (150 km), are shown. (For a tiny state like Israel, that is about as far as it can be.) However, unlike in *The Band's Visit*, this town's level of isolation is acceptable. In those early days, the new towns in the Negev (the Israeli desert) were indeed isolated, but here at least there is bus service to and from the town.

Forced togetherness is also a part of the film's representation of the town from the beginning. Upon her arrival, Sarah accidently interrupts Nicole, the other protagonist, who is bathing nude in the local water reservoir, effectively forcing her disturbing presence on her. Although the desert around it is spacious and wide, the buildings of the housing project are crowded together, standing one in front of the other so that families can peek into other families' flats—an opportunity taken advantage of several times in the film. The flats are small and stuffy, and conversations can be heard through the thin walls. Although Nicole has only one sister, they share a room, a fact that lays the foundation for the exhibitionistic show on masturbation that Nicole gives to her shocked, prudish sister. However, the most pervasive aspect of this forced togetherness is in the ethnic composition of the town. The residents frequently talk about the unsuccessful blending of the Moroccans and Indians who make up the population—a wide-scale forced togetherness that causes tension and sometimes even violence.

Nevertheless, the most developed feature of Bourekas Mizrahi representation in the film is the reduction of the romantic ethos. With two teenage girls at the film's center, romance stands out as one of the major themes. For Nicole, the sensual and romantic heroine of the film, the high priestess of love is Simone, the beautiful widow who lives in the apartment above hers. However, Simone—who tends to hang around in sexy underwear or a kimono, gives Nicole a garter for her birthday, and prefers Indian men because they "wrote the Kama Sutra"—is revealed to be more of a sexual high priestess than a romantic one. The wordless affair that she has with Sarah's handsome father, which ends with him leaving her, seems to prove it. As for

Nicole, she believes in romance. She falls in love with her literature teacher, an Ashkenazi man from Tel Aviv, and entices him to have an affair with her, but the romance does not fulfill her dreams. "I gave myself totally to him and feel empty inside," she complains in tears to Simone. "Men know nothing about love," answers Simone affectionately, while hugging her. "If you want love from them, you have to take it." But Sarah's father (Simone's lover) and the teacher (Nicole's lover) don't have a lot to give. In the end, Simone remains alone, and Nicole leaves the teacher and at her graduation party dances with Moshe, whose unromantic problem is that he suffers from a never-ending erection that cannot be hidden.

The three archetypical Bourekas features of isolation, forced togetherness, and reduction of the romantic ethos are also used in the representation of the Mizrahi community in *Aviva, My Love*. Tiberias, the town where the film takes place, is home to Aviva, the hardworking cook, would-be writer, and heroine of the film. Tiberias is not as isolated as the desert town of *Turn Left at the End of the World*, but the severity of its insulation from the cultural, financial, and academic center of Israel is heavily stressed: Aviva has to make the trek to Tel Aviv for her writing lessons and to meet her professor—a journey that she makes a few times in the film.

As in some Bourekas films thirty years earlier, forced togetherness is reinforced in the film through the fact that much of the community activity takes place on the street. When Aviva returns from work, she usually witnesses some human activity in the public areas near her home. One time, it's a cheerful band playing a Mizrahi song; another time, it's a street gang taking a bath together using garden hoses and wearing only their bathing suits. However, even more impressive is the neighborhood people inclination to have conversations from windows down to the street below, bringing their private conflicts into the public sphere—much as the residents of the Bourekas neighborhoods do. Anita, Aviva's sister, constantly quarrels with her husband this way. A more sophisticated way of doing the same, which adapted itself to the period (2006), takes place when Aviva uses her smartphone to have a conversation with Anita while standing near the open window looking at her down in the street. The exhibitionism of Violet, Aviva's disturbed mother, has no up-to-date parallel. From time to time, she sits on the windowsill and proclaims loudly to the whole neighborhood that she is going to jump. Shortly before committing herself to a mental hospital, she stands in the same window, naked, and shouts to the people of the neighborhood that she is "free," while they are being "strangled" by their lifestyles.

However, it seems that the more disturbing forced togetherness is the one that Aviva experiences at home. Claustrophobic quarters are one of the main reasons that she gives up her dream of becoming a writer: she cannot find a quiet spot to write at home. The housing project apartment, with the three tiny rooms, is overcrowded. There are three children in the house; two are ill-tempered teenagers, and everyone is always at home (a girl soldier on leave from the army, a boy who is in the induction age but was rejected by the army, and a little schoolboy on a summer long school vacation). Moni, her husband, is also always at home because he is unemployed. Aviva simply can't find a place for herself. The forced togetherness becomes unbearable, due to the fact that the teenage boy, like his grandmother, has exhibitionist tendencies. Every morning Aviva is embarrassed by bumping into him sitting in his underwear in the kitchen or the living room. This becomes even more disturbing when, encouraged by a psychologist, he starts wandering around the house completely naked.

Embarrassment of the same kind is experienced by the young son when he sees his father passionately kissing his aunt in the living room. The flat's lack of privacy is so severe that when confidentiality is critical, the family members go up to their building's roof to have their conversations. Aviva and Anita, her sister, do this several times, and the teenage daughter takes Aviva to the roof when she wants to announce to her, rather dramatically, that she is about to become a prostitute. The fact that the public space of the commune roof is being used as a secret sphere for highly private conversations blurs the borders between public and private in the same way that the public-private phone of *The Band's Visit* did, but here it is well immersed in the narrative and is presented as a reasonable solution to the stressful privacy issue of the home rather than proof of extreme oddness.

The reduction of the romantic ethos is quite obvious as a quality of the Mizrahi residents in *Aviva, My Love*. There are three couples in the film, none of which can serve as an example of romance or even good partnership. Aviva and Moni, her husband, could have been good friends, but two shadows darken their relationship. The obvious one is the unemployment that causes Moni, now supported by his wife, to lose his sexual attraction for her. In the only intimate scene that they have as a couple in the film, Moni is distracted by the cockroaches in the room instead of showing any

Figure 6.6. *Aviva, My Love* (2006). The roof as a refuge from the forced togetherness at home. Aviva (Aussie Levy) and her daughter, Oshrat (Dana Ivgi), on the roof of a pavilion. Photo: Yoni Hamenachem.

passion for his wife. However, the even darker shadow is the attraction Moni develops for Aviva's pretty married sister, Anita—an attraction that leads him to kiss her in his house in front of his young son. Even at the optimistic conclusion of the film, when Aviva seems to be in agreement with herself and her life, it is not romance or love for her husband that makes her happy but the harmony in the family, within which Moni appears to be more of a child than a man.

"Unromantic" would also describe Anita and her husband, Aryeh. They are trying unsuccessfully to have a baby while coping with other conflicts. Aryeh wants to move to another city to be near his mother, while Anita wants to stay near her sister, Aviva. Aryeh is also the jealous type and follows Anita everywhere. They quarrel frequently, and it seems as if he sometimes beats her. However, their dynamic is hardly as weird as that of Aviva's mother and father. Violet, the mentally ill mother, complains that the father always cheated on her, so she has stopped cooking for both of them. The husband is becoming addicted to collecting food recipes, but when the mother is hospitalized, she begins cooking for the patients in the mental hospital. "She likes it there," muses the husband sadly. "She will never return home."

But the Bourekas flavor of the interactions between men and women in the movie does not come so much from the reduction of romantic love as from the matriarchalism that structures the lives of the main characters. In *The Travels and Adventures of Benjamin the Third* by Mendele, the two heroes, Benjamin and Senderel, are both married, but since they are students at the *kollel*[6] and their wives both have jobs and manage the houses, it is their wives who are in control. Benjamin is afraid of his wife, and Senderel, whose nickname in the shtetl is "Senderel the Woman," is constantly beaten by his wife. Some Bourekas films, such as *Charlie and a Half* (1974) and *Aliza Mizrahi* (1967), have adopted this matriarchal paradigm and portray the Mizrahi family through it.[7] In *Charlie and a Half*, Charlie's mother is the provider for the family, while the father is a good-for-nothing idler who has to beg his wife for a dime. In *Aliza Mizrahi*, the eponymous wife is clearly in control, constantly yelling at her poor husband, who just wants to have some fun.

Aviva, My Love repeats this aspect of the Bourekas paradigm. While Aviva is the breadwinner and seems to be in control of the house, the unemployed Moni adopts feminine behaviors; he stays home most of the time, taking care of the children, and weeps when insulted by his former employer; when he goes to settle the score with him, he takes Aviva along as a shield. This matriarchal atmosphere is passed on to the next generation: while Aviva's daughter is demanding and takes responsibility for her mother's writing career, her son is the one who goes around the house naked, showing off his young body. Matriarchy also colors Aviva's parents' relationship. While the mother has stopped cooking, the father's feminine hobby is to fill large colorful folders with recipes from magazines. However, Anita and Aryeh seem to live their lives within the patriarchal paradigm at its worst. At first, it seems as though Anita is a battered woman; only later toward the end of the film, the truth comes to light: Anita is the violent one. Like Senderel's wife in *The Travels and Adventures of Benjamin the Third*, she beats her husband regularly. His feeble physical retaliation is only self-defense.

Overall, the Bourekas paradigm is kept alive in Israeli cinema through its appearance in contemporary post- and neo-Bourekas films. The Bourekas formula has persisted and may continue to persist in popular and mainstream Israeli cinema as long as three conditions continue to prevail:

(1) veteran Ashkenazi elites are in power in Israel; (2) the polarity between Ashkenazim and Mizrahim remains a dominant force in Israeli society; and (3) the negation of exile maintains some restrictive power. As long as these elements hold, Ashkenazi elites will have in the Bourekas paradigm a means for manipulating the Mizrahim through the politics of representation and will be dialectically manipulated by Mizrahim in turn to strengthen their distinctive Ashkenazi Zionist/Hebrew identity by secretly injecting Yiddish culture—in the form of Yiddish literature's representation paradigm of the shtetl—into filmic representations of Israeli Mizrahi reality.

NOTES

Preface

1. Concerning the use of this term, please see the introduction.
2. For the purposes of this study, Sephardim are the descendants of the Jews expelled from Spain and Portugal during the fifteenth and sixteenth centuries, who kept the Ladino language. In Israel, they are considered to be a subgroup of Mizrahim. The word *mizrahim* literally means "easterners." In Israeli discourse, the term basically refers to Jews of the Middle East, including North Africa, as well as Jews from the Balkans (Shemer 2013, 8). Please also see my discussion of the subject in the introduction and in chapter 3.

Introduction

1. This wave, called in Zionist history the Second Alliya (immigration), proved to be extremely important to Israel's history, since those people who arrived during this era created the institutions of the state that would soon govern.
2. This then spread to other locations and was called in Zionist history the Pogrom of 1921.
3. The prestate organized Jewish community in Palestine between 1920 and 1948.
4. Some Mizrahim, such as the Yemenites and the Sephardim, immigrated to Palestine before the first Zionist immigrants did, but they were poorly organized. Though the Sephardim had a long history of supporting Jewish political independence in Palestine through such figures as Dona Gracia Mendes (sixteenth century) and Benedictus de Spinoza (seventeenth century), when the World War I defeat of the Ottoman Empire, the loss of its political patronage, and its disappearance as a power in the Middle East and the Balkans left them bereft of political power (Kimchi 2017).
5. Only thirty-two films were produced from 1933 until 1964—the year *Sallah*, the first Bourekas film, was released (Schnitzer 1994).
6. Here and throughout the manuscript, I use the term *Bourekas* as a name for the cycle of films.
7. When *Sallah* was first released, 1,184,900 Israelis watched it, while the total population of Israel was 2,475,000, only about 70 percent of them Hebrew speakers (Gretz 1993, 55).
8. In May 2015, *Yediot Aharonot*, the most widely read daily newspaper in Israel, interviewed me and the Israeli actor most identified with Bourekas films, Ze'ev Revach, for a special holiday (Shavuot) item in honor of the fortieth anniversary of *Snooker* (1975), one of the major Bourekas films.
9. I would like to single out the contribution of one of these critics, Nisim Dayan, who, in his article on what he considered to be Bourekas films, pointed to shtetl culture as a possible source for these films—an approach this book also takes (see Dayan 1976).

10. A reference to the excellent reception of *Sallah* among Mizrahim can be found in the testimony given by the anthropologist Harvey Goldberg, who described watching *Sallah* with a group of Mizrahi youngsters from one of the villages of Lubian emigrants. Goldberg recounts an incident when, in 1964, while conducting research on a *moshav* (Israeli Jewish village) inhabited by Libyan emigrants of the group that had come to be known as the "cave dwellers," he went to Netanya one evening with some young men in their late teens and watched *Sallah* with them. To his surprise, the young men enjoyed the movie and laughed during it in a comfortable way (Goldberg 2002, 7).

11. A strategy first initiated by the Haskalah movement (Jewish Enlightenment) during the nineteenth century (Feiner 2002, 274–346).

12. In a way reminiscent of the American blaxploitation movies since, in most cases, the producers were white, although the directors were not always white.

13. According to Israel's governmental statistics bureau, in 1964 the population of Israel was about 2,500,000, but only 44 percent reported that Hebrew was their mother tongue. (*Source:* Israel statistical bureau website at https://www.cbs.gov.il/he/pages/default.aspx)

14. One aspect of Zionist ideology was the negation of all pre-Zionist diasporic Jewish cultural elements and placing them within an oxymoronic relationship with the Hebrew/Zionist Israeli culture (see Krakotzkin-Raz 1993).

15. At this juncture, the study is part of an exciting development in recent scholarship that scrutinizes the question of Ashkenazi identity in Israel and the role of Yiddish in Israeli culture. Here I refer to studies by the historian Rachel Rojanski of Haifa University, as well as to the work of scholars of Israeli and Jewish literature and culture, such as Dan Miron (Columbia University), Benjamin Harshav (Yale University), Yael Chaver (University of California, Berkeley), and Shachar Pinsler (University of Michigan).

16. In 2017, a musical version of *The Band's Visit* opened on Broadway. Among other accolades, it won the New York Drama Critics' Circle Award for Best Musical of 2017.

17. As a structural analysis, and since its focus is on conflicts that are typical both to the directors and to the examined films' discourses, not on narrative events, the study is closer to Lévi-Strauss's (1963) paradigmatic form of structural analysis than to Propp's ([1968] 2003) narrative syntagmatic structural analysis.

18. Christian Metz (1974, 38) concludes that because cinema has no double articulation and because it is an open system, it has no "*langue*." He then takes up the obvious question: If cinema has no language system, how do we understand films? To answer this, Metz distinguishes between meaning and signification; as in human and artificial languages, only the latter involves arbitrary (vs. natural), strict, and well-defined relations between the signifier and the signified to form the sign. Cinema, therefore, has the capability to create meaning and to be understood but not to signify.

1. Birth of the Bourekas

1. I consider Israeli cinema to include the films that were produced by Zionist institutions during the Yishuv period (1920–1948) before independence and all the films (sometimes even directed by non-Israelis) that were produced in Israel thereafter. In this chapter, early Israeli cinema therefore includes films from the groups that Shohat calls "Jewish Agency films" (from the 1930s and 1940s), the "national heroic genre" (mainly from the 1950s), and "bourgeois comedies" (early 1960s). See Shohat 1989, 21–119; and Gertz 1999, 381–403.

2. Ephraim Kishon was an author of Renaissance magnitude. A Holocaust survivor who immigrated to Israel from Hungary at age twenty-eight, he left behind a career as a successful writer of satire, learned Hebrew with phenomenal speed, and quickly became the most prominent writer of feuilletons and comedy in the Hebrew language; later he became the most famous Israeli writer in Europe. *Sallah*, his first film, won the Golden Globe Award in 1964. For more on Kishon, see London 1993.

3. Schnitzer (1994, 76) claims that *Sallah* is the most popular film in the history of Israeli cinema. It was also nominated for an Academy Award for Best Foreign Language Film in 1964, and it won two Golden Globes that year.

4. For example, Nehama Gannoth (*The People Have Decided: A High-Quality Movie*, 1964), a critic for *Al Hamishmar* (a now-defunct Israeli Zionist daily newspaper), wrote, "How is the Jewish National Fund presented [in the film]? As an organization that makes its fortune through deceit, planting forests in the name of the beloved of Jews? . . . And the parties? All of them—in the same bag of cheating and treachery."

5. See Ne'eman 1979, 17–21. For *Sallah*'s negation to Israeli cinematic discourse of its times, see also Kimchi 2011 Eng.

6. In this study, the signifier "subjectivity" is used just as in Michael Hardt and Antonio Negri's (2001, 21–22) *Empire*. In comparison to "identity," which indicates an already final and constructed set of personal characteristics, "subjectivity" denotes the process of the production of a person's identity or sense of self. Jewish diasporic subjectivity is considered here through the Zionist perspective, its exile-negated discourse, and, as early Israeli films saw it, as an identity that is structured from the characteristics attributed to Jews in European anti-Semitic discourse.

7. Within the framework of this study, Hebrew (Ivrit) is being used in the sense of Hebraic (Ivri). The signifier "Hebrew" is used in Zionist discourse to describe the Zionist characteristics of a phenomenon or a person. One such example is the name of the annual Israeli national song contest, Festival Hazemer Ha'ivri. In addition, the archaic and biblical/Canaanite connotations of this term differentiate these phenomena from the stereotypical characteristics associated with diasporic Jewish culture.

8. See especially in A. D. Gordon's writings and Aharonovitz 1929, 1.

9. See also Gertz 1999, 383, 386.

10. For criticism on the Zionist ethos of labor in *Sallah*, see also Ne'eman 1999, 17–19.

11. Such as the figures in *Kirya Ne'emana* (*The Faithful City*, 1952) or in *Dim'at Hanechama Hagedola* (*The Great Promise*, 1947).

12. For example, Sallah devotes the bulk of his time to finding ways to avoid any productive labor and is constantly busy looking for ways to make easy money through fraud—such as when he takes bribes from political activists during elections. He is also particularly attracted to deals in which trade—the traditional Jewish occupation—is involved.

13. Such scenes appear, for example, in the films *Adama* (*Tomorrow's a Wonderful Day*, 1946) and *Beit Avi* (*My Father's House*, 1946).

14. The Zionist discourse's stereotypical characteristics of the kibbutz at that time included pioneering, farming, a flourishing landscape, social justice, women's liberation, Hebrew labor, modesty, and self-reliance.

15. For Holocaust survivors and open space in Israeli cinema, please see also Kimchi 2017 Eng.

16. While early films depicted Israeli society as a utopian Zionist sphere with a great majority of Sabras of Ashkenazi origin and a marginal minority of others, *Sallah*, in sharp

contrast, draws a more realistic picture of a migrant society: multiethnic, multicultural, and diverse. *Sallah* presents a gallery of types totally different from the Israeli films that preceded it. There are no soldiers in *Sallah*, only a few Sabras, and most of the figures seem to be immigrants. This includes Sallah himself, his transit camp neighbors (including those who came from Europe), state officials, political party activists, his daughter's suitor, the kibbutz secretary, and the kibbutz accountant.

17. This representation follows the reality of Israeli society in the early 1960s, when the film takes place. Records from Israel's Central Bureau of Statistics show that in 1948 only 35 percent of the Jewish population were Sabras. This percentage declined throughout the 1950s, when about one million more immigrants came to Israel (see "7.2 Million Israelim" [7.2 million Israelis], *ynet*, October 9, 2007). https://www.ynet.co.il/articles/0,7340,L-3447922,00.html

18. In his biography, Kishon testifies to the existence of this conflict in his own family. His parents, he tells his biographer, forbade him to speak even one word of Yiddish, since Yiddish was the language of those other Jews with the beards, those who wear capotes, and "in their language and behavior put us modern Hungarians who believe in Moses to shame" (London 1993, 17, 20).

19. On a different level, this negation of the Hebrew/pre-Hebrew dichotomy in *Sallah* can be credited to Kishon's frustration and his problems identifying with this demand of the elites to Hebrew subjectivity (which he did not have) and with this subjectivity being a factor in determining one's status. He also struggled with the fact that as an immigrant who spoke Hebrew with a heavy Hungarian accent, this subjectivity excluded and degraded him.

20. See Schweitzer 2003, 33, 51.

21. A group to which Kishon belonged (London 1993, 171).

22. As Chetrit (2004) points out, many so-called Mizrahim were Palestinian natives for generations before the arrival of the Ashkenazi Zionists (we might think of the Sephardim of Jerusalem who came in the fifteenth and sixteenth centuries). Others immigrated to Israel before most of the Ashkenazi Zionists (e.g., Yemenite Jews who came at the end of the nineteenth century) and at the time of the film had already been native Israelis for a few generations. An echo of this phenomenon can be found in the fact that in *Sallah*, his older children's Hebrew is less accented than that of the older kibbutz members. This representation also goes hand in hand with the idea of the modernization approach that the later generations of the Mizrahim will assimilate into Israeli society better than their ancestors. On the reflection of the modernization approach in Bourekas dialogues, see also Kimchi (2011:105–125).

23. See Shohat 1989, 25–55.

24. The last claim is that made by Ne'eman (1979, 20).

2. A Thematic Analysis of Bourekas

1. Research indicates an inclination by film scholars all over the world to avoid offering a grounded, generic definition for a group of films they intuitively identify with a particular genre (westerns and musicals come to mind) (Altman 1999, 1–28). While using the genre's name to define these films, they do not really bother to systematically explain the features that allowed them to include them within its borders in the first place.

2. This group includes such critics as Yehuda Ne'eman and Nissim Dayan. They were later joined by Ya'akov and Nathan Gross (1991), Meir Schnitzer (1994), Moshe Zimmerman (2001), Nitzan Ben Shaul (1999), and Ariel Schweitzer (2003).

3. This is within the spirit of modernist film critique. For example, Schweitzer (2003, 119) analyzes films of that period according to Metz's (1974) assertions about modern cinema of the 1960s.

4. In an interview in 1993, Ne'eman, a leading critic of this group, was asked about this period. He said, "We searched for a model that we would be able to identify with. . . . We turned to the European cinema, especially to the French New Wave" (Schweitzer 2003, 52).

5. See Shohat 1989, 130.

6. For Nichols (2001, 1), popular fiction films' function is to "give a tangible expression to our wishes and dreams or our nightmares and dreams. They give a sense of what we wish or fear reality itself might be or become."

7. Dayan (1976) is the exception in this case, as he relates briefly and metaphorically to the ethnic aspects of Lupo in New York and Sallah in his article, "Back to the Ghetto Culture," discussed later in this chapter.

8. In a more recent article, Ne'eman (1999, 19) repeats this idea, although he refines it by saying that Bourekas films are *part* of a phenomenon that expressed the "destabilization of the utopist belief of Zionism."

9. Bourekas films, Ben Shaul says (1999, 130), "look for genre formulas (and in general, Hollywood formulas) that within a predictable plot construction contrast a limited number of locations, comic situations and stereotypes (poor/rich, man/woman, Mizrahi/Ashkenazi) that chase each other until all ends well. At that point, all the conflicts—economic, sexual, and ethnic—are laid to rest." It appears that Ben Shaul immediately realized the potential for error in his generalization. In the same article, he includes Boaz Davidson's *Half and Half (Hetzi-Hetzi)* in his Bourekas film corpus, a film that no other critic defines as such, given its major thematic and aesthetic distinctions.

10. Ben Shaul (1999, 128–35) takes a similar position.

11. The Israeli Ha'panterim Ha'shkhorim (Black Panther) movement of the 1970s highlighted the discrimination and oppression suffered by Mizrahim in Israel. Since it was a movement founded by uneducated youngsters in the poorer Mizrahi neighborhoods of Jerusalem (Chetrit 2004, 142–43), it shows that the Mizrahi masses were not persuaded by attempts within the Zionist discourse to represent Israeli reality as egalitarian and socially fluid. (See also the discussion on Mizrahim in chapter 3.)

12. See Gross 1991, 259.

13. At the same time, he does bring into focus the relevance of traditional Jewish culture for the Bourekas, a point that becomes crucial to this discussion.

14. "Candies for the masses," in the words of Schnitzer (1994, 17).

15. A discourse adopted by state institutions as an ideological/academic rationale for political action in the socioeconomic arena, which was used intensively from 1950 until 1970.

16. Their emphasis on intermarriage as a solution to the main conflict of the films' Mizrahi figures seems to echo writings of the previous group of critics. Indeed, common to both analyses is the assumption that the Bourekas express elite Zionist ideology and that they served as a kind of ideological state apparatus. However, while modern critics view what they see as the Bourekas' false presentation of Israeli reality as a sign of the ideological decadence of the Zionist elite, and as testimony to the diminution of true Zionist values by the Zionist establishment, Shenhav, Hever, and Mutsafi (2002) see them as an implementation of the Zionist elite's values at the time. The films constitute an apparatus that reproduces and distributes these values.

17. Shohat's (1999, 52) definition is as follows: "It is possible to see the Bourekas comic films from the sixties and seventies as allegories about the tension—as well as the reconciliation—between Ashkenazim and Mizrahim."

18. See Schnitzer 1994.

19. See Perchomovski 2016.

20. According to Dayan (1976), Ne'eman (1979), and Schnitzer (1994).

21. Despite apparently coining the demeaning term *Bourekas*, Davidson is the one director who did not refrain from defending the group against critical attacks (Shiran 1978).

22. Only in *Sallah* does a social worker appear, but she is a kibbutz member who volunteered for the job and is not connected with the authorities.

23. At first glance, there are three exceptions to this rule in the Bourekas corpus: *Aliza Mizrahi*, *Fortuna*, and *Salomonico*. But in these films, the alienation and the rift between the government as an employer and the Mizrahim remain. In *Aliza Mizrahi*, the heroine indeed works at a police station; however, she isn't exactly a police officer; she's the janitor. Later in this section, the study details the manner by which the film accentuates her exclusion and alienation within the establishment and the immediate and natural conflict between her and the policemen (the Ashkenazim). In *Fortuna*, the men in the main Mizrahi family do work at the Dead Sea Works (which then belonged to the government), but the rift between the Mizrahi characters and management turns into a real conflict that ends in a long strike. In *Salomonico*, the hero's (Reuven Yotam) governmental place of work—the Tel Aviv port—is shut down, and the hero is fired. Soon thereafter, Salomonico himself resigns from his new and depressing governmental workplace (the Ashdod port).

24. Support for the fact that this might be a theatrical characteristic of Bourekas can be gleaned from Shohat (1989, 136), who suggests that the carnival-like portrayal of the elite's representatives in Bourekas films, and the main characters' alienation from them, is one of their main appeals to Mizrahi audiences.

25. This seems to surpass cinematic realism. In Arieh Lahola's documentary about the ma'abara, *The City of Tents* (1953), a film made by the Israeli Film Service, the residents live not in stone or wooden houses but in tents or shacks made out of tin and cloth.

26. Here I agree with Roland Barthes, who in his *Image—Music—Text* (1977) describes how texts create meanings and points to the fact that any text is a fabric of signifiers that carry meaning. One subgroup of signifiers, he writes, is the "informants, who bring ready-made knowledge. . . ." "Informants serve to identify, to locate the story in time and space . . . to embed fiction in the real world. . . ." Analyzing informants will allow us to move from the level of the story to the level of the discourse that the films represent, since they are realist operators and as such possess undeniable functionality, not on the level of the story, but on that of the discourse (Barthes 1977, 96–97).

27. Ne'eman (1979, 21) is probably referring to these kinds of strategies when he writes about the "dramaturgy being replaced with straightforward shooting." This comment hints at his opinion that the Bourekas' cinematic choices are characterized by cinematic ignorance and time- and money-saving concerns. This book, however, does not purport that money is such a crucial consideration in the cinematic authors' aesthetic choices.

28. Filming with a very wide-angle lens, a technique used especially for capturing landscapes.

29. This impression also serves the humor in the film. In one of the scenes, Sallah and the kibbutz secretary go into a closet to change money. The closet is in the center of an open

space, so the cinematic sequence serves to highlight the difference between the free, vast surroundings and the two men's preference to lock themselves up in a cupboard.

30. The metonymic presentation of the ma'abara in *Sallah* is similar to that of the small Jewish town in Becker's *Two Kuni Lemel*. On the homology between the set of the Jewish town in *Two Kuni Lemel* and the original Jewish town, see Sharik 1966.

31. On composition in photography and painting, see Hans Krytler and Shulamit Kreitler's *The Psychology of the Arts* (1980).

32. "Shooting" refers to breaking up a scene into distinct shots (from various camera angles) that are taken from various perspectives.

33. Zooming in is the action of reducing the width of the lens and changing the angle of the camera, which results in focusing on a certain object within the frame.

34. We can glean support for this idea from previous critiques: Ne'eman (1979, 21) suggests that the Bourekas films present a competitive, capitalistic world that renounces the pseudo-socialist rhetoric of the elites. Ben Shaul (1999, 129) develops the idea of competition and formulates the role it plays in the Bourekas when characterizing them thematically as dealing with "competitive oppositions between ethnic, class-oriented and generational collectives," a theme illustrated in the plot by the characters "chasing each other around."

35. One might be tempted to claim that *Snooker* has the most developed motif of competition, yet it lacks one dimension of competition present in other films: the metonymic dimension. In contradiction to Ne'eman's statement regarding the socially manipulative role of the Bourekas and its ethnic context, in *Snooker* there seems to be no Ashkenazim. All the characters are Mizrahim, and so the competition stays within the Mizrahi community.

36. Shohat (1989, 135) argues that the interior filming of the houses in the Bourekas emphasizes the collectivism and the crowded atmosphere in the Mizrahi neighborhood. Both she and Dayan (1976, 55) claim that Bourekas films represent the Mizrahi neighborhood as a "ghetto." Although the use of the term *ghetto* refers, in this context, to "a crowded neighborhood," one cannot ignore the additional meaning—that of a place where the inhabitants are forcibly sequestered.

37. This spying phenomenon becomes a more extreme, vulgar invasion of the individual's privacy in Davidson's *Eskimo Limon*, a series of films (that began in 1978) in which teenagers incessantly spy on each other while having sex.

38. Ne'eman (1999, 17) claims that one of the Bourekas' functions as a popular model (which was created, in his opinion, as a reaction to the films of Zionist realism) has been to protest against the ideal of work—against the socialistic Zionist "labor religion." He also suggests that the protagonists' idleness in the Bourekas represents a popular rebellion against this Zionist utopia.

39. In one of the most unforgettable scenes in the film, Sallah tries to convince a man who has lost his dog (Gideon Singer) to buy a stray dog from him instead of trying to find the missing pet.

40. When he attempts to sell the dog and then his daughter, Sallah tries to profit from the lives of others. In doing so, he exhibits blatant ignorance and emotional numbness.

41. See also Shohat 1989, 91.

42. This character, Halfon, is apparently based on the character of Zachi (also played by Arieh Elias), Charlie's father in *Charlie and a Half*, which in turn was based on Aharon (also Arieh Elias), Aliza's husband in *Aliza Mizrahi*.

43. The only one who is seen around a synagogue in the Bourekas is Sallah in *Sallah*, but only for a minute and only once in the film.

3. Mizrahi Self-Representation Films

1. One of the definitions in the *Oxford English Dictionary* (1989) of *representation* is "the fact of standing for, or in place of, some other thing or person, esp. with a right or authority to act on their account; substitution of one thing or person for another." https://www.geneseo.edu/~johannes/Representation.html

2. Spivak, on the other hand, seems to minimize the importance of agency. The attempts of the subaltern for self-representation, which they expect to be more truthful, are in vain, she argues, since if a representation falls outside the lines laid down by the official institutional structures of representation, this act of representation is not heard. It is not recognized perhaps because it does not fit in with what is expected of the representation (1990b, 306).

3. *I Love You, Rosa* (*Ani Ohev Otach, Rosa*), *The House on Shlush Street* (*Habayit B'rechov Shlush*), and *Daughters, Daughters* (*Abu al Banat*) (Lubin 1999, 120–28).

4. Shohat (1989), although coming close to this kind of definition, never goes this far. She ignores the hypothesis that her own research seems to suggest: that adopting self-representation and the denial of self-representation are effective tools for investigating the Bourekas films further, as a group. This is again due to the fact that her study is a diachronic one, positioning itself as historical research intended to make chronological sense out of Israeli cinema history. Accordingly, it naturally strives for a meaningful presentation of Israeli cinematic evolution rather than for a deep and detailed description of each unit. Ne'eman (1979), like Shohat, seems to highlight the denial of self-representation as a fundamental feature of the Bourekas. Although not familiar with the postcolonial term, he suggests a Bourekas definition based on the denial of self-representation: "The Bourekas is an arrogant glance at true culture and tradition. This is an Ashkenazi gaze over the culture of another people" (Ne'eman 1979, 21). However, as is the case with Shohat, this insight remains unfocused. Ne'eman avoids using his perspective to further investigate the Bourekas.

5. Although essentialism in itself is not inherently "bad," as Diana Fuss (1989, xi) suggests in *Essentially Speaking*, "In and of itself, essentialism is neither good nor bad, progressive nor reactionary, beneficial nor dangerous. The question we should be asking is not 'is this text essentialist (and therefore 'bad')?' but rather, 'if this text is essentialist, what motivates its deployment?' How does the sign 'essence' circulate in various contemporary critical debates? Where, how, and why is it invoked? What are its political and textual effects?"

6. Hall's (1994, 230–31) conceptualization of cultural identities is as follows: "Once we avoid essentialist definitions of culture, we may tend to its fluid and evolving nature while still asserting some continuity, relative stability, and intra-ethnic commonalities."

7. The name is a play on words that uses the Latin expression *ars poetica* (a poem the uses poetic techniques to explain the art of poetry). While *poetica* means "poetic" in Hebrew, *ars* is Hebrew slang for an ignorant, vulgar, outlandish, or aggressive Mizrahi man.

8. Biton won the Israel Prize for Hebrew Literature and Poetry in 2016.

9. See also my article "The Evolution of the Mizrahim as an Ethnic Category in the Israeli Academic Discourse," *Moreshet Israel* 14 (February 2017): 311–31.

10. See Baer 1965.

11. See Pickar 2007.

12. A more recent example of this type of attitude by Mizrahi subjects to Mizrahi identity can be found in Yaron Shemer's (2013, 251–52) book on Mizrahi cinema. There, in the afterword, he describes Mizrahi filmmakers who objected to the appellation "Mizrahi filmmaker"

and insisted that they were "Israeli filmmakers," since they found the former expression meaningless.

13. This observation of Swirski's (1981, 4) explains why the discussion of ethnicity in Israel only emerged in the late 1950s, as observed by Avruch (1987, 228–333).

14. As Shemer (2013, 3) remarks, the group nowadays defined in Israel as Mizrahim has had many names in the past, such as Sephardim, Edot Hamizrah, and sometimes Yahadut Hamizrah ("Eastern Jewry").

15. In fact, Smooha (1970, 24) takes the initial step toward pointing to Mizrahim as an ethnic group rather than a class group when he uses the term *Mizrahim* instead of the former *Edot Hamizrah*. While *Edot Hamizrah* indicates an overall ethnic multiplicity and difference, alongside a religion-based homology, the term *Mizrahim*, which avoids multiplicity and religious context, suggests instead ethnic-based unity.

16. Swirski (1981) explains that the school of pluralism—to which Smooha's attitude belongs—was developed in the United States as a reaction to the "functionalist school," which believed that a society is a complex structure in which each part has a different function and is characterized by a high level of consent and coordination between its different components. By contrast, in the "pluralistic model," society is characterized by competition and conflicts between groups and involuntary subordination of all the groups to a powerful leading one.

17. For Shohat (2001, 145–50), the modernization approach forms part of this discourse, which is a local branch of the Eurocentric orientalist global discourse. One can view this approach as the religious branch of Zionist modernization: While the modernization approach stressed the "premodernity" of Mizrahim in such fields as education and technology, this group stressed the ancient, stagnated traditions. S. Shaked (1979, 10), for example, echoes some of the preconceptions that formed the basis of the modernist approach, saying that all eastern Jewish communities had their premodern backwardness in common, or, in his words, "stagnation in the attitude towards the adoption of modern technologies."

18. "In differentiating between the bad Orient (Muslim–Arab) and the good Orient (Jewish–Arab), Israel took upon itself to purify the Mizrahim from themselves and to redeem them from the original sin of belonging to the Orient. [Here Shohat means 'Near East'—R.K.] . . . From their high school history book, *The History of the Jewish People*, Mizrahi pupils learn nothing meaningful about *their* Jewish history, formed over more than a thousand years in a Muslim civilization" (Shohat 2001:151).

19. Alcalay (1993, 54–55) provides testimonies that insinuate, in his opinion, that if Levantine Jews had run Israeli politics instead of the Ashkenazim, the conflict with the Arabs would have been easier to solve because of the natural understanding and sympathy between Levantine Jews and Arabs. As an example, he cites a letter from Albert Antebi, a Palestinian Sephardic Jewish activist, to Zionist leaders about their misunderstanding of the Arabs and a lecture by Moshe Ventura, chief rabbi of Alexandria, on the mutual destiny of Jews and Muslims.

20. At about the same time (1998), Sami Chetrit edited the first anthology of Mizrahi literature: *One Hundred Years—One Hundred Writers* (*Mea Shanim—Mea Yotzrim*), published by Kedem (Chetrit 1999b).

21. See Hever 2002, 191–212.

22. As examples of films in which an actual journey takes place, Shemer cites *Galoot* (*Exile*), directed by Ben Tolila (2003); *Ancient Winds* (Benchetrit 2002); *The South* (Bar David

1998); *Taqasim* (Dror 1999); and *Father Language* (Kimchi 2006). As an example of films based on a journey into the past, he cites *Bayit* (Ofek 1994); *Cinema Egypt* (Kimchi 2001); *Mirrors* (Malessa 2004); *Maktub Aleik* (Basson 2005); *A Bit of Luck* (Revach 1992); and *The Barbecue People* (Ofek and Madmoni 2003).

23. "Contemporary Mizrahi filmmakers, most of whom are native-born Israelis, rarely have qualms about where home is even when they vehemently criticize the national Zionist enterprise and the role it assigned to Mizrahi people and culture" (Shemer 2013, 254).

24. This may correspond with the findings of Michael Inbar and Chaim Adler (1977), who, in comparing Jewish Moroccan brothers who immigrated to France and to Israel, found that emigrants to France were more socioeconomically mobile but also had less of a sense of belonging to their new society than those who moved to Israel, even when the latter were critical of their society.

25. And in Yossef's (2010, 46) words:

> The immigration experience of Mizrahim in Israel is based on the construction of mourning and melancholy. When a person leaves his homeland, he must mourn a wide range of losses: family, language, identity, status, property, etc. Eliminating the Arabism of the Mizrahim and their assimilation into the Israeli-Ashkenazi national narrative made this mourning forbidden and invisible, and led to ethnic melancholy. Mizrahi melancholy is double: The Mizrahi subject was tamed to reject and erase his Arab identity, and was also forced to re-identify with the loss of this identity, since he was denied the option of a full entrance into the Ashkenazi national ideal. These layers of loss were censored, forbidden, and muted in Israeli culture.

26. Shohat (1989, 132), Ben Shaul (1999, 130), and Schnitzer (1994, 17). Ne'eman (1979, 23), who wrote his article when Revach was just becoming a director, refers to Ovadia as a "Bourekas filmmaker."

27. These are not the only films made by the two. (Ovadia had made films in Iran and an earlier film in Israel whose production was still Iranian.) But they are the first two Israeli films by these directors and will serve here as examples of their work. The only film that Revach, who began his directorial career relatively late, directed during the Bourekas period was *Rak Hayom*.

28. To isolate the element of representation and distinguish it from other variables that might influence the evaluation of the films (such as the year of production), it was decided that the films in the control group must also be produced in the period of the Bourekas films cycle, that is, between 1964 and 1977. Revach, who joined the industry as a director rather late, managed to make only one film before 1977 (*Only Today*, 1976). Ovadia, on the other hand, made about nine films in the specified period, but it seemed fitting to keep to the rule of the first film in this case, too. The problem is that Ovadia's first film, *Lusted* (1968), is only partially an Israeli film, as it featured Iranian actors and had an Iranian crew. Keeping in mind that the culture reflected by the film is very important to this study's point of view, his second film, *Ariana* (1971), considered his first all-Israeli film, is analyzed instead.

29. This argument borrows from the literary theory of space. Gabriel Zoran (1997) identifies two fields through which the reader gleans information about the space of a novel: interior (meaning all the information one can receive about the space from what is written in the novel) and exterior (information about the space that one can gather by cross-referencing the information in the text with one's knowledge about the extratextual world). By indicating that the film identifies the "extratextual location," I mean that it gives enough information

about the location to make it possible for the viewer to locate the site of events in the real world. In classical Yiddish literature, it is impossible to know, for example, where towns like Kabtsiel or Batalon really are. Likewise, in the Bourekas, the cinematic sequence never allows spatial identification. The lack of a discernible extratextual location is one of the strategies that contributes to the feeling that the Mizrahi neighborhood is isolated.

30. Even in *Sallah*, it is clear that the official civil servant's offices are located outside the ma'abara.

31. Unlike the municipality's inspector in *Kazablan*, for example (see previous chapters).

32. In *Snooker* (1975), for example, none of the protagonists are seen in their houses; *Kazablan* (1972) does not present the protagonist's house as an actual space at all. In principle, it seems that the cinematic sequence in George Ovadia's films follows the protagonists' activity within their houses or in other closed spaces and uses these spaces to present the characters. Generally, the films' cinematic sequences present a preference for indoor shots. In *Badranit B'hatzot* (*Midnight Entertainer*, 1977), the protagonist's home is the main location for shooting. Only one outdoor shot reveals the Hatikvah neighborhood in Tel Aviv in which the story takes place.

33. Both in *Charlie and a Half* (1975) and *Sallah* (1964), the couples are not alone when they first meet. When Gila and Charlie meet in *Charlie and a Half*, Robert, Gila's fiancé, is there; in *Sallah*, the eponymous main character is present when Habuba and Ziggy first meet.

34. Shafik (2007, 256) remarks that according to Galal Sharqawi in the 1942–1943 season, more than 50 percent of Egyptian films involved seduced or raped women.

35. Typically, a Bourekas film represents a charming Mizrahi man who surpasses his Ashkenazi counterpart in the power of his masculine appeal, which allows him to compete with the Ashkenazi despite their socioeconomic differences. In contrast, *Only Today* presents a situation in which the Mizrahi man does not stand a chance in a sexual competition over a woman with an Ashkenazi man. In so doing, the film chooses to portray a more realistic state of affairs instead of the manipulative presentation in some Bourekas films; this has been perceived by modern critics of the Bourekas as "dishonest" (see Ne'eman 1979, 20).

36. This also resembles an Egyptian melodrama. Elsaesser (1985, 168) remarks that the images of sexual exploitation, cross-class seduction, and rape in Egyptian melodrama are metaphorical interpretation of class conflict.

37. Films such as *The House on Shlush Street* and *Daughters, daughters* represent a Sephardic-Mizrahi community nonreductively, and they construct their narratives around their male heroes' coming of age (see also Lubin 1999).

4. Bourekas and Classical Yiddish Literature

1. Since the study is about to claim a linkage between the Bourekas representation of Mizrahim and the representation in classical Yiddish literature of the shtetl Jews, any similar or homologous presentation in a different group of films might weaken the claim. Two groups of films have been suggested as sources of influence for the Bourekas: Egyptian (Arab) melodramas and blaxploitation films. The Egyptian melodrama seems closer to George Ovadia's films than to the Bourekas (see chapter 3). As for blaxploitation films, they do not show competition within the African American community, nor do they show community togetherness or reduction of the romantic ethos in the same way; they also do not typically end with intermarriage between a man from the minority group and a woman from the hegemonic group.

2. In the Mizrahi self-representation films, the focal conflict is male maturation, and the composition of the smaller units of the film (sequences and scenes) is varied according to their contribution to this central conflict.

3. In seeing these writers primarily as Yiddish writers, we follow here Ken Frieden (1995) and Dan Miron (1973). Indeed, all three writers were bilingual and wrote also in Hebrew, but their mother tongue was Yiddish, their writings reflected the Yiddish culture, and, as Miron (1996, 1) remarks, they each had an obligation to the Yiddish language.

4. The quarrelsome relationships between Israeli-Zionist discourse and Yiddish culture will be dealt with in the next chapter.

5. We will use the Hebrew version that was first translated by the writer and published as a series in the literary journal *Hashiloh* in 1897.

6. The Hebrew translations were more popular than their original versions in Yiddish; see Fishman and Fishman 1973. Although this book does not claim that the writings of classical Yiddish authors had a direct influence on authors of the Bourekas, it seems that one cannot totally ignore the importance of the fact that Yiddish culture penetrated Israeli Yiddish-negating discourse through these works' Hebrew translations. (See the discussion in the next chapter.). See also Peretz 1962. On the other hand, there are two short stories by Peretz whose Hebrew translations cannot be located: "Impressions of a Journey through the Tomaszow Region" and "The Dead Town." Therefore, in these two cases, I use the English translation that appears in Ruth Wisse's (1991) collection

7. I have translated the quotations from the Hebrew version. The page numbers here are also a translation, since the original pages were marked using Hebrew letters.

8. Stressing the language aspect of isolation in *Motl* is possible because the novel involves travel and immigration. Lack of knowledge of the country's language was one of the main criticisms of the Jewish Enlightenment movement (Haskalah). This aspect of detachment from the area's surroundings is very subtle in *In the Valley of Tears*.

9. Regarding density and transparency in literary space, see 1997.

10. However, classical Yiddish literature does not usually present things this way; it prefers to see the shtetl as a separate Jewish town (Miron 2000).

11. A derogatory term for a vulgar adult Jewish woman.

12. His excuse is that her denial of the Hassidic way of life makes it impossible to bless her, since "without faith, this thing can do harm, and she has no faith" in him and in his Hassidic ways (16).

13. Peretz 1962, 128–51.

14. Everyone in the shtetl comes to say farewell to the family embarking on their journey to the United States. In *Fortuna*, there is a scene that is very similar to this one (when, in the film, all the townspeople come out to welcome the visitor to Fortuna's family).

15. Zaki in *Charlie and a Half* and Aharon in *Aliza Mizrahi* also beg for money.

16. The meaning of the name Kabtziel in Hebrew is "the town of beggars."

17. Sallah in *Sallah* makes a living from playing backgammon with his neighbors. He also tries to make a living from pimping; he pimps dogs as well as his daughter's dowry. Flora, Charlie's mother in *Charlie and a Half*, earns her money as a fortune-teller, but not a very good one. Rabbi Gamliel in *Rabbi Gamliel* makes a living predicting the future. Sasson from *Charlie and a Half* is a petty criminal, although exactly what he does remains undisclosed. Charlie provides for himself by fraud, gambling, and blackmailing, while Gabriel in *Snooker* makes a living from fraud and blackmailing naïve people.

18. In the novel, the narrator tells the story of a Jewish prostitute, which shows the existence of Jewish prostitutes, brothels, and pimps in Kissalon.

19. This scene contains a clear analogy to the scene with the social worker's (played by Gila Almagor) visit to the ma'abara in *Sallah*. A character who represents modernity (the social worker) is treated with suspicion there also. Just as in "Impressions of a Journey," in *Sallah* the visitor is followed by a "handful of idlers" who listen to her conversations, curiously peering in and reacting to what is said and seemingly waiting for a conflict to arise.

20. With the exception of *Aliza Mizrahi* and *You can work it out Salomonico*, all Bourekas films have pairings at the core of their narratives and stress their economic aspect and the social benefit to the Mizrahi characters while downplaying its romantic aspects.

21. It may be that Sholem Aleichem was less interested in fighting religion than the others, because in his time, religion was declining in importance in many Jewish communities.

22. Examples of this can be seen in the completely nonobservant Charlie in *Charlie and a Half*, who has this habit, or Azriel in *Snooker*, who does the same thing. Residents of Bourekas neighborhoods also use expressions having to do with God—for example, Sallah in *Sallah*, Azriel in *Snooker*, and the fisherman in *Kazablan*.

23. Old Luria is a scholar and a very wealthy man in whose home the ceilings are more colorful than those in the beit midrash. After his father's death, Motl becomes his companion, and his job is to be with him at night. Luria enthusiastically studies the Rambam (Maimonides), but the problem is that his Rambam studies lead him to the conclusion that he must *eat* Motl. Mercy has nothing to do with it, says Luria to himself: "I'm fulfilling my will. . . . I'll eat him, my will is to eat him, I must eat him" (46). This reductive presentation of both a Jewish scholar and Judaism's foremost philosopher indicates religious decadence and the decline of religious faith in Kasrilevke.

24. Jewish religious elementary school.

25. In many of the stories that focus on very religious Hassidic characters—most of them true believers—the author pretends to praise the Hassidic characters while actually condemning them as fools who are weak, hypocritical, or antisocial.

26. *In the Valley of Tears* and "Between Two Mountains" tend to emphasize the deterioration of religion and religious observance, while *Motl* is more focused on the collapse of the shtetl's mutual aid system and its solidarity. *Motl* was written in 1916, while *In the Valley of Tears* was first published (as *The Wishing Ring*) in the 1860s.

27. See also Shenhav, Hever, and Mutsafi 2002. This aspect is discussed in detail in chapter 6.

5. The Dynamics of Continuity between Two Disparate Cultures

1. It was suggested by early critics that the source of the Bourekas films' Mizrahi representation could be Arab cinema. A hint of this can be found in Dayan's (1976) article on *Lupo*. However, it seems that our discussion of *Ariana* rules out this option (see chapter 3). Alternative sources of influence might have been film cycles relating to other minority groups, such as American blaxploitation films. However, those films do not show competition, isolation, or the romantic ethos negation that we find in the Bourekas and do not usually end with a comparable intermarriage between Black and white characters (Benshoff 2000).

2. I use "Israeli discourse" as a general phrase that includes all of the more specific intellectual pursuits (literary discourse, cinematic discourse, etc.) that take place within the

borders of the state of Israel. Zionist discourse and Hebrew literature discourse are therefore part of Israeli discourse.

3. A few occurrences in the historical development of Israeli culture and society show that the negation of exile's power as a leading ideology is gradually fading. Bar Ilan University opened Yiddish Literature and Language Departments in 1961, and secular institutions, such as Tel Aviv University, have recently begun to offer Yiddish and Ladino courses. Two documentaries released in the relatively recent past—*The Komediant* (Israel, 2000) and *The Ashkenazim* (Israel, 2005)—connect Yiddish culture to the Israeli Ashkenazi elite but no feature film has seriously done so yet. (Please see our discussion on chapter 6.) It seems that at the end of the process, we should expect the revival of classical Yiddish literature in Israeli discourse, especially the writings of Sholem Aleichem and Y. L. Peretz (who are *not* exile negators). One of the early signs of this development is the latest republication of all of Sholem Aleichem's writings in a new translation (by Arye Aharoni) in 1997, and, in fact, his stories continue to be translated and published as collections. The last one, translated by Dan Miron, was published in 2010 (*Sipurei Tohu*, 2010).

4. However, this triumph of Hebrew was neither complete nor immediate, since during the 1930s and early 1940s, the stream of immigrants arriving from eastern and central Europe brought Yiddish as their mother tongue to this Hebrew territory (Eretz Yisrael) and the status of Yiddish was raised (Chaver 2004).

5. For the complexity of the relationships between Yiddish and Hebrew, these words of Pinsker about Navot Yeshurun, a Hebrew poet, are revealing: "Yeshurun," says Pinsker, "describes Yiddish as 'a poor woman selling hot doughnuts in Warsaw's streets,' to support Hebrew, a 'respected, but half paralyzed' female relative." . . . "Yeshurun," continues Pinsker, "calls for a kind of revenge, in which the 'royal Hebrew'—now the official language of the State of Israel—needs to go and 'sell hot falafel in Dizengoff Street' [a main street in Tel Aviv] 'in memory of Yiddish'" (Pinsker 2014, 326).

6. Fishman and Fishman (1973, 1974) revealed what can be seen as the systematic institutional suppression of Yiddish language and culture in Israel in the 1960s and 1970s and a denial of any privilege for Yiddish in such fields as education, newspapers, radio, television, and theater.

7. Although for Miron (1987b), Peretz is not part of the history of Hebrew literature, for Shaked (2000, 24–28), he seems to be a milestone in its evolution. However, in a later book, Shaked, like Miron, ignores Peretz, presenting a narrative that goes from Mapu to Mendele and then to Brenner (Shaked 2005, intro.). The Zionist-Hebrew literary discourse regarded Peretz as important mainly to "Yiddish literary tradition, with which, as one of the spiritual fathers of the Bund, he was ideologically identified" (Shaked 2000, 24).

8. Wisse (1991, xiii–3) claims that Peretz shaped Yiddish literature into an expression and an instrument of national cohesion, one that would help the Jews compensate for the absence of such staples as political independence and territorial sovereignty in Europe.

9. Sholem Aleichem, *Ktavim*, trans. Aryeh Aharoni. Tel Aviv: Sifryat Ha'poalim (1997).

10. *Tuvia V'sheva Bnotav*, Menahem Golan (Israel, 1966).

11. Also confirming Sholem Aleichem's decent reception in Israeli discourse is the fact that Miron (1971) has devoted extensive research to his writings.

12. His works in Hebrew, about thirty stories written between 1888 and 1908, were collected by Hana Shmeruk and published in a book entitled *Ktavim Iverim / Sholem Aleichem (Sholem Aleichem / Hebrew Writings)*. Shmeruk (1976, 46) writes there that "the original story of Sholem Aleichem in Hebrew deserves a recognition of its value" (my translation). Shmuel

Werses (1996, 35) also claims that Sholem Aleichem's Hebrew writings deserve more attention.

13. Miron (1971, 80–87) finds that some of Sholem Aleichem's seminal works reflect one of the metanarratives of Zionist discourse: death and revival. Miron adopts Sholem Aleichem into Hebrew literature by explaining the author's influential works as a specific literary articulation of this narrative. Miron (1971, 86) finds "Tevye the Dairyman," *Motl*, and "Menachem Mendel" to be stories that reflect a metanarrative of hope, defeat, and recovery.

14. Brenner (1955, 107) criticizes him for being "a folk writer" with no "clear ideology." Brenner also could not forgive Sholem Aleichem for what he saw as an exilic conviction in his writings, instead of upholding the negation of exile.

15. In the end, Mendele wrote nearly as much in both languages. Some critics regard his Hebrew writings as his best work and see it as more sophisticated than his Yiddish offerings (Aberbach 1993, 21–23).

16. See, for example, Bartana 1979; Karib 1950; Miron 2000, 1–128; and Shaked 2005, 1–21.

17. He writes: "Let us go to the first artist in our new national literature, to the man who got into the center of things . . . and wrote for us three clear bright volumes on ourselves" (Brenner 1985, 58).

18. It seems that Mendele was aware of this demand of Hebrew literary criticism and made efforts to adjust the Hebrew versions of his novels accordingly. In his analysis of the title change that Mendele made to his originally Yiddish novel, *Fishke the Lame* (which became *The Book of Beggars* in Hebrew), Miron (1988) finds that the Hebrew title testifies to Mendele's more historical, national, and didactic intentions in the Hebrew version of the novel.

19. David Aberbach (1993, 35), for example, claims that Mendele did not take Zionism seriously.

20. The first edition of *Kol Kitvei Mendele*, which was published in Odessa between 1899 and 1902.

21. So, in a way, also says Shaked (2000, 11–21).

22. In Shaked's (2000, 22) account of the history of Hebrew literature, in contrast, Peretz is mentioned as one of the founders of the national literature, but not Sholem Aleichem. Shmuel Werses also gives Mendele a prominent position in the Hebrew literature narrative. In the introduction to his book on Hebrew literary history, *Mi Mendele Ad Hazaz* (Werses 1987, 10), he talks about Mendele as one of the fathers of Hebrew literature, among such others as Feierberg, Berdichevsky, Agnon, and Hazaz.

23. Hebrew writers, such as Devorah Baron (see Pinsker 2007, 145–46), also wrote about the shtetl, and their images of the shtetl were present in the Israeli discourse of the time, but their work is irrelevant to the discussion here. It is my main intention to show that the special paradigmatic representation of the shtetl that was typical of classical Yiddish writers, as analyzed in the previous chapter, had a considerable presence in Israeli discourse at the time.

24. However, as already mentioned, it did not begin this way. The first contact of Yiddish with the Israeli sphere created a problematic reality for its speakers. The fact that Yiddish speakers who came to Israel during the Yishuv period were typically forced to abandon this language (considered to be part of diasporic culture) in favor of Hebrew created an immediate ambivalence toward Yiddish among them. On the one hand, it was something that "had to be forgotten" (Chaver 2004), but on the other, it was the mother tongue, a reliable means of communication with parents and elderly individuals, and as such it held a positive aura of intimacy and identification with cherished people, as well as cultural and personal memories. Yiddish

soon gained the ambivalent position of a mother tongue both beloved and rejected. Although suppressed, it continued to reverberate and affect the nascent Hebrew culture. During the Yishuv period (1920–1948), the overwhelming majority of Israelis were Yiddish speakers, and they continued to speak their language because Hebrew was unable to function as a complete substitute; Hebrew lacked the ability to perform all the functions that Yiddish formerly fulfilled. And although Zionist historians would have liked to create a different impression, people whose mother tongue was Yiddish continued to utilize its long colloquial history and its well-established literary tradition and kept on producing Yiddish literature after immigrating to Israel. This odd situation of a Zionist, Yiddish-negating world—populated by Yiddish speakers and readers—changed with the mass emigration of the Middle Eastern, North African, and Sephardic Jews (Mizrahim) during the 1950s, but ambivalence toward Yiddish continued to secretly feed Hebrew culture. The simultaneous attraction and repulsion toward Yiddish, as well as the underground influence of Yiddish on the official Israeli discourse, seemed to reach its peak during the 1960s and 1970s. Many native Yiddish speakers were still alive in Israel then, and at the same time, the evident and unshakable success of Hebrew as a national language—and the triumph of the Hebrew Zionist culture over the Jewish diasporic one—permitted Zionist institutions to soften their negation of Yiddish and its culture. The differences between the modes of reception of the various writers show how they were the result of different relationships with ideologies that prevailed at the time in Israeli discourse.

25. Miron (2004, 9) does not mention any specific years, but he does mention the actor Shaike Ophir, who "was so good in using this [Yiddish] in the first days of the State of Israel." Ophir lived abroad during the 1950s and returned only at the beginning of the 1960s, with his career fading at the end of the 1970s.

26. In the same way, my article about *Sallah* sheds some light on the linkage between the construction of Hebrew subjectivity and the use of Yiddish as a minor language. My discussion there points to the fact that an arbitrary use of Yiddish vernacular was a secret component in the Hebrew subjectivity construction of the character of the kibbutz secretary, that is, the Zionist Ashkenazi character with the highest social status in the film (Kimchi 2011).

27. The fact that many of these books were written by non-Israeli Yiddish writers and were distributed in Jewish communities outside Israel may not shed light on the status of Yiddish in Israel, but it does explain Israel's role as a global center for Yiddish at the time.

28. For example, during the 1960s and 1970s, there were no film adaptations of stories by S. Y. Agnon, 1966 Nobel Prize laureate, who is considered by many to be the foremost Hebrew-Israeli writer of all time, and there was only one film adaptation of a book by Amos Oz, one of today's prominent Hebrew Israeli writers (*My Michael*, 1971).

29. The Jewish Enlightenment's main demand from the Jews was to assimilate into European culture and languages.

30. While Avraham Karib's (1950, 9–86) account of Mendele clearly indicates Mendele's source of bias in the presentation of the shtetl through Haskalah ideology, and while Miron (1971, 93) writes openly about how Haskalah ideology was crucial for Sholem Aleichem's creation of the dialogues of his characters, Shaked (2000, 25) seems to argue for Peretz's post-Haskalah sensibilities, stressing that Peretz was deeply influenced by the European literature of his time.

31. Ortsion Bartana (1979) also stresses the Haskalah ideology reflected by Mendele's writings, although he claims that Mendele's stories present a slightly different narrative than the fundamental "maskilic" one.

32. See Miron 1971, 93; 1973, 257–29.

33. By the "esthetic of ugliness," Miron (1973, 16) means the authors' decision to present the shtetl's surroundings as repulsive, both sociologically and physically, and through characters that sometimes lack basic human manners and are characterized by rudeness and ignorance.

34. Shin Niger (1961, 149) writes that Peretz's *Hassidism* ("Hassidut") stories are characterized by a hidden critique and irony regarding the Hassidic world, from a perspective of Haskalah ideology and, therefore, should be defined not as neo-Hassidism (as some other critics argue; see Frieden 1995) but as "neo-Maskilism."

35. Although the Jewish Enlightenment officially ended in 1881, Shmuel Feiner (2002) talks about "late Haskalah" or "post-Haskalah" as central ideological modes from 1880 until 1914. It also seems that the ending date of the Haskalah is not so clear-cut and that the dating of the Haskalah's period of major influence is vague. Uzi Shavit (1996, 133) mentions two periodicals that were still published long after the Haskalah officially ended—*Hamelitz*, published from 1860 until 1903, and *Ha'tsfira*, published from 1862 until 1931—and indicates that they "contributed" to the "development of the Haskalah and its literature . . . expanding the number of readers of Haskalah journalism."

36. See also my discussion on *Sallah* in chapter 1. For this matter, the figure of the writer Y'aakov Shabtai is revealing: on one hand, he was considered the most native Israeli writer and, on the other, one whose writings echo Yiddish literature and Jewish diasporic reality. Though almost all of Shabtai's fiction is set in Tel Aviv, the urban setting is radically transformed in the context of the extended family of immigrants and refugees. This focus enables the literary representation of "what has been exiled from the Zionist discourse: the Diaspora Jewish immigrants who were kept hidden behind the sabra's broad back" (Pinsker 2014, 347; Soker-Schwager 2006, 251). On the Jewish diasporic reality in Shabtai's novel *Zichron Dvarim* (1977), see also Kimchi 2003.

37. See the discussion on the director Ephraim Kishon in chapter1.

38. The fact that Yiddish cultural elements are projected into a Mizrahi community obviously reduces them.

39. We might think of such figures as the politicians, government officials, and kibbutz members in *Sallah*; the police chief in *Aliza Mizrahi*; Gila in *Charlie and a Half*; and Katz's daughters in *Katz and Carasso*. They are all Ashkenazi-inflected characters within the Bourekas who are being presented as Hebrew by the films.

40. The modernization approach is an academic-institutional theory that dominated the Israeli discourse of ethnicity between 1950 and 1970 and formed the major perspective through which Mizrahim were seen by Zionist institutions and integrated into Israeli society. Swirski claims that the modernization approach was not a discourse of ethnicity but of class. However, Avruch (1987, 228–333) refers to this as a "pseudo class" discourse, pointing out that it expresses an expectation that through the process of resocialization and acculturation, the Mizrahim would become cultural Ashkenazim, since the latter were presented by Israeli Zionist discourse as a model of modernity. Avruch (1987, 229) also quotes Ben Raphael, who claims, in the same spirit, that the progress that Mizrahim were expected to achieve through the modernization project was to become "similar to Ashkenazim."

41. Presenting Ashkenazim as modern also helped construct the Western identity of the Ashkenazim, taking part in what Chinski (2002) called Israeli art's "Sisyphean effort to construct the Western identity of the Ashkenazi elite" and present them accordingly.

42. Indeed, as I have shown in my article about the Bourekas film *Charlie and a Half* (Kimchi 2011a), through their dialogues, Bourekas films at the same time subvert the

modernization approach in their inner paradigm. Examination of the language capabilities of the various characters in the film shows that the language becomes less effective instead of improving with the progress of the generations; however, this representation does not subvert the idea of the homology between modernity and Ashkenaziness but in the end supports it, since it implies that modern Hebrew education and language capabilities are exclusive to Ashkenazim (Kimchi 2011a).

43. This is part of Bhabha's ongoing discussion about the use of the stereotyped representations of nonhegemonic communities. In his introduction to *The Other Question*, a discussion of the relationships between a certain reality and its artistic presentation, Bhabha (1983, 20) claims that criticism of representations of a nonhegemonic community should focus on the identification and understanding of subjectification realized through a discourse of stereotypes. Using Bhabha to see textual representations and their authority within colonist discourse highlights the ambivalence in the production of stereotypes of the colonized by the colonizer. The stereotype, claims Bhabha (1983, 18–36), is an impossible object; its impossibility derives from its ambivalence. It is through the stereotype that the colonizer constructs the identity of the colonized other—apparently from a position of power—but this construction is actually the projection of the colonizer's own threatened self.

44. Mizrahi moviegoers didn't have to be familiar with classical Yiddish literature to be flattered. It was enough that they saw themselves on-screen attending synagogue and praying to God in Hebrew (*Sallah*, *Fortuna*), receiving a blessing from the local rabbi (*Rabbi Gamliel*, *Snooker*), using godly language (*Charlie and a Half*, *Snooker*, *The Tzan'ani Family*, *Salomonico*, *Kazablan*), and so on—all some of the myriad Jewish elements that are part of the community's presentation in Bourekas films.

45. Evidently, most Mizrahi viewers could not precisely place the particular community either culturally or historically. However, my assumption is that they could tell that these were others; as can be seen in the films made by Mizrahi directors about the Mizrahi neighborhood, the self-image of the Mizrahim is totally different than the stereotype attached to them by the Bourekas. And since the Zionist ethnic discourse is binary (Ashkenazim-Mizrahim), they tended to interpret this otherness as Ashkenaziness.

46. The Fishmans mention the provocative request of the Black Panthers (the militant group that fought for social equality between Mizrahim and Ashkenazim in Israel during the 1970s) to Prime Minister Golda Meir to teach them Yiddish (Fishman and Fishman 1973, 29).

47. There is no doubt that the fact that Ashkenazi actors often played Mizrahi figures contributed to this kind of understanding (Shohat 1989, 138–39).

6. Bourekas Legacy

1. A few indicators point to the fact that the status of Yiddish culture is on the rise, although the number of Yiddish speakers in Israel is in severe decline. In the 1990s, the Knesset passed the Yiddish Heritage Law, which recognized the language's importance in Jewish culture and the need to preserve it; this law led to the creation of the National Authority for Yiddish Culture. Since then, Yiddish studies departments have opened in a few Israeli universities, and the number of students in them is continuously growing (Maltz 2012). In my research on Israeli cinema, I've seen that between 2008 and 2013, three Yiddish cospeaking Israeli feature films were made—more than during the previous three decades combined (Kimchi 2014).

2. Since the origins of Israeli Zionist culture lie—as this study shows—in Ashkenazi Yiddish culture, it is sometimes difficult to separate Zionist Israeli films, which ignore Ashkenazi ethnicity while adopting the negation-of-exile ideology, from Ashkenazi pseudo-ethnic films, admitting Ashkenazi ethnicity. The indication in this case would be the presence of Yiddish culture in the film. An extensive representation of Yiddish culture (not necessarily the language but a culture in the broadest sense of the word) would point to a film that depicts Ashkenazi ethnicity.

3. Indeed it is never mentioned in the film that the community presented is Ashkenazi, but since it is clearly a classic Hassidic community, and it is known historically that there are no classic Mizrahi Hassidic communities and that this is an exclusively Ashkenazi religious movement, one can conclude it is Ashkenazi. See Horovitz 2017 and Leon 2009.

4. Such as the conflict of the Georgian Israeli hero of *Late Marriage*, who is torn between his love for a native Israeli woman whom he would like to marry and his family's demand that he marry one of his own tribe. Cultural conflict of the same kind torments Vivian Amsalem, the heroine of the Alkabetz Brothers' trilogy, who is torn between the demands of the patriarchal men in her family—supported by their Moroccan Jewish heritage—and her desire to live as an independent, free, westernized Israeli woman.

5. As previously noted, a musical version of *The Band's Visit* opened on Broadway to critical acclaim, winning the New York Drama Critics' Circle Award for Best Musical of 2017.

6. A yeshiva for married men.

7. Although matriarchism may be typical of Ashkenazi culture and family (see Boyarin 1997), it is not typical for Mizrahim. See, for example, Lubin (1999) on Moshe Mizrahi's films.

BIBLIOGRAPHY

English

A. Classical Yiddish Literature and Its Reception

Aberbach, David. 1993. *Realism, Caricature, and Bias: The Fiction of Mendele Mocher Sfarim.* London: Littman Library of Jewish Civilization.
———. 2007. *Jewish Cultural Nationalism: Origins and Influences.* New York: Routledge.
Feiner, Shmuel. 2002. *Haskalah and History: The Emergence of Modern Jewish Historical Consciousness.* Oxford: Littman Library of Jewish Civilization.
Fishman, Joshua, and David Fishman. 1973. "Yiddish in Israel: The Press, Radio, Theatre, and Book Publishing." *Yiddish* 1–2:4–23.
———. 1974. "Yiddish in Israel: A Case Study of Efforts to Revise a Monocentric Language Policy." *Linguistics* 120:125–47.
Frieden, Ken. 1995. *Abramovitsh, Sholem Aleichem, and Peretz.* Albany: State University of New York Press.
———. 1996. Foreword to *A Traveler Disguised: A Study in the Rise of Modern Yiddish Fiction in the Nineteenth Century,* by Dan Miron, 9–11. New York: Schocken.
———. 2009. "Neglected Origins of Modern Hebrew Prose: Hassidic and Maskilic Travel Narratives." *AJS Review: The Journal of the Association for Jewish Studies* 3:3–43.
———. 2013. "Suppression of Yiddish by the Early Hasidim and Their Opponents." In *Between Yiddish and Hebrew,* edited by Shlomo Berger, 37–53. Amsterdam: Menashe Ben Israel Institute.
Kirshenblatt-Gimblett, Barbara. 1995. Introduction to *Life Is with People: The Culture of the Shtetl,* by Mark Zborowski, 9–30. New York: Schocken.
Miron, Dan. 1973. *A Traveler Disguised: A Study in the Rise of Modern Yiddish Fiction in the Nineteenth Century.* New York: Schocken.
———. 1996. *A Traveler Disguised: A Study in the Rise of Modern Yiddish Fiction in the Nineteenth Century.* New York: Schocken.
———. 2000. *The Image of the Shtetl and Other Studies of Modern Jewish Literary Imagination.* Syracuse, NY: Syracuse University Press.
———. 2010. *From Continuity to Contiguity: Toward a New Jewish Literary Thinking.* Stanford, CA: Stanford University Press.
Norich, Anita. 1984. "Portrait of the Artist in Three Novels by Shalom Aleichem." *Prooftext* 4:237–51.
———. 2014. *Writing in Tongues.* Seattle: University of Washington Press.
Oyerbach, Ephraim, Moshe Kalsh, and Moshe Shtarkman, eds. 1965. *Bibliographical Dictionary of Modern Yiddish Literature.* New York: Narstin.
Peretz, Isaac Leib. 1990. *The Y. L. Peretz Reader.* Edited by Ruth Wisse. New York: Schocken.
Peretz, Y. L. 2002a. "Bontsha the Silent." In *Yiddish Classic Course Pack,* edited by Anita Norich, 49–62. Ann Arbor: University of Michigan.

———. 2002b. "If Not Higher." In *Yiddish Classic Course Pack*, edited by Anita Norich, 37–48. Ann Arbor: University of Michigan.
Pinsker, Shachar. 2014. "That Yiddish Has Spoken to Me: Yiddish in Israeli Literature." *Poetics Today* 35 (1): 325–56.
Polonsky, Antony. 1993. *From Shtetl to Socialism: Studies from Polin*. Oxford: Littman Library for Jewish Civilization.
Polonsky, Antony, and Israel Bartal. 1999. *Focusing on Galicia: Jews, Poles, and Ukrainians, 1772–1918*. Oxford: Littman Library for Jewish Civilization.
Roskies, David, and Diane Roskies. 1975. *The Shtetl Book*. New York: Ktav.
Shaked, Gershon. 2000. *Modern Hebrew Fiction*. Translated by Yael Lotan. Bloomington: Indiana University Press.
Wisse, Ruth. 1991. *Y. L. Peretz and the Making of Modern Jewish Culture*. Seattle: University of Washington Press.
———. 2003. *The Modern Jewish Canon: A Journey through Language and Culture*. Chicago: University of Chicago Press.
Zborowski, Mark. 1995. *Life Is with People: The Culture of the Shtetl*. New York: Schocken.

B. Cinema, Postcolonial Discourse, Minority Discourse

Althusser, Louis. 1971. "Ideology and Ideological State Apparatus." In *Lenin and Philosophy and Other Essays*, 89–127. New York: Monthly Review.
Altman, Rick. 1999. *Film/Genre*. London: BFI.
Anassey, Douglas S. 1997. "Causes of Migration." In *Ethnicity Reader: Nationalism, Multiculturalism, and Migration*, edited by Montserrat Guibernau and John Rex, 257–69. Oxford: Polity.
Anderson, Benedict. 1991. *Imagined Communities: Reflections on the Origin and Spread of Nationalism*. London: Verso.
Astruc, Alexander. (1968) 2009. "The Birth of the New Avant-Garde: La Camera-Stylo." In *The French New Wave: Critical Landmarks*, edited by Graham Peter, 17–23. London: Palgrave Macmillan/British Film Institute.
Bakhtin, Mikhail. 1978. *The Formal Method in Literary Scholarship: A Critical Introduction to Sociological Politics*. Baltimore: Johns Hopkins University Press.
Barthes, Roland. 1977. *Image, Music, Text*. New York: Hill and Wang.
Bazin, Andre. 1967–1971. *What Is Cinema?* Berkeley: University of California Press.
Ben Shaul, Nitzan. 1993. *Expressions of the Siege Syndrome in Israeli Films*. Ann Arbor, MI: University Microfilms.
Benamou, Catherine L. 2007. *It's All True*. Berkeley: University of California Press.
Benshoff, Harry M. 2000. "Blaxploitation Horror Films: Generic Re-appropriation or Re-inscription." *Cinema Journal* 39 (2): 29–35.
Bhabha, Homi. 1983. "The Other Question." *Screen* 24:18–36.
———. 1990. *Nation and Narration*. London: Routledge.
———. 1994. *The Location of Culture*. London: Routledge.
———. 1998. "The White Stuff." *Artforum International* 36 (9): 21–33.
Bloom, Peter. 2003. "Beur Cinema and the Politics of Location: French Immigration Politics and the Naming of a Film Movement." In *Multiculturalism, Postcoloniality and Trans-*

national Media, edited by Robert Stam and Ella Shohat, 44–62. New Brunswick, NJ: Rutgers University Press.
Booth, W. C. 1961. *The Rhetoric of Fiction*. Chicago: University of Chicago Press.
Bordwell, David, and Kristin Thompson. 2008. *Film Art: An Introduction*. New York: McGraw Hill.
Boyarin, Daniel. 1997. *Unerotic Conduct: The Rise of Heterosexuality and the Invention of the Jewish Man*. Berkeley: University of California Press.
Cone, James H. 1991. *Martin and Malcolm and America: A Dream or a Nightmare*. Maryknoll, NY: Orbis.
Cutting J. E. 2016. "Narrative Theory and the Dynamics of Popular Movies." *Psychonomic Bulletin and Review* 23 (6): 1713–43.
Deleuze, Gilles, and Félix Guattari. (1975) 1986. *Kafka: Toward a Minor Literature*. Translated by Dana Polan. Minneapolis: University of Minnesota Press.
Elsaesser, Thomas. 1985. "Tales of Sound and Fury—Observations on Family Melodrama." In *Movies and Methods*, vol. 2., edited by Bill Nichols, 165–89. Berkeley: University of California Press.
Fanon, Frantz. 1967. *Black Skins, White Masks*. New York: Grove.
———. 1979. *The Wretched of the Earth*. New York: Grove.
Foucault, Michel. 1965. *Madness and Civilization: A History of Insanity in the Age of Reason*. Translated by R. Howard. London: Tavistock.
———. 1969. *The Archaeology of Knowledge and the Discourse on Language*. Translated from the French by A. M. Sheridan Smith. New York: Pantheon Books.
———. (1954) 1987. *Mental Illness and Psychology*. Translated by Alan Sheridan and foreword by Hubert Dreyfus. Berkeley: University of California Press.
———. 1997. *Ethics: Subjectivity and Truth*. New York: New Press.
Fuss, Diana. 1989. *Essentially Speaking: Feminism, Nature & Difference*. New York: Routledge.
Gellner, Ersent. 1997. "Nationalism as a Product of Industrial Society." In *Ethnicity Reader: Nationalism, Multiculturalism, and Migration*, edited by Montserrat Guibernau and John Rex, 52–69. Oxford: Polity.
Gelmis, Joseph. 1970. *The Film Director as Superstar*. New York: Pelican Books.
Gerstner, David A., and Janet Staiger. 2003. *Authorship and Film*. New York: Psychology Press.
Goldman, William. 1984. *Adventure in the Screen Trade: A Personal View of Hollywood and Screen Writing*. New York: Werner Books.
Gombrich, E. H. 1972. *The Story of Art*. London: Phaidon.
Grant, Barry Keith, ed. 2003. *Film Genre Reader 2*. Austin: University of Texas Press.
Hall, Stuart. 1994. "Cultural Identity and Diaspora." In *Colonial Discourse and Post Colonial Theory—a Reader*, edited by Williams Partick and Laura Chrisman, 227–37. London: Harvester Wheatsheaf.
———. 1996a. "Cultural Identity and Cinematic Representation." In *Black British Cultural Studies—a Reader*, edited by Houston A. Baker Jr., Manthia Diawara, and Ruth Lindeborg, 209–20. Chicago: University of Chicago Press.
———. 1996b. "Who Needs Identity." In *Questions of Cultural Identity*, 1–18. London: Sage.
———. 1997. *Cultural Representation and Signifying Practices*. Thousand Oaks: Sage.
Helkin, Simon. 1950. *Modern Hebrew Literature: Trends and Values*. New York: Schocken.
Jameson, Frederic. 1986. "Third World Literature in the Era of Multinational Capitalism." *Social Text* 15:65–88.

Kael, Pauline. 1971. *The Citizen Kane Book*. Boston: Little, Brown.
Katz, Sheila Hannah. (1996) 2007. "Adam and Adama, Ird and Arb." In *Gendering the Middle East: Emerging Perspectives*, edited by Deniz Kandiyoti, 85–103. London: I. B. Tauris.
Kimchi, Rami. 2017a. "Altering Hebrewness: The Case of Under the Domim Tree (Etzs Ha'domim Tafus." *Jewish Film and New Media* 5 (2): 143–60.
———. 2011. "A Turn towards Modernity: The Ideological Innovation of Sallah." *Shofar: An Interdisciplinary Journal of Jewish Studies* 29 (4): 1–22.
Klages, Mary. 2006. *Literary Theory: A Guide for the Perplexed*. New York: Continuum.
Lévi-Strauss, Claude. 1963. *Structural Anthropology*. New York: Basic Books.
Lynch, Gordon. 2009. "Cultural Theory and Cultural Studies." In *The Routledge Companion to Religion and Cinema*, edited by John Lyden, 275–91. London: Routledge.
Malou-Strandvad, Sara. 2012. "Organizing for the Auteur: A Dual Case Study of Debut Filmmaking." *MedieKultur: Journal of Media and Communication Research* 53:118–35.
Marsh, Clive. 2009. "Audience Reception." In *The Routledge Companion to Religion and Cinema*, edited by John Lyden, 255–74. London: Routledge.
Martin, Michael T., ed. 1995. *Cinemas of Black Diaspora: Diversity, Dependence, and Oppositionality*. Detroit: Wayne State University Press.
McIntyre, Philip. 2012. *Creativity and Media Cultural Production*. London: Palgrave Macmillan.
Metz, Christian. 1974. *Film Language: A Semiotics of the Cinema*. Oxford: Oxford University Press.
Naficy, Hamid. 2001. *An Accented Cinema: Exilic and Diaspora Filmmaking*. Princeton, NJ: Princeton University Press.
Naremore, James. 2005. "Citizen Kane: The Magician and the Mass Media." In *Film Analysis: A Norton Reader*, edited by Jeffery Geiger and R. L. Rutsky, 340–60. New York: W. W. Norton. .
Nichols, Bill. 2001. *Introduction to Documentary*. Bloomington: Indiana University Press.
Nocke, Alexandra. 2009. *The Place of the Mediterranean in the Modern Israeli Identity*. Leiden: Brill.
Peleg, Yaron. 2008. *Israeli Culture between the Two Intifadas: A Brief Romance*. Austin: University of Texas Press.
Propp, Vladimir. (1968) 2003. *Morphology of the Folktale*. Austin: University of Texas Press.
Rex, John. 1997. "The Concept of Multicultural Society." In *The Ethnicity Reader: Nationalism, Multiculturalism, and Migration*, edited by Montserrat Guibernau and John Rex, 105–220. Oxford: Polity.
Said, Edward. 1979. *Orientalism*. New York: Vintage Books.
———. 1993. "The Voyage in the Emergence of the Opposition." In *Culture and Imperialism*, 239–61. New York: Vintage Books.
Sarris, Andrew. 1968. *The American Cinema: Directors and Directions, 1929–1968*. New York: E. P. Dutton.
———, ed. 1971. *Hollywood Voices: Interviews with Film Directors*. Indianapolis: Bobbs-Merrill.
———. (1971) 2000. "Notes on the Auteur Theory in 1962." In *Film Culture Reader*, edited by Adams Sithey, 121–36. New York: Cooper Square.
Schatz, Thomas. 1981. *Hollywood Genres*. Philadelphia: Temple University Press.
Sellors, C. Paul. 2010. *Film Authorship: Auteurs and Other Myths*. London: Wallflower.
Shafik, Viola. 1998. *Arab Cinema: History and Cultural Identity*. Cairo: American University of Cairo Press.

———. 2007. *Popular Egyptian Cinema: Gender Class and Nation.* Cairo: American University of Cairo Press.
Shklovsky, Viktor. (1917) 1965. "Art as Technique: Four Assays." In *Russian Formalist Criticism*, edited by L. T. Lemon and M. Reis, 3–24. Lincoln: University of Nebraska Press.
Shoda, Yuichi, and Daniel Cervone. 2007. *Persons in Context: Building a Science of the Individual.* New York: Guilford.
Shohat, Ella. 1992. "Notes on the Post-Colonial." *Social Text* 31/32:99–113.
———. 1995. "The Struggle over Representation: Casting, Coalitions, and the Politics of Identification." In *Late Imperial Culture*, edited by Román de la Campa, E. Ann Kaplan, and Michael Sprinker, 166–78. London: Verso.
Spivak, Gayatri. 1990a. "Practical Politics of the Open End." In *The Post-Colonial Critic: Interviews, Strategies, Dialogues*, edited by Sarah Harasym, 95–113. New York: Routledge.
———. 1990b. "Questions of Multi-Culturalism." In *The Post-Colonial Critic: Interviews, Strategies, Dialogues*, edited by Sarah Harasym, 59–67. New York: Routledge.
Stam, Robert. 1983. "Colonialism, Racism, and Representation." *Screen* 24:2–20.
Stam, Robert, and Ella Shohat. 1994. *Unthinking Eurocentrism, Multiculturalism, and the Media.* London: Routledge.
Stier-Livny, Liat. 2019. "Mizrahi Jews and Holocaust Survivors in 1950s Israeli Cinema: A Revised Outlook." *Shofar: An Interdisciplinary Journal of Jewish Studies* 37 (2): 1–34.
Truffaut, François. 1967. *Hitchcock by François Truffaut.* New York: Simon & Schuster.
———. 1976. "A Certain Tendency of the French Cinema." In *Movies and Methods*, edited by Bill Nichols, 1:224–37. Berkeley: University of California Press.
Wimsatt, William K. 1954. *The Verbal Icon.* Lexington: University of Kentucky Press.
Wollen, Peter. 1972. *Signs and Meaning in the Cinema.* Bloomington: Indiana University Press.
———. 2002. "Who the Hell Is Howard Hawks?" *Framework* 43 (1): 9–17.

C. Mizrahi Ethnicity, Zionist Discourse, Israeli Culture, and Israeli Cinema

Alcalay, Ammiel. 1993. *After Jews and Arabs.* Minneapolis: University of Minnesota Press.
———. 1996. *Keys to the Garden.* San Francisco: City Lights.
Almog, Oz. 2000. *The Sabra: The Creation of the New Jew.* Translated by Haim Watzman. Berkeley: University of California Press.
Alush-Levron, Merav, 2015. "The Politics of Melancholy in the New Israeli Cinema, Social Identities." *Journal for the Study of Race, Nation and Culture* 21 (2): 169–85.
Avruch, Kevin. 1987. "The Emergence of Ethnicity in Israel." *American Ethnologist* 14 (2): 327–39.
Baehar, Moshe. 2008. "Mizrahim Abstracted: Action, Reflection, and the Academization of the Mizrahi Cause." *Journal of Palestine Studies* 37 (2):89–100.
Baer, Yitzhak. 1965. *The History of the Jews in Christian Spain.* Tel Aviv: Am Oved.
Chaver, Yael. 2004. *What Must Be Forgotten.* Syracuse, NY: Syracuse University Press.
Chetrit, Sami Shalom. 2010. *Intra-Jewish Conflict in Israel: White Jews, Black Jews.* London: Routledge.
Clifford, James. 1986. "Introduction: Partial Truth, in Writing Culture." In *The Poetics and Politics of Ethnography*, edited by James Clifford and George Marcus, 98–122. Berkeley: University of California Press.

Eyal, Gil. 2006. *The Disenchantment of the Orient: Expertise in Arab Affairs in the Israeli State*. Stanford, CA: Stanford University Press.
Foucault, Michel. 1972. *Histoire de la folie à l'age classique*. Paris: Editions Gallimard.
Freud, Sigmund. 1960. *Civilization and Its Discontents*. Translated by James Strachey. New York: Norton.
Gershenson, Olga. 2011. "Immigrant Cinema: Russian Israelis on Screens and behind the Camera." In *Israeli Cinema: Identities in Motion*, edited by Miri Talmon and Yaron Peleg, 134–48. Austin: University of Texas Press.
Gilmore, Leigh. 2008. *Autobiographics: A Feminist Theory of Women's Self-Representation*. Ithaca, NY: Cornell University Press.
Goldberg, Harvey, and Salomon Hagar. 2002. "From Laboratory to Field: Notes on Studying Diversity in Israeli Society." *International Social Science Review* 3 (1): 123–37.
Gottreich, Emily Benichou. 2008. "Historicizing the Concept of the Arab Jews in the *Maghrib*." *Jewish Quarterly Review* 98 (4): 433–51.
Hakak, Lev. 2002. *Modern Hebrew Literature Made into Film*. Lanham, MD: University Press of America.
Halkin, Shimon. 1950. *Modern Hebrew Literature: Trends and Values*. New York: Schocken.
Hardt, Michael, and Antonio Negri. 2001. *Empire*. Cambridge, MA: Harvard University Press.
Hever, Hannan. 1987. "Hebrew in an Israeli Arab's Hands: Six Miniatures of Anton Shamas' Arabesques." *Cultural Critique* 7:47–76.
Horowitz, Amy. 1999. "Israeli Mediterranean Music: Straddling Disputed Territories." *Journal of American Folklore* 445:450–63.
———. 2010. *Mediterranean Israeli Music and the Politics of the Esthetic*. Detroit: Wayne State University Press.
Inbar, Michael, and Chaim Adler. 1977. *Ethnic Integration in Israel: A Comparative Case Study of Moroccan Brothers Who Settled in France and in Israel*. Piscataway: Transaction Books.
Khazzoom, Aziza. 2008. *Shifting Ethnic Boundaries and Inequality in Israel; or, How the Polish Peddler Became a German Intellectual*. Stanford, CA: Stanford University Press.
Levy, Lital. 2008. "Historicizing the Concept of the Arab Jews in the *Mashrik*." *Jewish Quarterly Review* 98 (4): 452–69.
Loshitzky, Yosefa. 2001. *Identity Politics on the Israeli Screen*. Austin: University of Texas Press.
Shemer, Yaron. 2011. "Trajectories of Mizrahi Cinema." In *Israeli Cinema: Identities in Motion*, edited by Miri Talmon and Yaron Peleg, 120–33. Austin: University of Texas Press.
———. 2013. *Identity, Place, and Subversion in Contemporary Mizrahi Cinema in Israel*. Ann Arbor: University of Michigan Press.
Shohat, Ella. 2010. *Israeli Cinema: East/West and the Politics of Representation*. New York: I. B. Tauris.
Smoocha, Sami. 2004. "Jewish Ethnicity in Israel: Symbolic or Real?" In *Jews in Israel: Contemporary Social and Cultural Patterns*, edited by Uzi Rebhun and Haim Waxman, 47–80. Hanover, NH: Brandeis University Press.
Talmon, Miri, and Yaron Peleg. 2001. Introduction to *Israeli Cinema: Identities in Motion*, by Miri Talmon and Yaron Peleg, ix–xviii. Austin: University of Texas Press.
Weber, Max. 1997. "What Is an Ethnic Group?" In *Ethnicity Reader: Nationalism, Multiculturalism, and Migration*, edited by Montserrat Guibernau and John Rex, 15–27. Oxford: Polity.

Weitzner, Jacob. 2002. "Yiddish in Israeli Cinema." *Prooftexts* 22:186–99.
Yossef, Raz. 2006. "Restaging the Primeval Sense of Loss: Melancholia and Ethnicity in Israeli Cinema." *Third Text* 20 (3): 487–98.
———. 2010. *To Know a Man—Sexuality, Masculinity and Ethnicity in Israeli Cinema* [*La'da'at Gever-Miniyut Gavriyut ve'Ethniut Ba'kolnoa Ha'Israeli*]. Tel Aviv: Ha'kibutz Ha'meuhad.
Žižek, Slavoj. 1992. *Enjoy Your Symptom! Jacques Lacan in Hollywood and Out.* London: Routledge.
———. 1994."The Specter of Ideology." In *Mapping Ideology*, edited by Slavoj Žižek, 1–34. New York: Verso.
Zucherman, Ghil'ad. 2003. *Language Contact and Lexical Enrichment in Israeli Hebrew.* New York: Palgrave Macmillan.

Hebrew

Aharonovitz, Yossef. 1929. *The Writings of A. D. Gordon, 1925–1929* [*Kitvei Alef Daled Gordon*]. Tel Aviv: Ha'poel Hatsa'ir.
Almakayas, Carmen. 2014. "My Coalition—on My Heart in the East Coalition" ["Ha'koalitzia Sheli—Al Kohalitziat Libi Ba'mizrah"]. *Ha'kivun Mizrah* 26:13–16.
Alush-Levron, Merav. 2007. "On the Verge of the Orient: Identity and Liminality in Second- and Third-Generation Films, 1990–2007" ["Al Saf Ha'mizrah: She'ela Shel Zehut Be'sirtei Dor Sheni Shlishi 1990–2007"]. PhD diss., Bar-Ilan University.
Balas, Shimon. 1999. *Tel Aviv East* [*Tel Aviv Mizrah*]. Tel Aviv: Kedem.
Bartana, Ortsion. 1979. *Mendele Mocher Sforim: A Critical Reading in the Work of Avramovitch* [*Mendele Mokher Sfarin: I'un Bikorti Be'mihlol Yetsirato*]. Tel Aviv: Dekel.
Ben David, Yossef. 1952. "Ethnic Differences or Sociological Distinctions" ["Hevdelim Ethniyim O Shinuy Hevrati"]. *Megamot Gimel* 2:171–83.
Ben Sason, Haim Hilel. 1986. "Heritage of Oriental Jewry: The Issue, Its Problems and Its Options" ["Moreshet Yehudei Ha'mizrah: A'inian, Be'ayotav Ve'Efsharuyotav"]. In *Oriental and North African Jews*, edited by Robert Attal, 85–87. Jerusalem: Yad Ben Zvi.
Ben Shaul, Nitsan. 1999. "The Secret Connection between the Bourekas Films and the Personal Films" ["Hakesher Hasamuy Ben Sirtei Habourekas Ve'Hastratim Ha'ishiyim"]. In *Fictive Looks*, edited by Jad Ne'eman, Orly Lubin, and Nurit Gertz, 128–56. Tel Aviv: Open University Press.
Berdichevski, Micha Yossef. 1952. *All the Essays of Micha Yossef Ben Guryon* [*Kol Ma'amarei Micha Yossef Ben Guryon*]. Tel Aviv: Am Oved.
Bhabha, Homi. 2002. "The White Stuff" ["Ha'homer Ha'lavan"]. *Theory and Criticism* 20 (Spring): 283–88.
Biletski, Y. H. 1964. "A Different Opinion on Sallah Shabatti" ["De'a Aheret Al Sallah Shabatti"]. *Al Hamishmar*, June 30, 1964, 4–5.
Brener, Y. Haim. 1955. *All the Writings of Y. H. Brener* [*Kol Kitvei Y. H. Brener*]. Tel Aviv: Hakibbutz Ha'meuhad.
Burstein, Yigal.1990. *Faces as a Battlefield* [*Panim Kesde Krav*]. Tel Aviv: Ha'kibutz Ha'meuhad.
Chetrit, Shalom Sami. 1999a. *The Ashkenazi Revolution Died* [*Ha'mahapecha Ha'ashkenazit Meta*]. Tel Aviv: Kedem.

———. 1999b. *Literature Anthology: One Hundred Years—One Hundred Writers* [*Anthologia Lesifrut—Mea Shanim—Mea Yotsrim*]. Tel Aviv: Kedem.

———. 2004. *The Mizrahi Struggle in Israel, 1948-2003* [*Ha'ma'avak Ha'mizrahi Be'Israel, 1948-2003*]. Tel Aviv: Am Oved.

Chinski, Sara. 2002. "With Eyes Wide Closed: About the Symptomatic Albinism in the Field of Israeli Art" ["Be'einaim Atsumot Lirvaha: Al Tismonet Ha'lavkanut Ha'nirkeshet Bisde Ha'amanut Ha'israelit"]. *Theoria U'bikoret* 20 (Spring): 57–86.

Dayan, Nisim. 1976. "Back from the Bourekas to the Ghetto Culture" ["Me'habourekas Behazara Letarbut Ha'getto"]. *Kolnoa* 11 (Fall): 51–55.

Duvdevani, Shmulik. 2010. *First Person Cinema* [*Guf Rishon Mazlema: Kolnoa Ti'udi I'shi Be' Israel*]. Jerusalem: Keter.

Eilon, Amos. 1988. *The Israelis* [*Ha'Israelim: Avot U'banim*]. Jerusalem: Adam.

Eisenshtadt, Shmuel. 1948. *Introduction to the Sociology of Mizrahi Congregations* [*Mavo Le'heker Ha'mivne Ha'hevrati Shel Adot Ha'mizrah*]. Jerusalem: Szold Institute.

Eizenshtat, Shmuel. 1967. *Israeli Society: Background, Developments, and Problems* [*Ha'hebra Ha'Israelit: Reka, Hitpathoyot U'beayot*]. Jerusalem: Magnes.

Frankenstein, Karl. 1957. *Poverty, Disturbed State, Primitivism* [*Oni Mufraut Primitiviut*]. Jerusalem: Szold Institute.

Frieden Ken. 2002. "Parody and Hagiography in I. L. Peretz's Neo-Hassidic Stories" ["Parodia ve-hagiographia: sippurim hasidiim-keveyakhol shel I. L. Peretz"]. *Khulyot* 7:45–52.

———. 2006. "A Critical Perspective on 'Mendele's Nusah'" ["'Nusah Mendele' be-mabat bikorti"]. *Dappim le-Mehkar be-Sifrut* 14–15:89–103.

Frishman, David. 1964. *All David Frishman's Writings* [*Kol Kitvei David Frishman*]. Jerusalem: M. Newman.

Gannoth, Nehama. 1964. "The People Have Decided: A High-Quality Movie" ["Ha'am Hehlit—Seret Elit"]. *Al Ha'mishmar*, May 4, 1964.

Gertz, Nurit. 1993. *A Story from the Movies: Israeli Literature and Its Film Adaptations* [*Sipur Mehasratim: Siporet Israelit Ve'ibude'a Le'kolno'a*]. Tel Aviv: Open University Press.

———. 1999. *The Others in Israeli Films of the '40s and '50s* [*Ha'aherim Ba'sratim Ha'israelim Bi'shnot Ha'arbaim veha'hamishim*]. Tel Aviv: Open University Press.

———. 2004. *A Different Choir: Shoah Survivors, Foreigners and Others in Israeli Literature and Cinema* [*Makhela Aheret: Nitsolei Shoa, Zarim Va'aherim Ba'kolnoa Uba'sifrut Ha'israelim*]. Tel Aviv: Am Oved.

Goldberg, Ze'ev. 2002. "On Y. L. Peretz's Relationships to Zionism" ["Al Yahaso Shel Y. L. Perets La' Ziyonut"]. *Khulyot* 7 (Autumn): 53–82.

Gross, Ya'akov, and Nathan. 1991. *The Hebrew Film: Milestones in the History of Moving Pictures in Israel* [*Haseret Ha'ivry:Prakim Betoldot Ha'reinoa Veha'kolnoa Be'israel*]. Tel Aviv: Writers Addition.

Gurmezano, Yitshak. 2004. *On the Way to the Stadium* [*Ba'derech La'itstadion*]. Tel Aviv: Kedem.

Hever, Hannan. 2002. Hever, Hannan, Yehouda Shenhav, and Pnina Motzafi-Haller, eds. 2002. *Mizrahim in Israel: A New Study* [*Mizrahim Be' Israel—Iyon Mehudash*]. Jerusalem: Van Leer Institute.

———. "We Didn't Come through the Sea" ["Lo Bano min Hayam"]. In *Mizrahim in Israel: A Critical Observation into Israel's Ethnicity*, edited by Hannan Hever, Yehouda Shenhav, and Pnina Motzafi-Haller, 191–212. Jerusalem: Van Leer Institute.

Horovitz, Ariel. 2017. "From Eastern Europe to the Heart of the East" ["Mi'mizrah Europa Le'lev Ha'mizrah"]. *Makor Rishon*, Shabbat supplement, 27 (1).
Karib, Avraham. 1950. *Can't Hold It, so I'll Speak [Adabra Ve'Yirvach Li]*. Tel Aviv: Am Oved.
Karif, Moshe. 2005. *Hamizrahit: The Story of the Mizrahi Democratic Rainbow and the Social Struggle in Israel, 1995–2005 [Hamizrahit: Sipora shel Hakeshet Hamizrahit ve'ha'ma'avak He'hevrati Be'israel, 1995–2005]*.Tel Aviv: Globs - Hasifriya.
Kimchi, Rami. 1997. "The Burial of the Bourekas" ["Kvurat Ha'bourekas"]. *Maznaim* 71 (9): 20–22.
———. 2000. "Israeli Literary Republic" ["Republika Sifrutit Israelit"]. *Hakivun Mizrah* 1 (Fall): 4–11.
———. 2003. "The Jewish Memory of Jabes and Shabtai" ["Ha'zicharon Ha'yehudi shel Jabes ve'shabtai"]. *Iton 77* (280): 12–20.
———. 2011a. "The Unclosed Gap" ["Ha'pa'ar Shelo Nisgar"]. *Blshanut Ivrit* 65 (Winter): 105–25.
———. 2012. *The Israeli Shtetls [Shetel Be'eretz Israel: Sirtei Ha'bourekas U'mekorotiehem Be'sifrut Yiddish Klassit]*. Tel Aviv: Resling.
———. 2013. "Notes on the Acceptance of Yiddish Classical Literature in Israel of the Sixties" ["He'arot Lehitkabluta shel Sifrut Yiddish Klassit Bishnot Ha'shishim"]. *Moreshet Israel* 10 (Fall): 140–59.
———. 2014. "Israeli Cinema, 2008–2013: Data and Tendencies" ["Ha'kolnoa Ha'israeli 2008–2013, Netunim U'megamot"]. *Shnaton Ha'tikshoret Le'israel*, May 2014, 108–16.
———. 2017. "Mizrahim and Mizrahi Culture in Israeli Academic Discourse" [Mizrahim Vetarbut Mizrahit Ba'shiah Ha'academi Ha'israeli]. *Moreshet Israel* 14 (February): 311–31.
Klaussner, Yossef. 1956. *Creators of an Era and Era Successors [Yotsrei Tekufa U'mamshihey Tekufa]*. Tel Aviv: Masada.
———. 1958. *The History of New Hebrew Literature [Historia Shel Ha'sifrut Ha'ivrit Ha'hadasha]*. Jerusalem: Achiasaff.
Krytler, Hans, and Shulamit Krytler. 1980. *The Psychology of the Arts [Ha'psichologia Shel Ha'amanuyot]*. Tel Aviv: Sifriyat Ha'poalim.
Leon, Nissim. 2009. *Soft Ultra Orthodoxy: Religious Renewal in Mizrahi Judaism [Harediut Raka: Hithadshut Dathit Ba' Yahadut Ha'mizrahit]*. Jerusalem: Yad Ben Zvi.
London, Yaron. 1993. *Kishon: Biographical Dialogue [Kishon—Du Siah Biography]*. Tel Aviv: Sifriyat Ma'ariv.
Lubin, Orly. 1992. "From the Margins to the Center: The Subversion of the Transit Camps' Movies" ["Min Ha'shulayim La'mercaz—Hathranutam Shel Sirtei Ha'ma'abarot"]. *Zmanin* 39–40:141–49.
———. 1999. "Nationalism, Women and, Ethnicity" ["Leumiut Nashim Ve'etniyut"]. In *Fictive Looks*, edited by Yehuda Ne'eman, Nurit Gertz, and Orly Lubin, 120–27. Tel Aviv: Open University Press.
———. 2002. *Woman Reads a Woman [Isha Koret Isha]*. Tel Aviv: Ha'kibutz Ha'meuhad.
Maltz, Judy. 2012. "Yiddish Is Dead. Long Live Yiddish!!!" ["Ha'Yiddish Metha. Tehi Ha'Yiddish"]. *Ha'aretz*, December 21, 2012.
Mendele Mocher Sforim. 1966. *All Mendele's Mocher Sforim's Writings [Kol Kitvei Mendele Mocher Sforim]*. Tel Aviv: D'vir.
Meshulam, Ed. 1966. "Our Name Is Fortuna" ["Kor'im Lanu Fortuna"]. *Davar*, January 25, 1966, 7–8.

Miller, Marc. 2005. "Sholem Aleykhem the Modernist? The Subjectivity of Reality in the Letters of Menakhem mendl and Sheyne-sheyndl" ["Shalom Aleichem Modernist? Ha'subyektiviut shel Ha'metsiut be'Michtavei Menchem Mendel Ve Sheyne Sheyndl"]. *Khulyot* 9 (Summer): 83–95.

Miron, Dan. 1971. *Essay Chapters* [*Pirkei Masa*]. Tel Aviv: Am Oved.

———. 1987a. *If Not Jerusalem* [*Im Lo Tihye Jerushalaim*]. Tel Aviv: Am Oved.

———. 1987b. *One at the Time* [*Bodedim Be'moadam*]. Tel Aviv: Am Oved.

———. 1988. "The Sentimental Education of Mendele Mocher Sforim" ["Ha'hinuh Ha' sentimentali shel Mendele Mocher Sforim"]. In *The Book of Beggars*, 201–68. Tel Aviv: Am Oved.

———. 2004. *The Dark Side of Shalom Aleichem's Laughter* [*Ha'tsad Ha'hashuch Bitshoko shel Shalom Aleichem*].Tel Aviv: Am Oved.

———. 2012. *From Ear to Mouth: Conversations about Shalom Aleichem's Art of Monologue Writing* [*Mi'pe Le' Ozen: Shihot be'Amanut Ha'Monolog Shel Salom Aleichem*]. Tel Aviv: Afik.

Ne'eman, Yehuda. 1979. "Cinema: Ground Zero" ["Darga Efes Be'kolnoa"]. *Kolnoa* 5 (Fall): 18–23.

———. 1999. "The Modernists: The Genealogy Scroll of the New Sensitivity" ["Ha'modernim: Megilat Ha'yohasin Shel Ha'regishut Ha'hadasha"]. In *Fictive Looks*, edited by Yehuda Ne'eman, Nurit Gertz, and Orly Lubin, 9–32. Tel Aviv: Open University Press.

Niger, Shin. 1961. *The Life and Work of Y. L. Perez* [*Hayav Ve'yetsirato Shel Y L Perez*]. Tel Aviv: D'vir.

Ontokovsky, Yael. 1975. "I'm Tired of Doing Films for Critics" ["Nima's Li La'asot Sratim Le'mevakrim"]. *Kolnoa* 6/7:25–55.

Pasolini, Paolo Pier. 1974. "The Poetic Cinema" ["Ha'kolnoa Ha'piuti"]. *Kolnoa* 1:43–61.

Perchomovski, Maret. 2016. *Book of Israeli Film* [*Sefer Ha'kolnoa Ha'israeli*]. Accessed January 21, 2022. http://www.cinemaofisrael.co.il/וְכות--סיניע/.

Peretz, Y. L. 1962. *The Writings of Y. L. Peretz* [*Kol Kitvei Y. L. Peretz*]. Tel Aviv: D'vir.

Pickar, Ariel. 2007. *The Teachings of Rabbi Ovadia Yosef in an Era of Change—Research and Cultural Criticism*. Tel Aviv: Bar Ilan University Press.

Pinsker, Shachar. 2007. "An Old House: A New Country" ["Bait Yashan-Eretz Hadasha"]. *Davka* 3 (July): 46–49.

———. 2008. *Yiddish as a Double Agent in Israeli Culture* [*Yiddish Ke'sochen Kaful Ba'tarbut Ha'israelit*]. Tel Aviv: Beit Leivik.

———. 2018. "Vos vil ikh ton? Yosl Bergner, Yiddish, and the 'Father Tongue'" [*Vos vil ikh ton? Yosl Bergner, Yiddish Ve' shfat Av.*]. In *The World of Yosl Bregner*, edited by Uri Hollander. Tel Aviv: Hakibutz Ha'meuhad.

Raz-Krakotzkin, Amnon. 1993. "For the Criticism of the Negation of Exile in the Israeli Culture" ["Le'bikoret Shlilat Ha'galoot Batharboot Hayisraelit"]. *Theoria Ubikoret* 4 (Fall): 23–55.

———. 1994. "For the Criticism of the Negation of Exile in the Israeli Culture: Exile within Sovereignty" ["Le'bikoret Shlilat Ha'galoot Batharboot Hayisraelit—Galot Betoch Ribonut"]. *Theoria Ubikoret* 5 (Fall): 113–35.

Ross, Nikham. 2008. "Scholarly Personality in Peretz's 'Between Two Mountains'" ["Ha'ma'avak Al tadmito shel Ha'lamdan Ha'yeshivati"]. *Khuliyot* 11 (Summer): 37–60.

Sadan, Dov. 1994. *Researches in Hebrew Literature* [*Mehkarim Besifrut Ivrit*]. Tel Aviv: Tel Aviv University Press.

Schnitzer, Meir. 1994. *Israeli Cinema* [*Ha'kolnoa Ha'Israeli*]. Tel Aviv: Kineret.
Schweitzer, Ariel. 2003. *The New Sensitivity: Israeli Cinema in the 1960s and 1970s* [*Ha'regishut Ha'hadasha—Kolnoa Israeli Bi'shnot Ha'shishim Ve'Hashivim*]. Tel Aviv: Bavel.
Shaked, Gershon. 1998. *Hebrew Literature, 1880–1980* [*Ha'siporet Ha'ivrit 1880–1980*]. Jerusalem: Keter.
———. 2005. *Mendele: Before Him, after Him* [*Mendele: Lefanav, Aharav*]. Jerusalem: Magnes.
Shaked, Shaul. 1979. "Traditions of Oriental Jewry's Study: Tendencies and Problems" ["Al Moreshet Yahadut Hamizrah Umehkara: Megamot U'be'ayot"]. *Pe'amim* 1:8–20.
Shalit, David. 2006. *Screening Power* [*Makrinim Koach*]. Tel Aviv: Resling.
Shalom Aleichem. 1997a. *Menahem Mendel*. Translated by Arye A'haroni. Tel Aviv: Sifriyat Ha'poalim.
———. 1997b. *Monologues and Train Stories* [*Monologim Ve'sipurei Rakevet*]. Translated by Arye A'haroni. Tel Aviv: Sifriyat Ha'poalim.
———. 1997c. *Motl, Peysi the Cantor's Son* [*Motl Ben Peysi Ha'hazan*]. Translated by Arye A'haroni. Tel Aviv: Sifriyat Ha'poalim.
———. 1997d. *Sempenyue, Sender Blank, Tevye the Milkman*. Translated by Arye A'haroni. Tel Aviv: Sifriyat Ha'poalim.
———. 2005. "Dryfoos in Katriellivke" ["Dryfoos Be' Katrielivka"]. In *The Town of the Small People*, translated by Beni Mar, 53–60. Tel Aviv: Yediot Aharonot.
———. 2010. *Sorties of Chaos* [*Sifurei Tohu*]. Translated by Dan Miron. Jerusalem: Keter.
Shmeruk, Hana. 1976. *Shalom Aleichem: Hebrew Writings* [*Shalom Aleichem: Ktavim Ivriym*]. Jerusalem: Biyalik Institution.
Sharik, Yossef. 1966. "Building Kabtsanesk" ["Bonim et Kabtsanesk"]. *Ha'aretz*, June 1, 1966.
———. 1970. "The Hero that Reached Adulthood" ["Ha'gibor She'egia Le'bagrut"]. *Ha'aretz*, November 5, 1970.
Shavit, Uzi. 1996. *In the Dawn: The Jewish Haskalah in the Russian Empire of the 19th Century* [*Ba'alot Ha'shachar—Ha'haskala Hayehudit Ba'imperia Ha'rusit Ba'me'a Ha 19*]. Tel Aviv: Hakibutz Hameuhad.
Shenhav, Yehuda. 2001. "Comments on Identity and Politics of Identities" ["Hearot Al Zehut Upolitika Shel Zehuyut"]. *Teoria U'bikoret* 19 (Fall 2001): 1–5.
———. 2003. *The Arab Jews: Nationality, Religion, and Ethnicity* [*Hayehudim Ha'arvim: Leumiyot, Dath, Ethniyot*]. Tel Aviv: Am Oved.
———. 2005. "On Hybridization and Purification: Orientalism as a Discourse with Wide Margins" ["Al Hakla'a Ve' Tihur: Oriyentalism Keshi'ah im Sula'im Rehavim"]. *Theory and Criticism* 26:5–11.
Shiran, Shaul. 1978. "An Interview with Boaz Davidson" ["Reayon Im Boaz Davidson"]. *Kolnoa* 5/6:23.
Shohat, Ella. 1989. *Israeli Cinema: History and Ideology* [*Kolnoa Israeli Historia Ve'idiologia*]. Tel Aviv: Breirot.
———. 1999. "The Politics of Israeli Cinema: Critical Readings / Master Narrative" ["Ha'politika Shel Ha'kolnoa Ha'israeli: Kriot Bikortiyot / Narrative Al"]. In *Fictive Looks*, edited by Yehuda Ne'eman, Nurit Gertz, and Orly Lubin, 44–66. Tel Aviv: Open University Press.
———. 2001. *Forbidden Memories* [*Zichronot Asurim*]. Tel Aviv: Kedem.

Smooha, Sami. 1970. *Ethnic Gap in Israel* [*Pa'ar Adati Be'israel*]. Tel Aviv: Tel Aviv University Press.
Soker-Schwager, Hana. 2007. *The tribal sorcerer from workers' dormitories-Ya'akov Shantai in Israeli culture*. Tel Aviv: Hakibutz Hameuhad.
Stahl, Avraham. 1979. *Interethnic Tensions within the Jewish People* [*Metahim Adatiyim Be'am Israel*]. Tel Aviv: Am Oved.
Swirski, Shlomo. 1981. *Not Faltering but Oppressed* [*Lo Nehshalim Ela Menuchshalim*]. Haifa: Haifa University Press.
Truffaut, François. 1987. *The Films of My Life* [*Hasratim Behayay*]. Tel Aviv: Masada.
———. 2004. *Hitchcock*. Tel Aviv: Bavel.
Unger, Henry. 1991. *Moving Pictures and Philosophy* [*Kolnoa Ve'philosophia*]. Tel Aviv: D'vir.
Utin, Pavlo. 2008. *The New Israeli Cinema: Conversations with Filmmakers* [*Ha'Kolnoa Ha'Israeli He'hadash: Sihot Im Bamaim*]. Tel Aviv: Resling.
Werses, Shmuel. 1979. "Mendele, the Legend Writer within the Light of *In the Valley of Tears*" ["Mendele Ba'al Ha'agada Le'or Emek Habacha"]. *Bikoret U'parshanut* 13/14:35–71.
———. 1987. *From Mendele to Hazaz* [*Mi'mendele ad Hazaz*]. Jerusalem: Magnes.
———. 1996. *From One Language to Another: Works and their Incarnation in out Literature* [*Mi'lashon El Lashon: Yetziroth Ve' gilgoleihen Be'sifroteinu*].
Weinreich, Max. 2002. "Ashkenaz: The Yiddish Period in Jewish History" ["Ashkenaz: Ha'tkufa Ha' Yiddit Behistoriya Ha'Yehudit"]. *Khulyot* 7 (Autumn): 371–80.
Werses, Shmuel. 1979. "Mendele, the Legend Writer within the Light of In the Valley of Tears" [("Mendele Ba'al Ha'agada Le'or Emek Habacha")]. *Bikoret U'parshanut* 13/14:35–71.
———. 1987. *From Mendele to Hazaz* [*Mi'mendele ad Hazaz*]. Jerusalem: Magnes.
Yudel, Mark. 1961. *Y. L. Peretz and His Work* [*Y. L. Peretz Ve'yetsirato*]. Tel Aviv: D'vir.
Zimmerman, Moshe. 2001. *Sines of Cinema: The History of Israeli Cinema 1896–1948* [*Simanei Kolnoa: Toldot Ha'kolnoa Ha'israeli Ben Hashanim 1896–1948*]. Tel Aviv: Tel Aviv University Press.
———. 2007. *The Hidden Films* [*Hasratim Hasmuyim Min Ha'ayn*]. Tel Aviv: Resling.
Zoran, Gabriel. 1997. *Text, World, Space: On the Ways of Space Planning in Literature* [*Text, Olam, Merhav: Al Darkei Ha' irgun shel Ha'merhav Be'sifrut*]. Tel Aviv: Tel Aviv University Press.

INDEX

Page numbers in *italics* refer to illustrations

Aberbach, David, 161n19
acculturation, 117, 163n40
Adler, Chaim, 156n24
aesthetic organization (formation), 72, 88, 89
Agnon, S. Y., 161n22, 162n28
albinism (sociological), 6, 109
Alcalay, Ammiel, 63–65, 155n19
Aleichem, Sholem, 1, 5, 91, 92, 102, 104, 110, 112, 115, 159n21, 160n3, 160n11, 161n14, 162n30; and Hebrew literature, 111, 126, 160n12, 161n13, 161n22; and Yiddish culture, 113, 116
Aliza Mizrahi (1967), 33, 40, 46–47, 49, 57, 145, 152n23, 153n42, 158n15, 159n20, 163n39
Althusser, Louis, 13
Altman, Rick, 4
Alush-Levron, Merav, 65
Amichay, Yehuda, 114
anarchy, 22, 88
Ancient Winds (2002), 155n22
anthropology, 62, 63, 91, 115; colonial, 59
anti-Semitic discourse, 1, 15, 17, 26, 149n6
Arabs, 2, 4, 26, 63, 139, 140, 155nn18–19, 156n25; Arab cinema, 157n1, 159n1; Arab countries, 2; Arab culture, 63, 64, 66, 83, 136; Arab music, 17, 73, 83, 84, 134, 137
Ariana (1971), 67, 68–69, 71–74, 77–79, 80–81, 82, 83–84, 85, 156n28, 159n1
Ars Poetica, 61, 154n7
Ashkenazi, 2, 5, 12, 14, 15, 20–21, 154n4, 156n25, 163n39, 163n42, 165n3; agency, 60–61, 68, 83, 90, 118, 127; audiences, 9, 118, 119, 122–23, 125; community, 121, 122, 123, 128–29, 165n3; cultural background, 7–8, 26, 60, 89, 90, 149n16; culture, 60, 61, 90, 118, 123, 126, 127, 129, 130, 165n7; diasporic, 8, 9, 23, 26, 116, 117, 119, 124; elites, 3, 4, 6, 8, 9, 10, 12, 15, 22, 23, 26, 62, 108, 109, 116, 117, 119, 120, 121, 122, 124, 126, 128, 146, 160n3, 163n41; ethnicity, 128, 129, 165n2; European, 2, 31, 116; families, 53, 55, 140; identity, 8, 10, 12, 15, 23, 65, 117, 122, 123, 124, 126, 127, 146, 148n15; neighborhoods, 130; non-Zionist, 24; relationship with Mizrahim, 3, 4, 9, 10, 12, 13, 20, 22, 24, 26, 27, 30–32, 33, 61, 64, 72, 73–74, 76–77, 85, 117, 119–20, 121–22, 123, 124, 125, 130, 146, 151n9, 152n17, 163, 164nn45–47; representation of, 32, 60, 122; shtetl, 6, 119, 121, 123; space, 68; subjectivity, 60, 119, 124; Zionists, 19–20, 24, 116, 117, 150n22, 162n26. *See also* Ashkenazi Zionist elites; assimilation: to Ashkenazi culture; directors: Ashkenazi; discourse: Ashkenazi; films: Ashkenazi; filmmakers: Ashkenazi; hegemony: Ashkenazi; non-Ashkenazi
Ashkenazim, 21–22, 32, 43, 44, 48, 53, 55, 59, 63, 68, 70, 73, 74, 76, 77, 78, 80, 84, 105, 106, 118, 119, 122, 125, 131, 132, 139, 140, 142, 152n23, 153n35, 155n19, 157n35, 163nn40–42
Ashkenazim, The (2005), 160n3
Ashkenazi Zionist elites: as colonial rulers of Israeli sphere, 4, 6, 8, 9, 10, 12, 13, 15, 62, 120–22, 121, 124, 125; and construction of Mizrahi subjectivity, 120–22; diasporic subjectivity, 124; and Hebrew/pre-Hebrew dichotomy, 15, 17, 19–20, 26, 121, 122; hegemony, 12, 23; ideology and needs of, 1, 3, 13, 22, 29–30, 119, 120, 121, 125–26, 151n16; and Israeli cinema, 3, 13; and modernity, 3, 21–22, 26, 27, 120, 124–25, 163n41; and negation of exile, 6, 10, 109–10, 117, 128–29; and socioeconomic status, 22, 24, 62, 124–25; stereotyping of Mizrahim, 66; Western identity of (Chinski), 109, 124,

Ashkenazi Zionist elites (*continued*)
163n41; and Yiddish culture, 6, 10, 108, 109, 113–20, 123, 125, 126, 127, 128, 130, 160n3; and Yiddish language, 24, 108, 113–14; and the shtetl, 6, 119–20, 121, 122, 123, 124, 127. *See also* Hebrew: Hebrew-Jewish dichotomy; Yiddish: and oedipal guilt of Zionist Ashkenazi elites

assimilation, 115, 116, 120, 121; to Arabness, 123; to Ashkenazi culture, 129, 156n25; to European culture, 23, 106, 162n29; to Hebrew subjectivity, 15, 18, 24; to Israeli society, 30–31, 32, 92, 124, 125, 130, 150n22; to local Jewry, 61; to modernity, 21–22, 26, 104, 106; and romantic ethos, 53, 57; to Zionism, 26. *See also* Mizrahim: assimilation of

astrology, 80, 95, 102
auteur cinema, 3
auteur theory, 6, 7, 10, 11, 12
author, as absent from text. *See* Barthes, Roland: author absence in films
author, cultural identity of, 7, 11, 12, 26, 28, 35, 59–60, 66, 89, 93, 126; in film theory, 7, 11–12, 37, 59–60; and Hebrew/pre-Hebrew distinction, 20; in Mizrahi-directed vs. Bourekas films, 71–72, 81–82, 85–86, 87
authorities, 14, 35, 36, 56, 57, 88, 92, 136, 152n21. *See also* government: government officials; police; social workers
Avidan, David, 114
Aviva, My Love (2006), 9, 139, 142–45
Avruch, Kevin, 155n13, 163n40

Baba Joon (2015), 128
Balkans, 147n2, 147n4
Band's Visit, The (2007), 10, 131, 134–37, 141, 143, 148n16, 165n5
Barbecue People, The (2003), 155n22
Baron, Devorah, 161n23
Bartana, Ortsion, 162n31
Barthes, Roland, 11, 12, 91, 126, 152n26; author absence in films, 7, 11, 126
Bayit (1994), 155n22
beauty, 40, 41, 72
begging, 49, 51, 57, 100; beggars, 49, 51, 57, 90, 95, 158n16

Ben David, Yossef, 62
Ben Raphael, Eliezer, 163n40
Ben Shaul, Nitzan, 30, 150n2, 151nn9–10, 153n34
"Between Two Mountains" (Y. L. Peretz), 91, 92, 96, 100, 103, 104, 105, 159n26
Bhabha, Homi, 6, 8, 9, 120–21, 122, 164n43
Birstein, Yossl, 127
Bit of Luck, A (1992), 155n22
Biton, Erez, 61, 154n8
Blacks, 4, 6
Bloom, Peter, 11
Bourekas films: aesthetics in, 4, 28, 29, 39–40, 72, 88, 89, 107, 151n9, 152; ambivalence in subordinate Mizrahi stereotype, 121, 164n43; Ashkenazi audiences' reactions to, 9, 30–31, 118–19, 122–23, 124–25; Ashkenazi cultural agency in, 7, 8, 26, 27, 59–60, 61, 89, 90, 127, 154n4; Ashkenazim as modern in, 20–22, 26, 27, 85, 106, 119–20, 123, 124–25, 163n41, 163n42; assimilation of shtetl in, 106, 118; audience reaction to, 3, 8, 30, 122–23, 125; authorities absent or subverted in, 14, 32, 35–36, 56, 57, 88, 92, 135, 152n22; box office success of, 4, 8, 12, 24; cinematic sequence reduced in, 37–40, 52, 56, 88, 89; and colonial mimicry (Bhabha), 9, 121–22; competition in, 41–42, 43–44, 48, 56, 76–77, 79, 87–88, 89, 94–95, 96–97, 104, 105, 106, 153nn34–35, 155n16, 157n1, 159n1; corpus, 4–5, 7–8, 12, 13–14, 30, 32–34; critical response and analysis, 4–5, 14, 28–33, 34, 59–60, 88–89, 150n2, 151n9, 151n16, 152n21, 157n35, 159n1; critical success of, 3–4; definitions/characteristics of, viii, 3, 4–5, 5–6, 7–8, 28, 30, 32–33, 34–57, 60, 68, 87–89, 104–6, 151n9, 152n17; extratextual locations obscured in, 34–35, 68, 156n29; as fetish, 121; forced togetherness and crowding in, 45, 46, 57, 78–79, 136, 141, 143, 153n36, 157n1; idleness, crime, and underemployment/unemployment in, 17, 18, 41–42, 44, 45, 48, 49–50, 50, 51, 57, 79, 100, 136, 152n23, 153n38, 158n17, 159n19; isolation/insularity of communities in, 34, 36, 41, 56, 88, 90, 93, 94, 97, 104, 105–6, 135, 140, 142, 156n29,

159n1; Mizrahi audiences' reactions to, 4, 8–9, 30–31, 32, 123–24, 125, 152n24; and Mizrahi identity (Bhabha), 6, 8–9, 65, 120–22, 164n43; Mizrahi neighborhood as hybrid identity in, 1, 39, *41*, 40–41, 56, 70–72, 93–94; Mizrahi neighborhood ontology in , viii, 3, 4, 5, 6, 7–8, 12, 33, 34–37, 39–40, 41, 46–47, 48, 49–51, 56–57, 60, 67, 68–69, 70–72, 79, 87, 90–97, 100–1, 118; modernist critical discourse of, 3, 4, 28–31, 33; modernization approach in, 29, 31, 32, 119–20, 123–24, 150n22, 163n40, 163n42; modern/premodern dichotomy in, viii, 6, 8, 9, *21*, 25, 20, 23, 26, 27, 31, 34, 85, 88, 89, 104, 119–20, 121, 122, 123–25 (*see also* Bourekas: Ashkenazim as modern in); and negation of exile, 6, 8, 9, 10, 32, 117, 124, 127, 146; negation of Mizrahi self-representation in, 7, 59; neglect and chaos in, 18, 36–40, 56, 72, 88, 89, 94; origin of name, vii; paradigmatic representation of Mizrahim/Mizrahi neighborhoods, 3, 4, 5–6, 8, 9–10, 12, 34–57, 60, 67–68, 74, 83, 87, 88, 89, 90, 91, 104–5, 106, 107, 108, 115, 118, 119, 120, 121, 122, 124, 125–26, 131, 132, 135, 136, 139, 142, 146; police absence in (*see* Bourekas: authorities absent or subverted in); and postcolonial critical discourse, 4, 5, 8–9, 11, 31–33, 58–59, 60–61, 88–89, 154n4; as projection mechanism for Zionist elites, 6, 9, 118, 119, 120, 123, 125, 127, 163n38, 164n43; public/private borders blurred in, 46, 57, 98, 135, 143; religion devalued in, 51, 52, 57, 102, 103, 104, 105–6, 139, 159n22; rhetoric of degeneration and neglect in (*see* Bourekas: neglect and chaos in); romantic ethos reduced in, 53, *54*, 55, 57, 131, 132, 133, 139, 141, 142, 143, 159n1; shtetl/Mizrahi neighborhood differences, 93, 94, 97, 99, 104, 105–6; shtetl/Mizrahi neighborhood homologies, viii, 5–6, 8, 90–97, 100–1, 104–5, 106–7, 108, 118, 119, 125–26, 147n90; superstition vs. religion in, 21, 51, *52*, 57, 102, 104, 105–6; as twisted representation of Mizrahim, 8, 9, 17, 90, 118
Brenner, Yossef Haim, 112, 160n7, 161n14

cafés, 47, 49, 71, 75
cameras, 39, 40, 69, 87, 135; camera angles, 153n32; handheld, 39; positioning of, 38; movements of, 40, 73, 131; zooming, 153n33
Canaan, 64, 149n7
capitalism, 14, 29, 30, 153n34
carnival, 32, 152n24
Catholicism, 61
chaos, 37, 40, 88, 94
Charlie and a Half (1974), 34, 35, 36, 37, 39, 40, 44, *45*, 46, 47, 49, *50*, 51, *52*, 53, 55, 57, 68, 71, 76, 81, 140, 145, 153n42, 157n33, 158n15, 158n17, 159n22, 163n39, 163n42, 164n44
Chaver, Yael, 148n15
Chetrit, Sami Shalom, 30, 31, 67, 150n22, 155n20
Chinski, Sara, 109, 163n41
Christianity, 61, 64, 94
cinema, 1, 3, 7, 11, 28, 37–38, 39, 40, 53, 55, 71, 72, 84, 87, 89, 93, 107, 122, 148n18, 151n3, 152n25, 152n27, 159n1; accented, 64, 65; cinematic apparatus, 37–38, 56; cinematic author, 12, 26, 28, 35, 37–38, 39, 40, 44, 46, 49, 53, 55, 56, 57, 81, 85, 86, 87, 88, 89, 94, 138; cinematic composition, 38–39, 56, 69, 73, 87, 89, 158n2; cinematic discourse, 3, 5, 9, 12, 16, 81, 83, 148n17, 159n2; cinematic editing, 38, 40, 87; cinematic language, 37, 89; cinematic paradigms, 14, 22; cinematic rhetoric, 24, 37, 40, 56, 72, 73, 81, 82, 88, 90; cinematic sequence, 19, 37, 39, 40, 44, 56, 71, 72, 81, 84–88, 89, 93, 136, 152n29, 156n29, 157n32, 158n2; cinematic strategies, 37, 87; cinematic tactics, 16, 22, 27; cinematic texts, 5, 10, 35; commercial, 29, 113; early Israeli, 13, 15, 18, 19–20, 22–23, 24, 26–27, 28, 151n4; European, 3, 4, 28, 151n4; Israeli, 1, 2–3, 4, 7, 9, 10, 12, 13, 14, 15, 16, 18, 19, 22–24, 26–27, 28, 29, 30, 32, 58, 65, 66, 91, 111, 113, 115, 118, 121, 127, 130, 145–46, 148n1, 149n3, 154n4, 164n1; Mizrahi, 64, 65, 66, 154n12
Cinema Egypt (2001), 155n22
City of Tents, The (1953), 152n25
class, 7, 53, 62, 76, 83, 84, 85, 155n15, 163n40; collective, 62, 153n34; conflict, 84, 85, 157n36; ideology, 11; mobility, 29,

class (*continued*)
    30; struggle, 31; and directors, 7, 11; disadvantaged, 29; and film, 11; low, 33; lower middle, 21, 22; middle, 68; ruling class, 1, 13; working, 62, 136
Colombian Love (2004), 9, 138–40
colonialism, 2, 26; colonial mimicry, 9, 121–22; colonial power, 121, 122, 123, 125, 164n43; colonial rule, 6, 10, 62, 65, 125. *See also* anthropology: colonial; postcolonialism
comedies, 3, 5, 28, 30, 33, 82, 107, 149n2; bourgeois, 28, 148n1; ethnic, 29; folk, 3, 27
community, 157n1, 164n43; Jewish, 8, 23, 51, 53, 61, 90, 92, 103, 107, 120, 147n3; premodern, 8, 27, 89, 104, 119, 126; sense of, 93; shtetl, 91, 92, 93, 97, 98, 99, 101–2, 104–5, 108, 115, 121. *See also* Ashkenazi: community; Mizrahim: community; representation: of Jewish community
competition: between Ashkenazim and Mizrahim, 73–77, 85, 157n35; in business, 29, 42, 53, 73–76; commercial, 95, 96; and crime, 45; financial, 42, 44, 48, 73; romantic, 42, 43, 53; sexual, 74, 76, 77, 97, 157n35. *See also* Bourekas films: competition in
conflict, 1, 5, 8, 11, 23, 42, 45, 46, 47, 57, 60, 87, 89, 92, 128, 129, 130, 135, 144, 148n17, 151n9, 151n15, 152n23, 155n16, 155n19, 158n2, 159n19; between Ashkenazim and Mizrahim, 3, 8, 13, 33, 74, 85; cultural, 108, 110, 129, 136, 165n4; family, 137, 150n18; personal, 46, 47, 79, 97, 103, 140, 142; political, 108, 110; sociological, 108, 110. *See also* class: conflict; Jewish-Palestinian conflict
control over open spaces. *See* open spaces: new Hebrew control over
crime, 36, 49–50, 84; petty, 44, 45, 49, 57, 100. *See also* competition
critics, 3, 4, 5, 8, 14, 147n9, 149n4, 150n2, 151n4, 163n34; and Bourekas films, 28–29, 30, 33, 33–34, 36, 37, 41, 59, 67, 151n9, 151n16, 157n35, 159n1; critical reception, 4; and Hebrew literature, 108, 111–12, 161n15, 161n18; and Mizrahi culture, 65, 89; modernist, 29, 30; postcolonial, 31, 88–89;
postmodern, 121; and Yiddish literature, 106, 110, 114, 115. *See also* critique
critique, 163n34; of Bourekas films, 28, 68, 153n34; modernist, 29, 151n3; postcolonial, 31, 33; poststructuralist, 7, 10, 11. *See also* critics
crowding, 40, 41, 88, 98. *See also* togetherness
culture, 62, 154n4, 154n6, 156n28; cultural continuity, 108, 126, 154n6; Israeli, 32, 61, 66, 127, 129, 148nn14–15, 156n25, 160n3, 165n2; Jewish, 9, 109, 127, 128, 148n15, 149n7, 151n13; material, 93; Near Eastern, 43. *See also* Arabs: Arab culture; Ashkenazi: culture; directors: and culture; Europe: European culture; Hebrew: culture; Mizrahi: culture; shtetls: shtetl culture; Yiddish: Yiddish culture

Davidson, Boaz, 34, 44, 151n9, 152n21, 153n37
Dayan, Nissim, 29, 37, 67, 147n9, 150n2, 151n7, 153n36, 159n1
decadence, 30, 39, 88, 94, 109, 151n16, 159n23
Deleuze, Gilles, 10
directors, 5, 6, 7, 10, 11, 23, 49, 89, 108, 118, 148n12, 148n17, 152n21, 156nn26–28; agency of, 8, 59, 89, 107; Ashkenazi, 6, 8, 12, 57, 59, 60, 67, 89, 107, 118, 121, 124, 125, 126; as cinematic author, 7, 11, 12, 59, 90; and culture, 7, 11; and identity, 11, 60; Mizrahi, 8, 59, 60, 67, 83, 107, 128, 164n45
discourse, 60, 64, 102, 151n15, 152n26, 164n43; anticolonial, 65; anti-Semitic, 15, 17, 26, 149n6; Ashkenazi, 116, 122; colonial, 2, 26; European modernist, 4, 28; gender, 66; hegemonic, 66; and identity, 10, 66; ideological, 3, 33; Israeli, 60, 61, 62, 65, 66, 91, 107–8, 109, 110, 113, 114, 115, 117, 147n2 (Preface); 158n6, 159n2, 160n3, 160n11, 161nn23–24, 163n40; Jewish, 116, 149n6; literary, 111, 112, 114, 126, 159n2, 160n7; Mizrahi, 65; orientalist, 26, 31, 155n17; political, 3, 33; postcolonial, 8, 63; postmodern, 66; Third World, 66; Yiddish, 114. *See also* cinema: cinematic discourse; modernism: modernist discourse; postcolonialism:

postcolonial discourse; Zionism: Zionist discourse
discrimination, 2, 63, 122, 151n11
disorientation, 19, 20, 39, 70, 88, 89
diversity, cultural/ethnic, 9, 127, 149n16
Dubnov, Shimon, 110

early Israeli cinema. *See* cinema: early Israeli
Eastern European elites. *See* European Ashkenazi elites; Ashkenazi Zionist elites
Egypt, 64, 85, 134, 135, 136, 137, 157n34. *See also* melodramas: Egyptian
Egyptian melodramas. *See* melodramas: Egyptian
Eilon, Amos, 90
Eisenshtadt, Shmuel, 62
elites, 1, 150n19, 152n24, 153n34; Israeli, 13, 24, 118, 124; Jewish, 116. *See also* Ashkenazi: elites; power: of Zionist elites; Zionism: Zionist elites
Elsaesser, Thomas, 157n36
Eskimo Limon (1978) 153n37
essentialism, 60, 65, 154nn5–6
ethnicity, 9, 62, 83, 127, 155n13, 163n40. *See also* Ashkenazi: ethnicity; diversity: cultural/ethnic; films: ethnic, pseudo-ethnic; Mizrahim: as ethnic group
Europe, 1, 3, 38, 40–41, 95, 110, 117, 122, 149n2, 149n16, 160n8; eastern, 1, 6, 12, 22, 60, 62, 90, 103, 109, 116, 127; central, 22, 62, 160n4; European culture, 23, 43, 106, 162n29; European languages, 114, 116, 162n29; Europeans, 116, 123, 124; western, 43, 61, 94. *See also* Ashkenazi: European; cinema: European; discourse: European modernist; Jews: European; literature: European
European Ashkenazi elites, 116
exclusion, 65, 69, 150n19, 152n23. *See also* inclusion
exhibitionism, 46, 57, 136, 137, 141, 142, 143
exile, 32, 64, 65, 66, 109, 110, 112, 163n36; negation of exile ideology, 6, 8, 9, 10, 32, 108, 109, 111, 112, 115, 117, 124, 127, 128, 129, 146, 148n14, 149n6, 160n3, 161n14, 165n2
extratextual location, 34–35, 68, 69, 156n29

families, 32, 42, 71, 81, 84, 117, 163n36, 165n7; bourgeois, 83; Jewish, 23. *See also* Ashkenazi: families; conflict: family; Mizrahim: families
Farewell Baghdad (2013), 128
Father Language (2006), 155n22
Father of the Girls (1973), 157n37
Feiner, Shmuel, 163n35
fetish, 121
Fiddler on the Roof (1971), 1, 5, 91
film cycles, 3, 12, 159n1; Bourekas, 14, 32, 33, 59, 68, 107, 124
filmmakers, 64; Ashkenazi, 9, 59, 127; Bourekas, 125, 156n26; immigrant, 128; Israeli, 24, 154n12; Jewish, 13; Mizrahi, 64, 65, 66, 154n12, 156n23
films, 3, 6, 7, 10, 11, 14–15, 28, 64–65, 66, 130–31, 145–46, 148nn17–18, 160n3, 163n39; Ashkenazi, 128, 165n2; blaxploitation, 148n12, 157n1, 159n1; Egyptian, 85, 157n34; ethnic, 128, 129; film adaptations, 1, 91, 115, 162n28; filmgoers, 29, 30, 32–33, 68; film industry, 24, 115; film scholars, 4, 28, 150n1; film text, 7, 11, 12, 31, 152n26; French New Wave, 28, 151n4; of identity, 128; Israeli, 3, 4, 7, 12, 13, 14, 16–17, 19–20, 22, 23, 27, 29, 33, 58, 113, 115, 147n5, 148n1, 149n6, 149n16, 156n28, 164n1, 165n2; Mizrahi self-representation, 12, 77, 86, 87, 88–89, 90, 128, 158n2; national heroic, 28, 148n1; neo-Bourekas, 9–10, 12, 130, 138, 139, 145; popular, 5, 11, 28, 29, 151n6; post-Bourekas, 9–10, 12, 130, 139, 140, 145; pseudo-ethnic, 128, 129, 130, 165n2. *See also* cinema; comedies; film cycles; filmmakers; melodramas; *and titles of individual films*
First World, 4, 31, 64
Fishman, David, 113, 114, 116, 160n6, 164n46
Fishman, Joshua, 113, 114, 116, 160n6, 164n46
folklore, 31
Fortuna (1966), 30, 32, 43, 53, 59, 76, 81, 97, 140, 152n23, 158n14, 164n44
fragmentation, 64, 66
Frankenstein, Karl, 62
fraud, 15, 16, 18, 49, 51, 57, 80, 84, 149n12, 158n17
Freud, Sigmund, 66, 118

French new wave cinema. *See* films: French New Wave
Frieden, Ken, 111, 158n3
functionalist school, 155n16
Fuss, Diana, 154n5

Gannoth, Nehama, 149n4
gender, 66, 83
gentiles, 109
Gett: The Trial of Vivian Amsalem (2014), 128
ghettos, 37, 153n36
Gilmore, Leigh, 66
God, 51, 93, 102–3, 104, 130, 133, 159n22, 164n44
Goldberg, Harvey, 148n10
gossip, 47, 48, 78, 79, 98, 99
government, 35, 69, 70, 113, 131, 152n23; government health system, 69; government officials, 16, 17, 18, 36, 48, 92, 163n39. *See also* authorities
Greece, 64
Gross, Nathan, 150n2
Gross, Ya'akov, 150n2
Guattari, Félix, 10

halacha (Jewish law), 128
Halkin, Shimon, 110
Hall, Stuart, 11, 60, 65
halutz (pioneer), 14
Ha'panterim Ha'shkhorim (the Black Panthers), 30, 67, 151n11, 164n46
Hardt, Michael, 149n6
harmony, 9, 13, 39, 69, 75, 90, 101, 110, 121, 144
Harshav, Benjamin, 148n15
Hasmonean kingdom, 108–9
hatzofe l'beit Yisrael. *See* Israeli nation watcher: Hebrew national literature as
Hebrew, 44, 149n7, 163n39; culture, 2, 64, 66, 127, 149n14, 161n24; Hebrew-Jewish dichotomy, 24, 26; Hebrewness, 9, 14, 15, 20, 22, 27; Hebrew/pre-Hebrew dichotomy, 17, *18*, 18, 19, 20, 22, 26, 118, 150n19; Hebrews, 14–15, 17, 18, 113, 123, 125; identity, 18, 108, 113, 117, 119, 146; language, 7, 15–16, 19–20, 24, 108, 109–10, 111, 116–17, 127, 133, 136, 147n7, 148n13, 149n2, 150n19, 150n22, 154n7, 158n3, 158n16, 160nn4–5, 160n12, 161n24, 163n42, 164n44; society, 128; subjectivity, 15–16, 17, 18, 23, 24, 26, 27, 109, 113, 117, 118, 119, 120, 123, 124, 125, 150n19, 162n26; translations, 91, 112, 115, 117, 118, 158n6. *See also* hegemony: Hebrew; Jews: pre-Hebrew; labor: Hebrew; literature: Hebrew; Yiddish: and Hebrew
Hebrew identity/subjectivity. *See* Hebrew: identity; Hebrew: subjectivity
Hebrew labor, as Zionist trope, 16, 149n14; subversion of in *Sallah*, 18
Hebrew/pre-Hebrew dichotomy. *See* Hebrew: Hebrew/pre-Hebrew dichotomy
Hebrew University, 70
hegemonic discourse, 66
hegemony, 8, 65–66, 157n1; Ashkenazi, 3, 12, 23, 61; Eurocentric, 63; Hebrew, 64, 66; Israeli, 64, 66; nonhegemonic communities, 164n43
Half and Half (*Hetzi-Hetzi*, 1971) 151n9
Hever, Hannan, 4, 31, 64, 65, 151n16
historians, 63, 161n24
historical vs. a-historical character of the shtetl, 106, 115–16, 164n45
Holocaust, 2, 15, 16, 19, 149n2
homeland, 1, 64, 65, 66, 156n25
hospitals, 70, 75, 139; mental, 132–33, 142–43, 144–45
host country, 128, 129
House on Shlush Street, The (*Habayit B'rechov Shlush*, 1973), 67

identity, 3, 9, 74, 149n6, 156n25; of colonized, 120, 121–22, 164n43; cultural, 11–12, 23, 60; films of identity, 128; identity politics, 10, 62; Israeli, 124; Jewish, 26, 123; Western, 109, 124, 163n41. *See also* Ashkenazi: identity; directors: and identity; films: films of identity; Hebrew: identity; Jews: and identity; Mizrahim: identity
ideology, 13, 58, 90, 112, 161n14; capitalist, 29, 30; Eurocentric, 89; national, 111. *See also* class: ideology; exile: negation of exile ideology; Jewish Enlightenment: ideology of; Zionism: Zionist ideology
idleness, 15, 16, 48, 49, 51, 100, 101, 153n38; idlers, 48, 49, *50*, 80, 90, 100, 101, 145, 159n19. *See also* Bourekas films:

idleness, crime, and underemployment/ unemployment in immigrants, 14, 16, 17, 23, 32, 64, 139, 149n16, 150n17, 150n19, 160n4, 163n36; Ashkenazi, 6, 24, 26; immigrant status, 20; Mizrahi, 2, 3, 32, 66, 140; non-Zionist, 16, 24; Zionist, 147n4. *See also* filmmakers: immigrant; immigration

immigration, 2, 23, 62, 66, 147n1 (Introduction), 150n22, 156nn24–25, 158n8, 161n24; Second Aliyya, 147n1 (Introduction). *See also* immigrants

Inbar, Michael, 156n24

inclusion, 8–9, 65, 125

independence, Israeli, 1, 110, 148n1; War of Independence, 2

India, 122; Indians, 141

In the Valley of Tears (*B'emek Habacha*, Mendele Mohher Sfarim), 91, 92, 93, 94, 95, 97, 100, 101, 102, 104, 105, 158n8, 159n26

isolation, 8–9, 34, 105, 106, 128. *See also* shtetls: isolation of

Israeli nation watcher, Hebrew national literature as, 108, 110, 111

Jaffa, 2, 55, 135

Jerusalem, 72, 85, 127, 150n22, 151n11; Old City, 69–70, 72–73

Jewish Diaspora, 61; subjectivity, 15, 16, 17, 19, 23, 24, 26, 109, 149n6. *See also* Ashkenazi: diasporic; Jews, diasporic

Jewish Diasporic identity/ subjectivity. *See* Jewish Diaspora: subjectivity

Jewish Eastern European elite, 116

Jewish Enlightenment (Haskalah), 115, 148n11, 158n8, 162n29, 163n35; ideology of, 116, 162nn30–31, 163n34

Jewish National Fund, 14, 149n4

Jewish-Palestinian conflict, 2, 3

Jews, 1, 14, 15, 16, 94, 98, 100, 108, 109, 116, 123, 147n2 (Preface), 149n4, 150n18, 160n8, 162n29; American, 18; and Arabs, 26, 63; diasporic, 15, 16, 26, 117; European, 1, 2, 110, 121; and identity, 26, 123; Levantine, 155n19; Near Eastern, 117; North African, 117; pre-Hebrew, *18*, 18, 19, 20, 22, 26, 118, 150n19; premodern, 124; shtetl, 157n1;

traits of, 15, 97, 149n6; Yemenite, 147n4, 150n22. *See also* Ashkenazi; Jewish Diaspora; Jewish Enlightenment; Jewish National Fund; Jewish-Palestinian conflict; Mizrahim; Sabras; Sephardim

Judeo-Arabic, 114

kabbalah, 48, 51

Kadosh (2000), 128, 129

Karib, Avraham, 116, 162n30

Katz and Carasso (1971), 33, 36, 40, 42, 43, 48, 53, 55, 81, 88, 140, 163n39

Kazablan (1973), 30, 34, 35, 36, 37, *38*, 39, 51, 53, 55, 57, 71, 76, 81, 140, 157nn31–32, 159n22, 164n44

kibbutz settlement, 14, 17, 19, 20, *21*, 22, 35, 38, 53, 149n14, 149n16, 152n29, 162n26; kibbutz members, 14, 17, 19, 20, 21, 22, 23, 26, 48, 150n22, 152n22, 163n39

Kishon, Ephraim, 13, 23, 33, 118, 149n2, 150nn18–19, 150n21

Komediant, The (2000), 160n3

labor: distribution of, 2, 20, 63; Hebrew, 16–17; productive, 16, 100, 116, 149n12; Zionist ideal of, 17, 153n38

Ladino, 114, 147n2 (Preface), 160n3

Lahola, Arieh, 152n25

Late Marriage (2001), 128, 165n4

Levantines, 58, 64, 136, 155n19

Lévi-Strauss, Claude, 148n17

Light Out of Nowhere (*Or Min Ha'efker*, 1973), 67

Likud Party, 30, 33

literature, 10, 109, 163n35; European, 162n30; Hebrew, 64, 91, 110, 111–12, 114, 115, 118, 126, 127, 159n2, 160n7, 161n13, 161n15, 161n18, 161nn22–23; Jewish, 148n15; Mizrahi, 64, 65, 155n20; national, 108, 110, 161n17, 161n22. *See also* Aleichem, Sholem: and Hebrew literature; critics: and Hebrew literature; critics: and Yiddish literature; Yiddish classical literature

Lovesick in Housing Complex C (1995), 10, 132

Lubin, Orly, 32, 59, 67

Lupo in New York (1976), 29

Lusted (1968), 156n28

ma'abara (transit camp), 14, 19, 34, 35, 36, 37–38, 40–41, 46, 48, 71, 152n25, 153n30, 157n30, 159n19

"making the desert bloom": as Zionist trope, 16; subversion in *Sallah*, 17, 18

Maktub Aleik (2005), 155n22

male-female bond, 53, 80, 81

marriage, 43, 48, 53, 56, 74, 80, 81, 83, 128, 133; arranged, 101; bourgeois, 83; and instrumental attitude toward, 53, 56, 83, 133; interclass, 30; intermarriage, 30, 119, 151n16, 157n1, 159n1

Martin, Michael, 11

maskilim (believers in Haskalah ideology), 116

matchmaking (*shidduch*), 42, 51, 53, 54, 57, 82

matriarchy, 137, 139, 145, 165n7; matriarchs, 129

Meir, Golda, 164n46

melancholy, 66, 156n25

melodramas, 3, 5, 27, 28, 32, 33, 81, 82, 107, 131; Egyptian, 83, 84, 85, 157n36, 157n1 (chap. 4); noncomedic, 32

Mendes, Dona Gracia, 147n4

metonymy, 7, 16, 19, 21, 37, 40, 44, 58, 71–72, 97, 105, 129, 138, 153n30, 153n35

Metz, Christian, 148n18, 151n3

mezuzah, 51, 102

Middle East, 61, 64, 66, 83, 84, 147n2 (Preface), 147n4, 161n24

Midnight Entertainer (*Badranit B'hatzot*, 1977), 85, 157n32

Miron, Dan, 106, 111, 112, 113, 115–16, 117, 148n15, 158n3, 160n3, 160n7, 160n11, 161n13, 161n18, 162n25, 162n30, 163n33

Mirrors (2004), 155n22

Mizrahi, Moshe, 59, 67, 77, 86

Mizrahi cinema. *See* cinema: Mizrahi

Mizrahi culture. *See* Mizrahim: culture

Mizrahi literature. *See* literature: Mizrahi

Mizrahim: 2, 4, 5, 6, 8, 29, 30–31, 58, 147n2 (Preface), 147n4 (chap. 1), 148n10, 150n22, 151n11, 154n7, 155n14, 155n18, 156n25, 161n24, 163n40, 165n7; assimilation of, 24, 31, 106, 124, 125, 156n25; audiences, 4, 8, 24, 30, 32–33, 122–24, 125, 152n24, 164nn44–45; and authorities, 36, 162n23; characters, 8, 13, 22, 24, 34, 41, 43, 44–45, 48, 69, 74, 76, 80, 84, 85, 122, 132, 136, 138–39, 145, 151n16, 153n35, 157n35, 159n20; as class category, 29, 30, 31, 33, 62–63, 68, 72, 84, 85, 155n15, 163n40; community, 3, 6, 7, 8, 9, 33, 34, 36, 41, 46, 47, 48, 53, 56, 57, 59, 67, 68, 69, 70–72, 73, 78, 79, 80, 85, 87, 88, 89, 90, 100, 106, 107, 108, 121, 122, 124, 125, 136, 138, 140, 142, 153n35, 157n37, 163n38, 164nn44–45; culture, 31, 56, 59, 61, 63–64, 65, 66–67, 85, 89, 130, 156n23; as ethnocultural category, vii, 3, 12, 13, 22, 29, 31, 62, 63, 80, 155n15; families, 5, 22, 33, 34, 35, 56, 59, 60, 67, 71, 73–74, 87, 89, 122, 138–40, 145, 152n23, 156n25; identity, 12, 64, 65–66, 67, 154n12; immigrants, 2, 3, 32, 66, 140, 156n25; and isolation, 41, 56, 69, 70, 88, 90, 97, 104, 135, 140–41, 142, 156n29, 159n1; and Levant culture, 58, 63–64, 136, 155n19; living spaces, 5, 6, 9, 35, 36–37, 69, 70, 71, 72, 73, 74, 78, 85, 87; and "Love of Israel" approach (Shohat), 63; marginalization of, 12, 13, 64, 66; and melancholy, 66, 156n25; and modernization approach, 29, 31, 32, 62–63, 119–20, 123, 124, 150n22, 155n17, 163n40; neighborhoods, 4, 5, 6, 8, 12, 30, 33, 34–37, 39, 40–41, 44, 46, 47, 48, 49–50, 51, 56, 57, 60, 67, 68–70, 71–77, 79, 80, 85, 87, 89, 90, 91, 92, 93, 94, 100, 104, 105, 106, 107, 108, 118, 119, 122, 125, 131–32, 135–36, 139, 142–43, 151n11, 153n36, 156n29, 159n22, 164n45; oppression of, 30, 66, 151n11; poetry, 61; political struggles of, 3, 30, 33, 58–62, 67; as premodern Jews, 6, 8, 9, 20, 25, 26, 27, 31–32, 34, 62, 85, 88, 89, 119, 121, 124, 155n17; reality, 10, 89–90, 127, 146; relationship with Ashkenazi, 3, 4, 9, 10, 12, 13, 20, 22, 24, 26, 27, 30–31, 33, 61, 64, 73, 74, 76–77, 85, 117, 119–20, 121–22, 123, 124, 125, 130, 146, 151n9, 152n17, 163, 164nn45–47; representation of, 3, 4, 6, 8, 9–10, 12, 20, 27, 32, 32–33, 34–35, 40, 41, 51, 56, 57, 58–60, 67, 71–72, 76, 77, 83, 85, 87, 88–90, 91, 107, 125, 138, 139, 140, 141, 142, 146, 157n1, 157n37, 157n1 (chap. 4), 158n2, 159n1; self-representation in *Ariana*, 68–70, 71–72, 73–74, 77–78, 79, 80, 81,

82–83, 84–85, 156n28; self-representation in Mizrahi-directed films, 59, 65–66, 67–68, 83–84, 88–89, 90, 128, 154n2, 154n4, 158n2; self-representation in *Only Today*, 69–70, 72–73, 74, 75, 75–76, 77, 78–80, 82, 82, 84, 85–86, 156n28; underrepresentation in Israeli cinema, 7, 22, 59, 154n4. *See also* cinema: Mizrahi; directors: Mizrahi; filmmakers: Mizrahi; films: Mizrahi self-representation; immigrants: Mizrahi; literature: Mizrahi

Mizrahi subjectivity, construction of, 120–22

modernism, 29, 104, 114; modernist critique, 29, 30, 31, 33, 151n3; modernist discourse, 3, 4, 28. *See also* modernity; modernization

modernity, 21–22, 25, 26, 27, 31, 62, 83, 97, 106, 119, 159n19, 163n40, 163n42; premodernity, 20, 23, 25, 26, 119, 155n17. *See also* modernism; modernization

modernization, 116, 124; modernization approach, 31, 32, 62–63, 119–20, 123, 124, 150n22, 155n17, 163n40; modernization theory, 89. *See also* modernism; modernity

morals: moral distinctions, 84; moral judgments, 28, 31; moral values, 29

Moroccans, 29, 73, 141, 156n24; Moroccan culture, 128, 165n4

Motl Ben Peysi Hahazan (Shalom Aleichem, Motl, Peysi the Cantor's Son), 91, 92, 115

mottled entity, 6, 9, 122

multiculturalism, 60, 64, 65, 66, 149n16

musicals, 1, 5, 33, 148n16, 150n1, 165n5

Muslims, 155nn18–19; Muslim Arabs, 2, 155n18

Mutsafi, Pnina, 32, 65, 151n16

My Father's House (Beit Avi, 1946), 149n13

Naficy, Hamid, 11, 64, 65, 128

narrative, 5, 16, 19, 51, 53, 75, 77, 81, 82, 83, 85, 87, 89, 108, 135, 140, 143, 148n17, 160n7, 161n13, 161n22, 162n31; metanarrative, 4, 60, 161n13; national, 156n25

National Authority for Yiddish Culture, 164n1

nationalism, 85, 110

nativism, 2

Ne'eman, Yehuda, 4, 29, 30, 33, 34, 36, 89, 150n24 (chap. 1), 150n2 (chap. 2), 151n4, 151n8, 152n27, 153nn34–35, 153n38, 154n4, 156n26

neglect, 18, 36, 37, 38, 39–40, 56, 72, 88, 92, 94, 136

Negri, Antonio, 149n6

neighborhood, 3, 94, 157n32; as hybrid entity, 40; representation of, 60, 71–72, 73, 89, 94, 104; reductive representation of, 85, 87, 113, 119, 123; space, 39–40, 70–72, 94. *See also* Ashkenazi: neighborhoods; Mizrahim: neighborhoods; neighbors

neighbors, 21–22, 40–41, 42, 42, 46, 48, 70, 75, 78, 95, 96, 98, 99, 149n16, 158n17; neighborly relations, 56–57, 85, 97, 99. *See also* Ashkenazi: neighborhoods; neighborhood; Mizrahim: neighborhoods

neo-Marxism, 66

Nes Ba'ayara (Miracle in Our Shtetl, 1966), 115

Niger, Shin, 163n34

non-Ashkenazi, 2, 61, 62, 117, 123

North Africa, 61, 117, 147n2 (Preface), 161n24

nostalgia, 113

oedipal behavior, 77, 120; guilt, 116, 117, 119, 120, 123

Only Today (Rak Hayom, 1976), 67, 69, 70, 72–73, 74, 75, 75–76, 77, 78–80, 82, 82, 84, 85–86, 156nn27–28, 157n35

open spaces: fear of, in anti-Semitic discourse, 15; Holocaust survivors' fear of, 19; new Hebrew control over, 15, 18–19; pre-Hebrew fear of, 19; Zionist control over, 15, 16

Ophir, Shaike, 162n25

orientalism, 2, 4, 8–9, 26, 31, 32, 34, 120, 155n17

Ottoman Empire, 61, 147n4

Ovadia, George, 67, 83, 85, 156nn26–28, 157n32 (chap. 3), 157n1 (chap. 4)

Oz, Amos, 162n28

pairings, 5, 56, 57, 92, 101, 105, 159n20

Palestine, 1–2, 13, 109, 147nn3–4

Panterim Hashkorim movement. *See* Ha'panterim Ha'shkhorim (the Black Panthers)
parody, 116, 132–33
patriarchy, 20, 97, 137–38, 145, 165n4
patriotism, 65, 85
Peretz, Y. L., 5, 91, 92, 94, 97, 99, 100, 101, 104, 106, 110–11, 112, 116, 130, 158n6, 160n3, 160nn7–8, 161n22, 162n30, 163n34
Pinsker, Shachar, 148n15
pluralism, 155n16; pluralistic model, 63, 155n16
pogroms, 2, 99, 147n2 (Introduction)
police, 29, 36, 49, 50, 57, 92, 95, 152n23, 163n39
pornography, 131–33
postcolonialism, 32, 66, 88, 89, 154n4; postcolonial approach, 31, 32, 60, 63; postcolonial discourse, 8, 63; postcolonial studies, 5, 11, 58; postcolonial theories, 4. *See also* critique: postcolonial
power, 10, 37, 41, 157n35; of authority, 6; dynamics of, 3; inequalities, 58; political, 58, 147n4; of religious leaders, 103; of Zionist elites, 27
privacy, 45–46, 47, 98–99, 143, 153n37; right to privacy, 45. *See also* Bourekas films: public/private borders blurred in; space; Yiddish classical literature: public/private boundaries
projection, 118, 120, 164n43. *See also* Yiddish literature: projection of shtetl onto Mizrahim
propaganda: orientalist, 32; Zionist, 2, 31
Propp, Vladimir, 11, 148n17
protest, 14, 30, 65, 66, 153n38; political, 67

Rabbi Gamliel (1975), 34, 35, 43, 48, 49, 51, 57, 71, 76, 158n17, 164n44
rape, 83, 84, 129, 157n34, 157n36
Raz-Krakotskin, Amnon, 108
reality, 36, 71, 94, 110, 115, 120, 131, 151n6, 161n24, 163n36, 164n43; Israeli, 10, 22, 62, 127, 150n17, 151n11, 151n16
rebbe, 96, 99–100, 103
refugees, 2, 163n36

religion, 51, 102, 153n38, 155n15, 159n21, 159n26; Jewish, 57, 102, 104
representation, 7, 23, 38, 40–41, 58, 59, 60, 66, 85, 87, 90, 93, 105, 107, 113, 135, 150n17, 150n22, 154nn1–2, 156n28, 163n36, 163n42, 164n43, 165n2; of Jewish community, 107, 120; representational paradigms, 125, 126, 131, 132, 161n23; self-representation, 7, 12, 58, 59, 68, 77, 83, 86, 87, 88–89, 90, 128, 154n2, 154n4, 158n2; underrepresentation, 20, 22. *See also* Ashkenazim: representation of; Mizrahim, representation of; neighborhood: representation of; shtetl: representation of
Revach, Ze'ev, 47, 54, 67, 69, 70, 82, 83, 85, 147n8, 155n22, 156n26, 156n28
rivalry, 43, 44, 46, 48, 74, 87, 96
Rojanski, Rachel, 148n15
romance, 40, 53, 80–83, 131, *134*, 140, 141–42, 144, 159n20; romantic atmosphere, 72, 81, *82*, 82; romantic behavior, 77, 80–81; romantic ethos, 53, *54*, 57, 81, 131, 132, 133, 139, 141, 142, 143, 157n1, 159n1; romantic love, 57, 83–84, 85, 101, 102, 132, 133–35, 139, 140, 145; romantic potential, *55*, 55, 81, 83, 88, 101. *See also* competition, romantic

Sabras, 16, 22, 24, 26, 149n16, 150n17
Said, Edward, 120
Sallah (*Sallah Shabati*, 1964), 1, 4, 7, 13–15, analysis, 16–27, *25*, 33, 34, 35, 36, 37, 38, 40–41, *41*, 45–46, 48, 49, 51, 53, 57, 59, 68, 71, 79, 81, 92, 97, 101, 118, 119, 140, 147n5, 147n7, 148n10, 149nn2–3, 149n12, 149n16, 150n19, 150n22, 151n7, 152n22, 152n29, 153n30, 153nn39–40, 153n43, 157n30, 157n33, 158n17, 159n19, 159n22, 162n26, 163n39, 164n44; and Hebrew labor, 16–17; plot, 14–15; and Zionist tropes and ideology, 16, 18
Salomonico (1972), 30, 34, 35, 36, 48, 51, 152n23, 164n44
Sarris, Andrew, 11
satire, 103, 116, 149n2
Schnitzer, Meir, 29, 149n3, 150n2, 151n14

Schweitzer, Ariel, 150n2, 151n3
seclusion, 56, 68, 78
Second Temple, 109
Sephardic culture. *See* Sephardim: culture
Sephardim, 61, 62, 117, 147n2 (Preface), 147n4 (Introduction), 150n22, 155n14, 155n19, 157n37, 161n24; culture, 59, 60–62, 117, 147n2, 150n22
Sforim, Mendele Mocher (Shalom Yaakov Abramovitz), 5, 90, 110, 111, 112, 126
Shabtai, Y'aakov, 163n36
Shafik, Viola, 83, 84, 157n34
Shaked, Gershon, 160n7, 161nn21–22, 162n30
Shaked, Shaul, 155n17
Sharqawi, Galal, 157n34
Shavit, Uzi, 163n35
Shemer, Yaron, 4, 11, 64–65, 154n12, 155n14, 155n22
Shenhav, Yehuda, 4, 31, 65, 151n16
Shiva (2008), 128
Shmeruk, Hana, 160n12
Shohat, Ella, 4, 31, 32–33, 34, 36, 50, 57, 58–59, 60, 63, 88, 148n1, 152n17, 152n24, 153n36, 154n4, 155nn17–18
shtetl, 1, 5, 6, 8, 23, 41, 90, 92, 93, 95, 97, 99, 100, 101, 103, 104–5, 106, 107, 108, 109, 111, 112, 115, 119, 121, 127, 145, 159n26, 161n23, 162n30, 163n33; isolation of, 92–93, 94, 101, 105, 106; residents of, 8, 92, 98, 100, 105, 157n1, 158n14; representation of, 6, 8, 12, 90, 91, 92, 93, 97, 104, 106, 108, 115–16, 118, 119, 124, 146; shtetl culture, 91, 147n9; shtetl space, 91, 94, 116. *See also* Ashkenazi, shtetl
signifiers, 7, 10, 29, 37, 40, 62, 72, 148n18, 149nn6–7, 152n26; signification, 10, 148n18
Smooha, Sami, 63, 155nn15–16
Snooker (1975), 30, 34, 35, 39, 40, 44, 47, 49, 50, 51, 54, 55, 55, 57, 71, 87, 133, 135, 139, 147n8, 153n35, 157n32, 158n17, 159n22, 164n44
social workers, 25, 35, 36, 45, 57, 101, 152n22, 159n19
sociologists, 59, 62–63
South, The (1998), 155n22
space, 7, 19, 21, 22, 37, 38, 39, 40, 55, 56, 64, 65, 71–72, 73–74, 83, 87, 88, 93, 152n26, 156n29, 157n32; hybrid, 1, 38, 93; open, 15, 16, 18–19, 35, 149n15, 152n29; private, 45, 56, 57, 71, 78, 79, 97, 98, 135, 136, 138, 142, 143; public, 45, 46–47, 57, 78, 79, 97, 98, 135, 136, 138, 142, 143; spatial continuity, 88, 89
Spain, 61, 147n2 (Preface)
Spinoza, Benedictus de, 147n4
Spivak, Gayatri, 154n2
stereotypes, 29, 151n9, 164n43, 164n45; colonized, 120–21
subalterns, 58, 154n2; subaltern groups, 58, 59
subjectivity, 116, 149n6. *See also* Hebrew, subjectivity; Jewish Diaspora, subjectivity
superstition, 20, 51, 52, 57, 80, 102, 103, 104, 105
Swirski, Shlomo, 62, 63, 155n13, 155n16, 163n40
synagogues, 22, 51, 103, 104, 153n43, 164n44
syuzhet, 5

Take a Wife (2005), 128
Taqasim (1999), 155n22
Tel Aviv, 35, 47, 68, 69, 127, 141, 142, 152n23, 157n32, 160n3, 160n5, 163n36
television, 4, 160n6
text analysis, postcolonial attitudes. *See* postcolonialism
Third World, 4, 31, 64, 65, 66, 83, 84
This Is Sodom (2010), 10, 131–32, *134*
To Fill the Void (2011), 128, *129*
togetherness, 78–79, 93, 98, 99–100, 105, 157n1; forced, 45, 46, 56–57, 77–79, 101, 105, 135, 136, 137, 140, 141, 142, 143, *144*
Tomorrow's a Wonderful Day (*Adama*, 1946), 149n13
Topol, Chaim/Haim, 1, *18*, 25
tropes, 16, 17, 51, 121
Truffaut, François, 7
Turn Left at the End of the World (2004), 9, 139, 140, 142
Tuvia and His Seven Daughters (*Tuvia Ve'sheva Benotav*, 1968), 115
Two Kuni Lemel (1968), 40, 153n30
Tzanani Family, The (1976), 34, 35, *42*, 42, 46, 47

ugliness, 37, 39–40, 94, 116, 163n33
universities, 70, 111, 114, 164n1
Ushpizin (2006), 128–30

voyeurism, 46

Weitzner, Jacob, 113
Werses, Shmuel, 160n12, 161n22
Westernization, 6, 121, 122, 123, 124, 165n4
Wisse, Ruth, 116, 160n8

Yediot Aharonot, 147n8
Yiddish: culture, 6, 8, 9, 10, 60, 91, 108, 113, 114, 115, 116, 117–19, 120, 123, 124, 125, 126, 127, 128, 130, 146, 148n15, 158nn3–4, 158n6, 160n3, 160n6, 161n24, 163n38, 164n1, 165n2; and Hebrew, 108, 109, 110, 160n5; in Israeli cinema, 9, 10, 18, 19, 20, 24, 60, 90–91, 108, 113, 115, 117–20, 122, 123, 124, 125, 127, 130, 145–46, 150n18, 164n44, 164n1, 165n2; in Israeli culture, 6, 8, 9, 10, 24, 91, 107–8, 109–15, 116–20, 123, 124, 125, 127, 128–29, 146, 148n14, 150n18, 158n4, 158n6, 160nn3–4, 160n6, 161n24, 162n25, 162n26, 164n46, 164n1, 165n2; language, 8, 18, 17, 19, 23, 24, 60, 92, 108, 109, 110, 111, 112, 113, 114, 115, 118, 120, 127, 150n18, 158n3, 158n6, 160n4, 160n6, 161n24, 162nn25–26, 164n46 (chap. 5), 164n1 (chap. 6); and oedipal guilt of Zionist Ashkenazi elites, 116, 116–17, 118–19, 120, 123; oppression of, 8, 108, 115; poetry, 114; as vernacular, 113, 116–17, 118, 128, 162n26; writers, 1, 5, 6, 8, 90–91, 94, 106, 110, 111, 112, 114, 116, 125, 126, 158n3, 158n6, 161n23, 162n27. *See also* Yiddish classical literature; Yiddish Heritage Law
Yiddish classical literature, 6, 10, 114–15, 158n10, 163n36; aesthetic of ugliness in the shtetl, 94, 116, 163n33; authorities/police absent or subverted in shtetl, 92–93; and Bourekas films, 6, 12, 118, 126, 146, 156n29, 157n1, 158n6, 164n44; Bourekas films/shtetl differences, 92, 93, 94, 104, 105–6; Bourekas films/shtetl similarities, 8, 12, 91–105; competition in the shtetl, 94–97; forced togetherness and crowding in, 93, 98, 99–100, 101, 105, 157n1; and Haskala ideology, 115–16; as ideological apparatus, 106, 111, 112, 115, 116, 120, 160n8; and idleness in the shtetl, 95, 100–1, 159n19; isolation of shtetl in, 91–92, 93; and negation of exile, 108–9, 111, 117; and paradigmatic representation of the shtetl, 12, 90, 104–5, 118, 121, 122, 124, 125, 146, 156n29, 161n23; projection of shtetl onto Mizrahim, 6, 104–5, 108, 118, 120, 121, 123, 124–24; public/private boundaries blurred in, 97–99; reception in Israel, 107–15, 160n3; religion devalued in, 139; romantic ethos reduced in, 101–2; and shtetl as ahistorical, 106, 115–16; superstition vs. religion in, 102–4
Yiddish Heritage Law, 164n1
Yishuv, 2, 3, 13, 109, 148n1, 161n24
Yossef, Raz, 66, 156n25
You Can Work It Out, Salomonico (1975), 34, 159n20
Yung Yisroel, 114

Zach, Nathan, 114
Zimmerman, Moshe, 4, 29, 150n2
Zionism, 1, 2, 3, 22, 30, 32, 64, 89, 109, 112, 113, 116, 117, 118, 119, 121, 123, 124, 125, 126, 148n1, 149n6, 149n16, 151n8, 153n38, 155n17, 156n23, 161n19, 163n40; non-Zionism, 16, 24, 29, 113; pre-Zionist culture, 9, 32, 128, 148n14; Zionist culture, 161n24, 165n2; Zionist discourse, 2, 4, 9, 14, 23, 31, 32, 58, 85, 109–10, 112–13, 118, 124, 149n7, 149n14, 151n11, 158n4, 159n2, 161n13, 163n36, 163n40, 164n45; Zionist dogma, 3, 13; Zionist elites, 3, 4, 9, 15, 16, 17, 19, 20, 22, 23, 24, 26–27, 29, 30, 62, 66, 108, 109, 113, 116, 117, 120, 151n16; Zionist ethos, 14, 17, 22, 26–27, 108, 127; Zionist history, 1, 59, 147nn1–2, 161n24; Zionist ideology, 3, 8, 14, 15, 19, 22, 27, 28, 29–30, 31, 32, 58, 86, 108, 110, 111, 128, 148n14, 151n16; Zionist leaders, 2, 155n19; Zionist movement, 2, 14–15; Zionist narrative/master narrative, 32; Zionist project, 1, 2, 113; Zionists, 6, 14–15, 24, 117, 119, 150n22; Zionist tropes, 16, 17; Zionist values, 29–30, 151n16. *See also* Ashkenazi: Zionist elites; Ashkenazi:

Zionists; assimilation, to Zionism; immigrants, Zionist; labor: Zionist ideal of; propaganda: Zionist

Zionist discourse. *See* Zionism: Zionist discourse

Zionist narrative. *See* Zionism: Zionist narrative/master narrative

Zionist tropes. *See* Zionism: Zionist tropes

Zoran, Gabriel, 156n29

RAMI KIMCHI teaches film and television in the School of Communications at Ariel University and has held guest appointments at the University of Michigan and University of California, San Diego. He is an international award-winning filmmaker and culture critic. He is the author of *The Israeli Shtetls: Bourekas Films and Yiddish Classical Literature*.

www.ingramcontent.com/pod-product-compliance
Lightning Source LLC
Chambersburg PA
CBHW030653230426
43665CB00011B/1081